Please scan to download
'Dreaming of Eden' by Skillet

This book is dedicated to Steve Noblett, who woke me to
the knowledge of the invisible Kingdom, and its ongoing
invasion of the Earth.
--John

I'd like to thank John Cooper for letting me be apart of
a piece of creation that means so much to him and his
mission on earth. I'd also like to thank our publisher
Josh Frankel who's been a great friend and a brother,
who has always believed in me and encouraged me
to be better and to push forward.
--Chris

EDEN:
A SKILLET GRAPHIC NOVEL

Written by John Cooper and Random Shock

Drawn By Chris Hunt

Colored By Fred Stresing & Meg Casey

Lettered By Justin Birch

Designed By Tyler Boss

Published By Z2 Comics

Publishers Josh Frankel and Sridhar Reddy

Special Projects Coordinator Josh Bernstein

Special Thanks to Kevin Chiaramonte

I fell in love with super heroes before I could ride a bike. My best friend and I used to dress up in our underoos (for those who were born after the 80's, underoos were super hero styled underwear). I would run around the neighborhood in nothing but my underoos and my Batman cape that my mom hand-made for me. Something about being powerful and virtuous-and apparently colorful-made me feel like I could change the world around me. It wasn't until I was about 10 years old that I fell in love with comics. Like most things in my childhood, I was influenced by my older brother who would religiously go to the comic shop and buy books. I wanted to be like him of course. I also should mention the fact that In the mid 80's, it was not "cool" to be in to comics. If you were a comic nerd, you had to love it enough to pay the price on your social status. I have always believed that if you were proud of who you are then you shouldn't be ashamed of what you love. And with my mom in the hospital battling cancer, I had bigger problems in my life than other people's opinions. I needed an escape. I needed a place to feel powerful. Like the world could be made right again. Where good wins. All the hours reading and drawing comics provided a small measure of hope in my life.

When I got a call asking if I'd be interested in discussing a possible graphic novel, I jumped at the chance. This was a bucket list item for me! I wrote a concept and some themes that I would want to say—and we were off to the races. Meeting with writers and artists was nothing short of thrilling for this comic nerd.

Since that original conversation, to what the book has now become, I have fallen in love with the world of Eden. This book has the same DNA as my music. It's exciting and theatrical, with a tinge of the supernatural. But mainly, behind it all, there is a feeling that is hard to put into words-some fans call it hope, or love, or community. I just say that Eden, like our music, has a feeling like you've heard this song before, but it was so long ago that you just cannot remember the words. But as it continues to play, you find yourself singing along. And the song you are singing feels like home.

--John L. Cooper

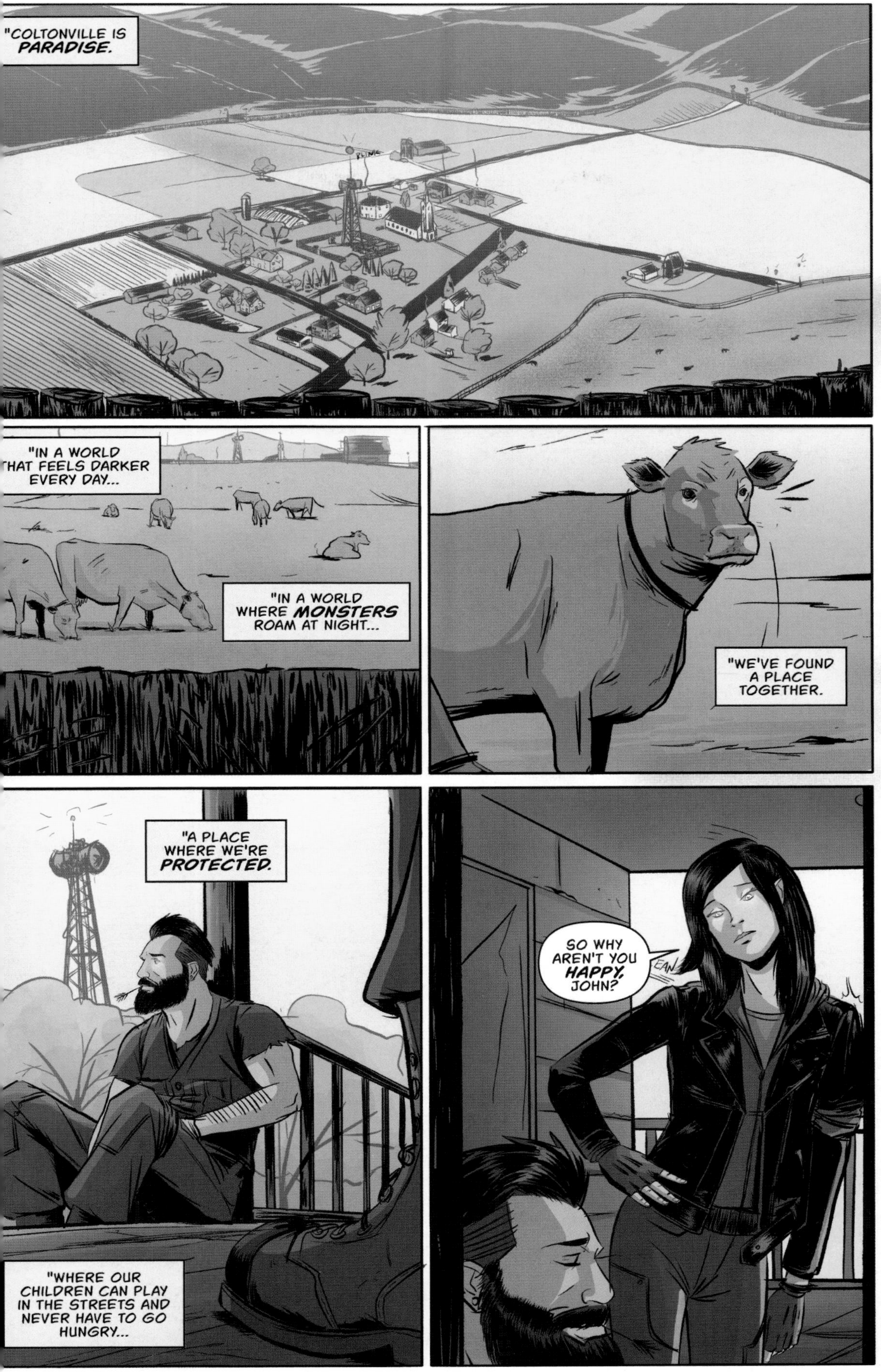
"COLTONVILLE IS PARADISE.
"IN A WORLD THAT FEELS DARKER EVERY DAY...
"IN A WORLD WHERE MONSTERS ROAM AT NIGHT...
"WE'VE FOUND A PLACE TOGETHER.
"A PLACE WHERE WE'RE PROTECTED.
"WHERE OUR CHILDREN CAN PLAY IN THE STREETS AND NEVER HAVE TO GO HUNGRY...
SO WHY AREN'T YOU HAPPY, JOHN?

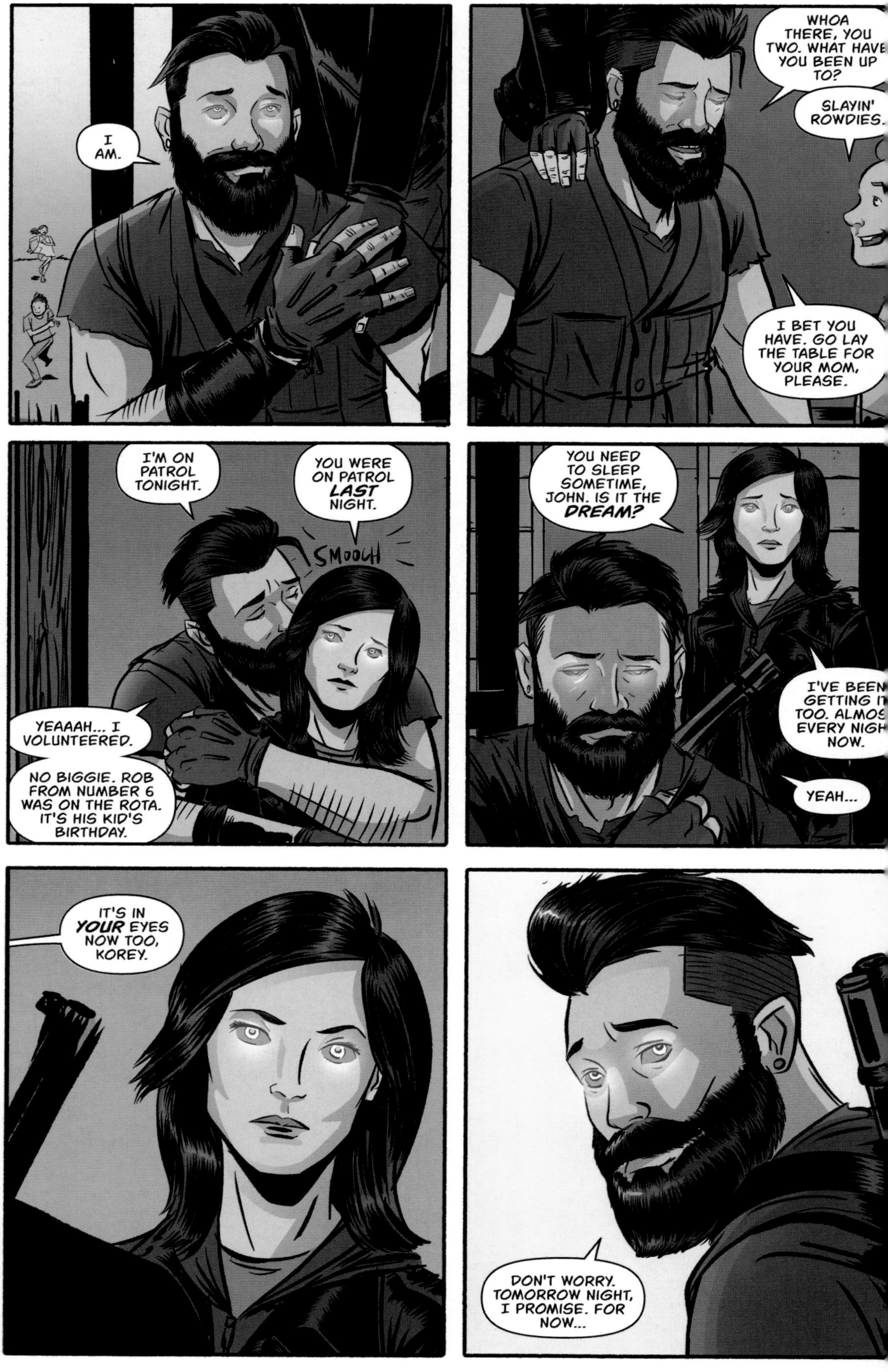
I AM.
WHOA THERE, YOU TWO. WHAT HAVE YOU BEEN UP TO?
SLAYIN' ROWDIES.
I BET YOU HAVE. GO LAY THE TABLE FOR YOUR MOM, PLEASE.
I'M ON PATROL TONIGHT.
YOU WERE ON PATROL LAST NIGHT.
SMOOCH
YEAAAH... I VOLUNTEERED.
NO BIGGIE. ROB FROM NUMBER 6 WAS ON THE ROTA. IT'S HIS KID'S BIRTHDAY.
YOU NEED TO SLEEP SOMETIME, JOHN. IS IT THE DREAM?
I'VE BEEN GETTING IT TOO. ALMOST EVERY NIGHT NOW.
YEAH...
IT'S IN YOUR EYES NOW TOO, KOREY.
DON'T WORRY. TOMORROW NIGHT, I PROMISE. FOR NOW...

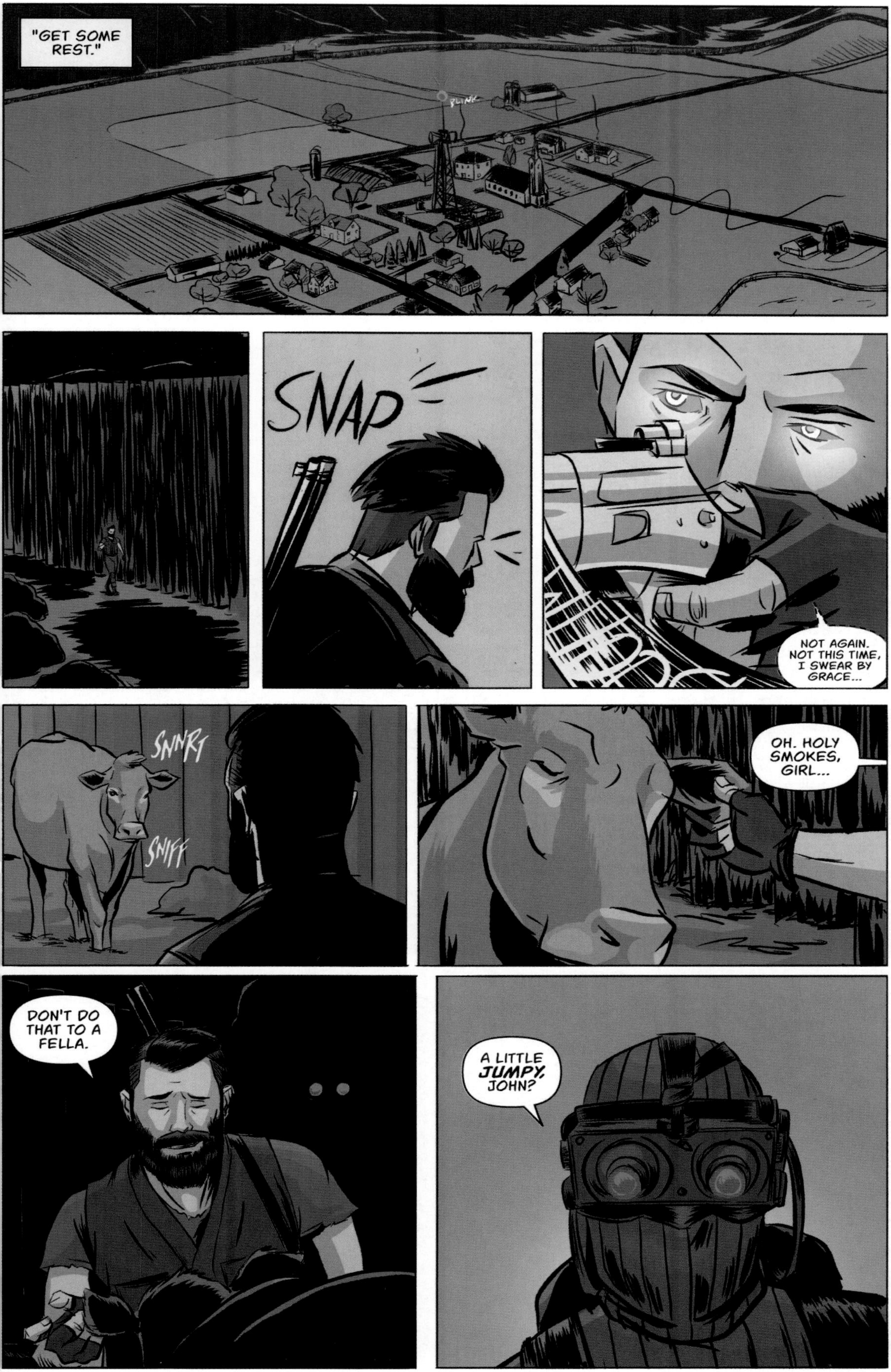
"GET SOME REST."
BLINK
SNAP
NOT AGAIN. NOT THIS TIME, I SWEAR BY GRACE...
SNNRT
SNIFF
OH. HOLY SMOKES, GIRL...
DON'T DO THAT TO A FELLA.
A LITTLE JUMPY, JOHN?

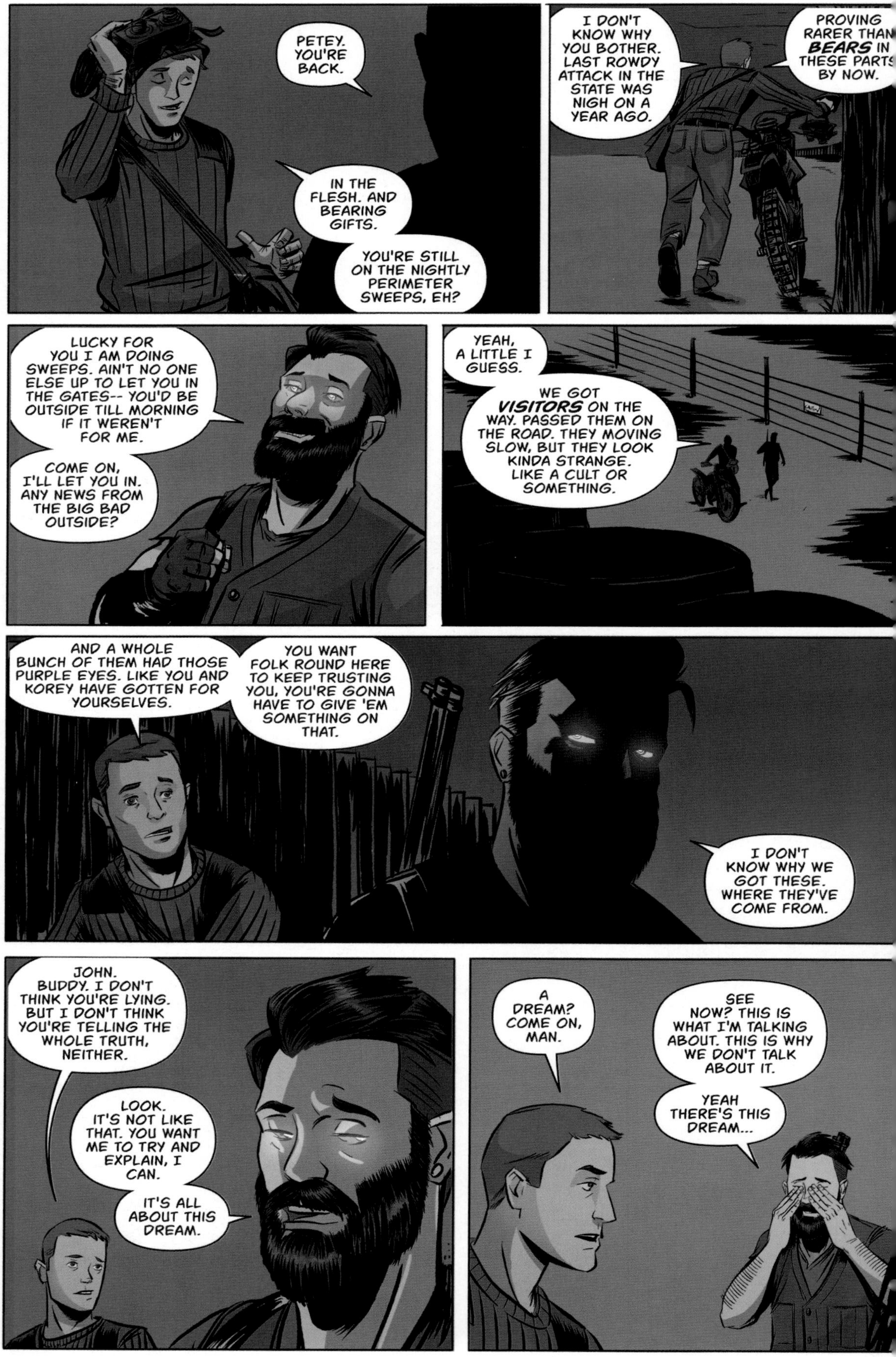
PETEY. YOU'RE BACK.
IN THE FLESH. AND BEARING GIFTS.
YOU'RE STILL ON THE NIGHTLY PERIMETER SWEEPS, EH?
I DON'T KNOW WHY YOU BOTHER. LAST ROWDY ATTACK IN THE STATE WAS NIGH ON A YEAR AGO.
PROVING RARER THAN BEARS IN THESE PARTS BY NOW.
LUCKY FOR YOU I AM DOING SWEEPS. AIN'T NO ONE ELSE UP TO LET YOU IN THE GATES-- YOU'D BE OUTSIDE TILL MORNING IF IT WEREN'T FOR ME.
COME ON, I'LL LET YOU IN. ANY NEWS FROM THE BIG BAD OUTSIDE?
YEAH, A LITTLE I GUESS.
WE GOT VISITORS ON THE WAY. PASSED THEM ON THE ROAD. THEY MOVING SLOW, BUT THEY LOOK KINDA STRANGE. LIKE A CULT OR SOMETHING.
AND A WHOLE BUNCH OF THEM HAD THOSE PURPLE EYES. LIKE YOU AND KOREY HAVE GOTTEN FOR YOURSELVES.
YOU WANT FOLK ROUND HERE TO KEEP TRUSTING YOU, YOU'RE GONNA HAVE TO GIVE 'EM SOMETHING ON THAT.
I DON'T KNOW WHY WE GOT THESE. WHERE THEY'VE COME FROM.
JOHN. BUDDY. I DON'T THINK YOU'RE LYING. BUT I DON'T THINK YOU'RE TELLING THE WHOLE TRUTH, NEITHER.
LOOK. IT'S NOT LIKE THAT. YOU WANT ME TO TRY AND EXPLAIN, I CAN.
IT'S ALL ABOUT THIS DREAM.
A DREAM? COME ON, MAN.
SEE NOW? THIS IS WHAT I'M TALKING ABOUT. THIS IS WHY WE DON'T TALK ABOUT IT.
YEAH THERE'S THIS DREAM...

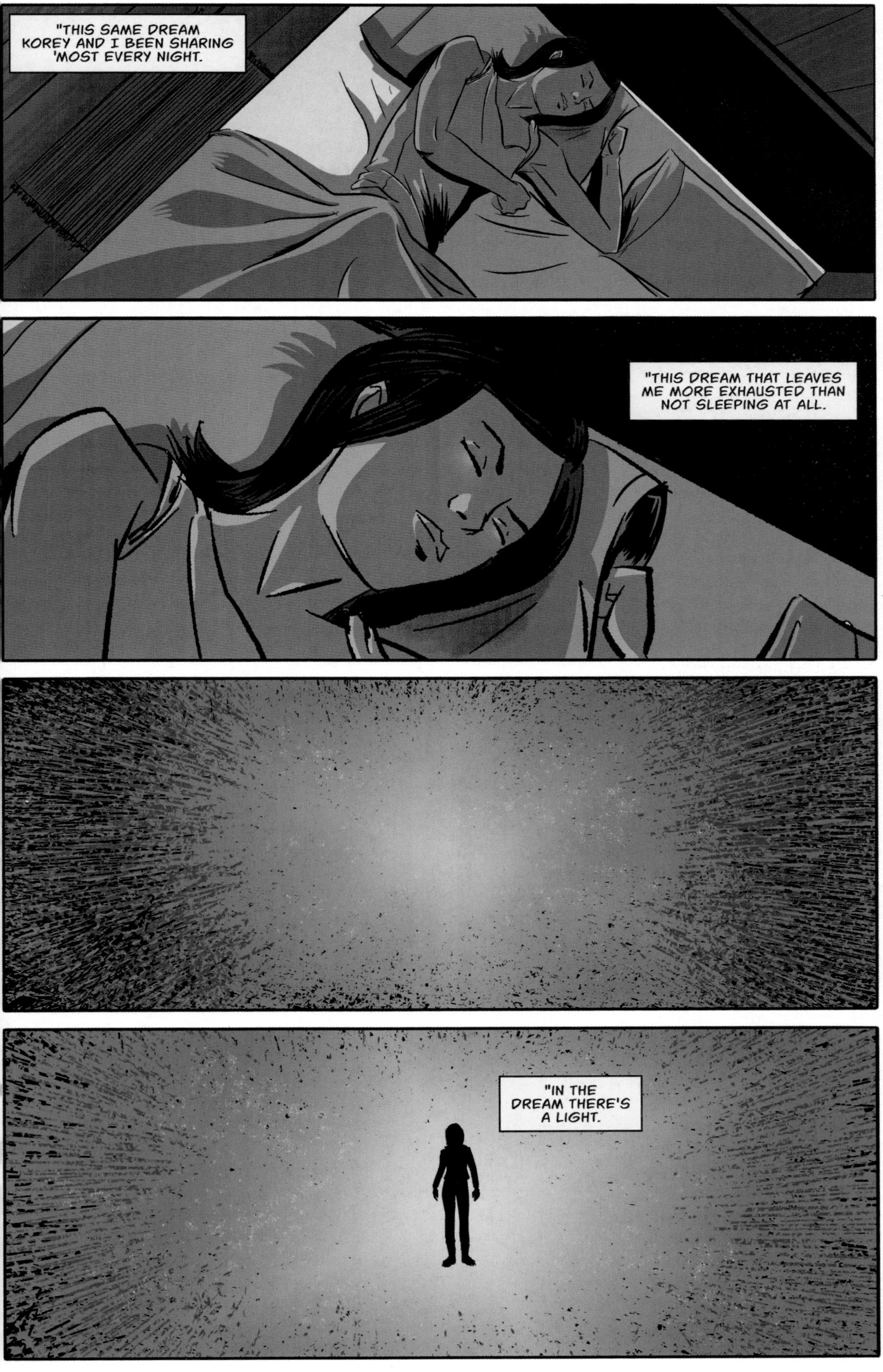
"THIS SAME DREAM KOREY AND I BEEN SHARING 'MOST EVERY NIGHT.
"THIS DREAM THAT LEAVES ME MORE EXHAUSTED THAN NOT SLEEPING AT ALL.
"IN THE DREAM THERE'S A LIGHT.

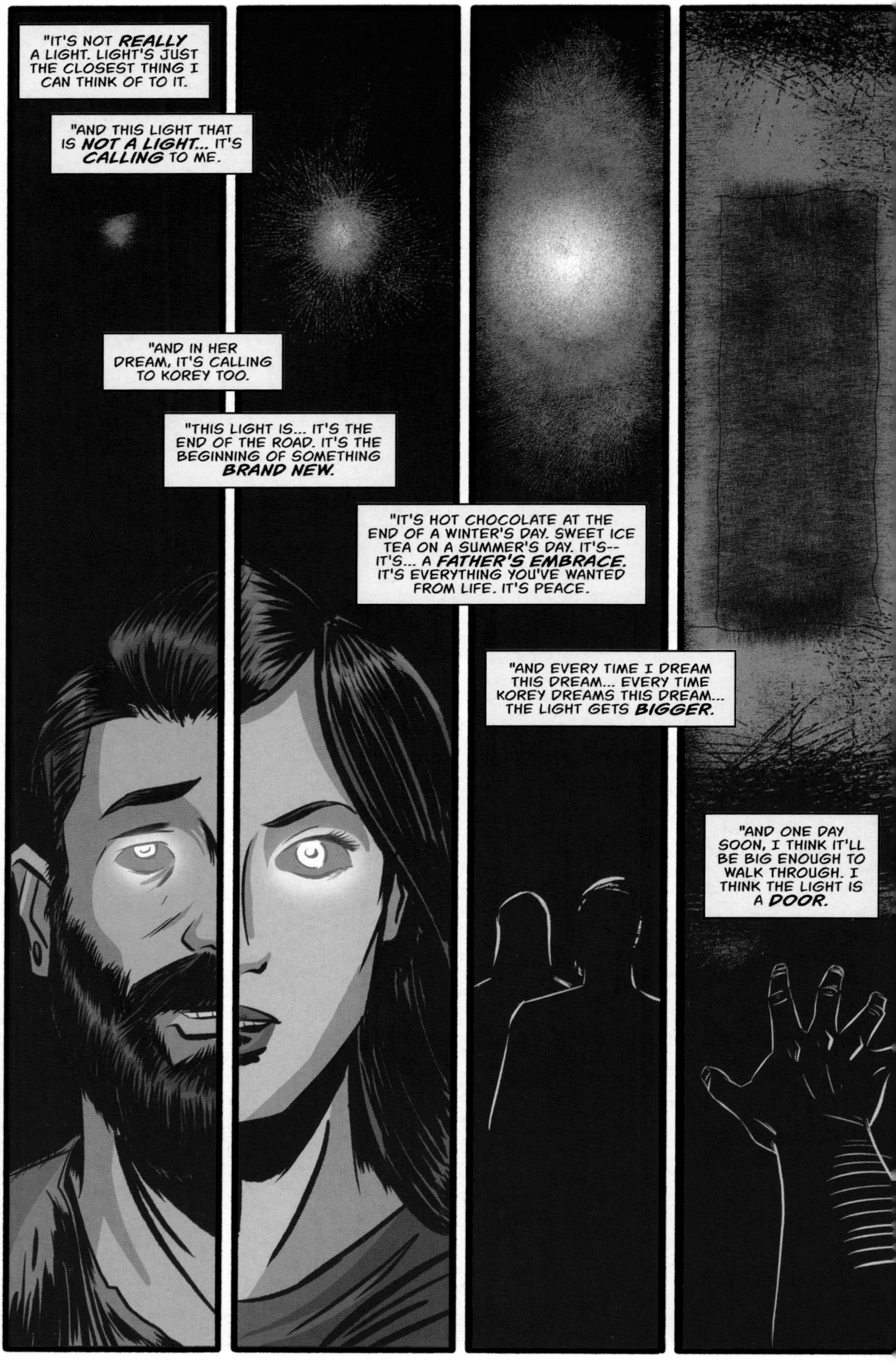
"IT'S NOT REALLY A LIGHT. LIGHT'S JUST THE CLOSEST THING I CAN THINK OF TO IT.
"AND THIS LIGHT THAT IS NOT A LIGHT... IT'S CALLING TO ME.
"AND IN HER DREAM, IT'S CALLING TO KOREY TOO.
"THIS LIGHT IS... IT'S THE END OF THE ROAD. IT'S THE BEGINNING OF SOMETHING BRAND NEW.
"IT'S HOT CHOCOLATE AT THE END OF A WINTER'S DAY. SWEET ICE TEA ON A SUMMER'S DAY. IT'S-- IT'S... A FATHER'S EMBRACE. IT'S EVERYTHING YOU'VE WANTED FROM LIFE. IT'S PEACE.
"AND EVERY TIME I DREAM THIS DREAM... EVERY TIME KOREY DREAMS THIS DREAM... THE LIGHT GETS BIGGER.
"AND ONE DAY SOON, I THINK IT'LL BE BIG ENOUGH TO WALK THROUGH. I THINK THE LIGHT IS A DOOR.

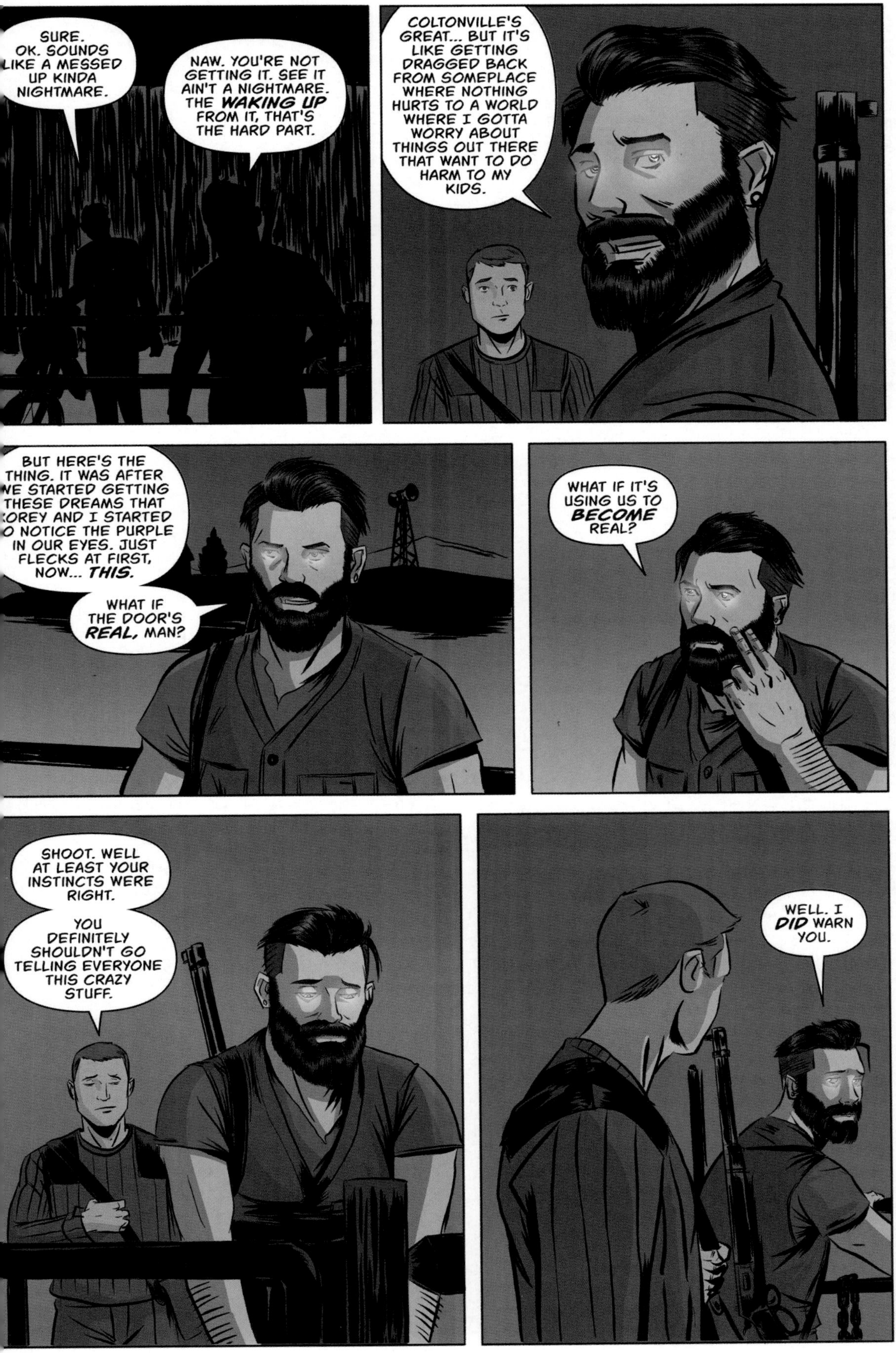
SURE. OK. SOUNDS LIKE A MESSED UP KINDA NIGHTMARE.
NAW. YOU'RE NOT GETTING IT. SEE IT AIN'T A NIGHTMARE. THE *WAKING UP* FROM IT, THAT'S THE HARD PART.
COLTONVILLE'S GREAT... BUT IT'S LIKE GETTING DRAGGED BACK FROM SOMEPLACE WHERE NOTHING HURTS TO A WORLD WHERE I GOTTA WORRY ABOUT THINGS OUT THERE THAT WANT TO DO HARM TO MY KIDS.
BUT HERE'S THE THING. IT WAS AFTER WE STARTED GETTING THESE DREAMS THAT COREY AND I STARTED TO NOTICE THE PURPLE IN OUR EYES. JUST FLECKS AT FIRST, NOW... *THIS.*
WHAT IF THE DOOR'S *REAL,* MAN?
WHAT IF IT'S USING US TO *BECOME* REAL?
SHOOT. WELL AT LEAST YOUR INSTINCTS WERE RIGHT.
YOU DEFINITELY SHOULDN'T GO TELLING EVERYONE THIS CRAZY STUFF.
WELL. I *DID* WARN YOU.

MAYBE THESE FOLKS YOU SAY ARE ON THEIR WAY KNOW MORE ABOUT IT.

EVEN IF THEY DO, I SAY WE SET 'EM ON THEIR WAY.

THAT AIN'T THE WAY WE DO THINGS. THEY'LL BE TIRED FROM THE ROAD. PROBABLY HUNGRY.

NORMALLY I'D AGREE. BUT I ONLY SAW THEM FROM AFAR, BUT I STILL GOT THIS REAL BAD FEELING.

I THINK THIS LOT COULD BE MORE DANGEROUS THAN ANY--

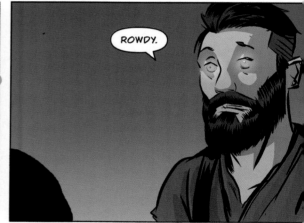

ROWDY.

RIGHT.

WHIP

NO, PETE...

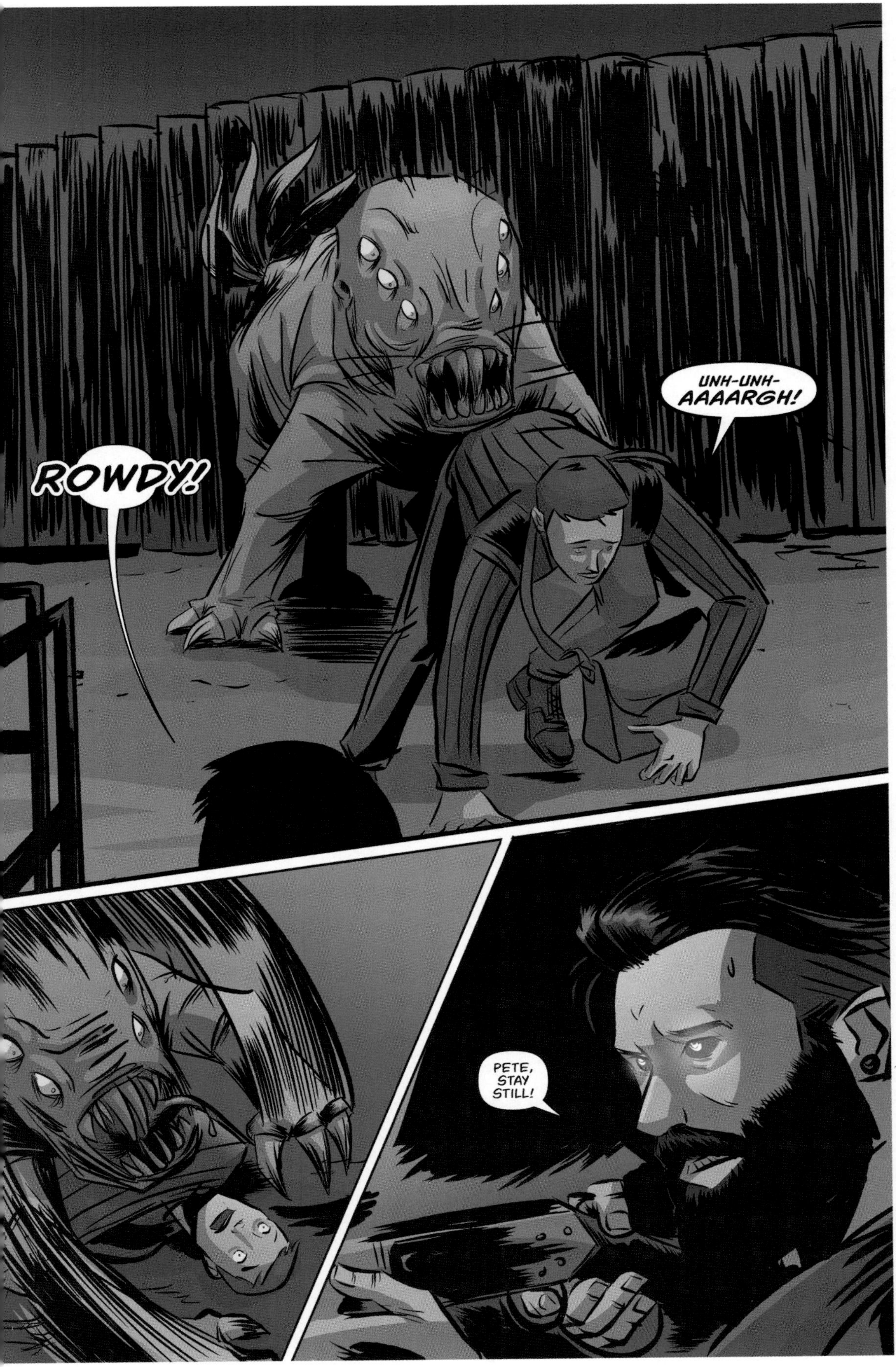
UNH-UNH-
AAAARGH!
ROWDY!
PETE,
STAY
STILL!

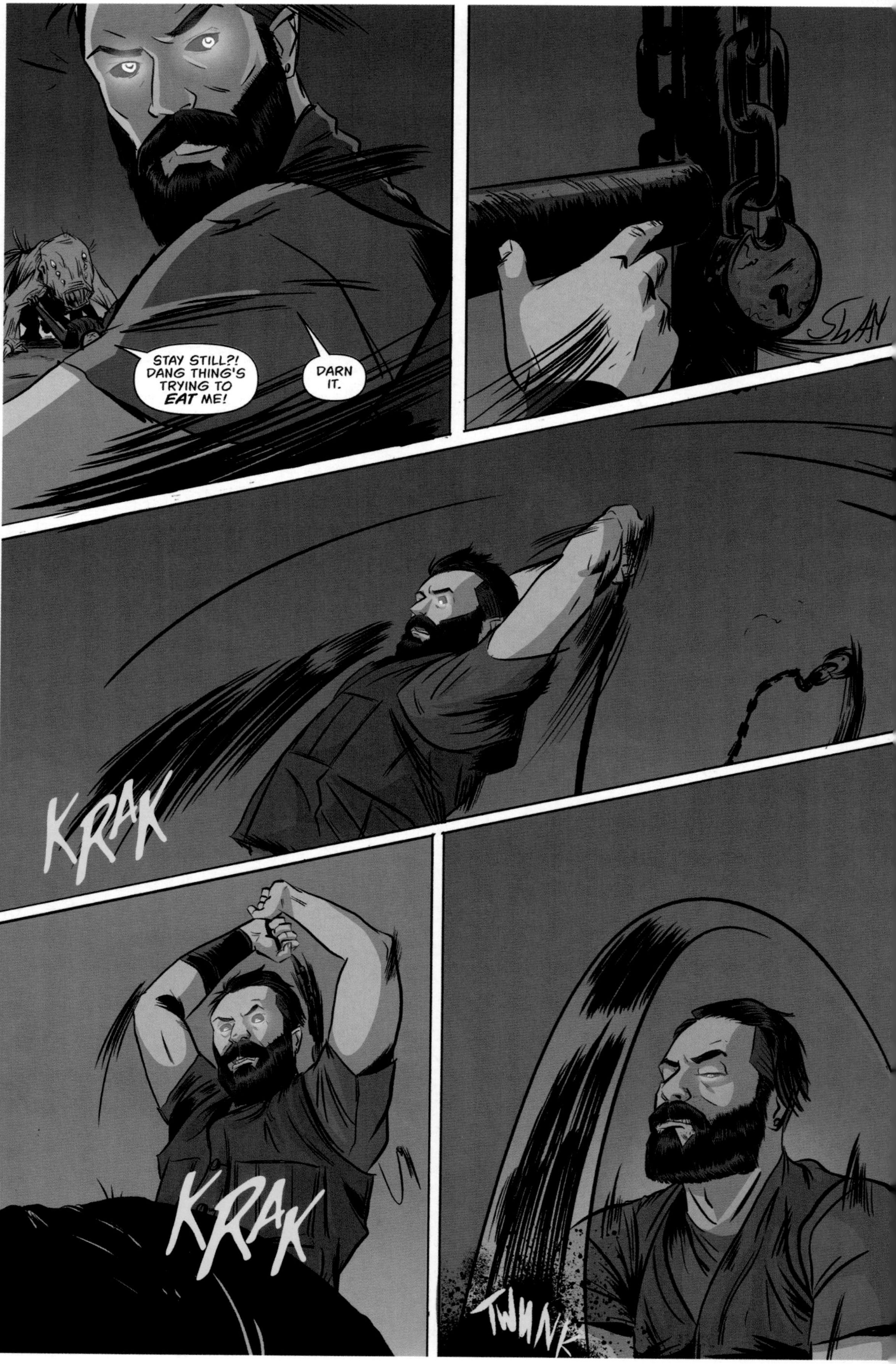
STAY STILL?! DANG THING'S TRYING TO EAT ME!
DARN IT.
SWAY
KRAK
KRAK
TWUNK

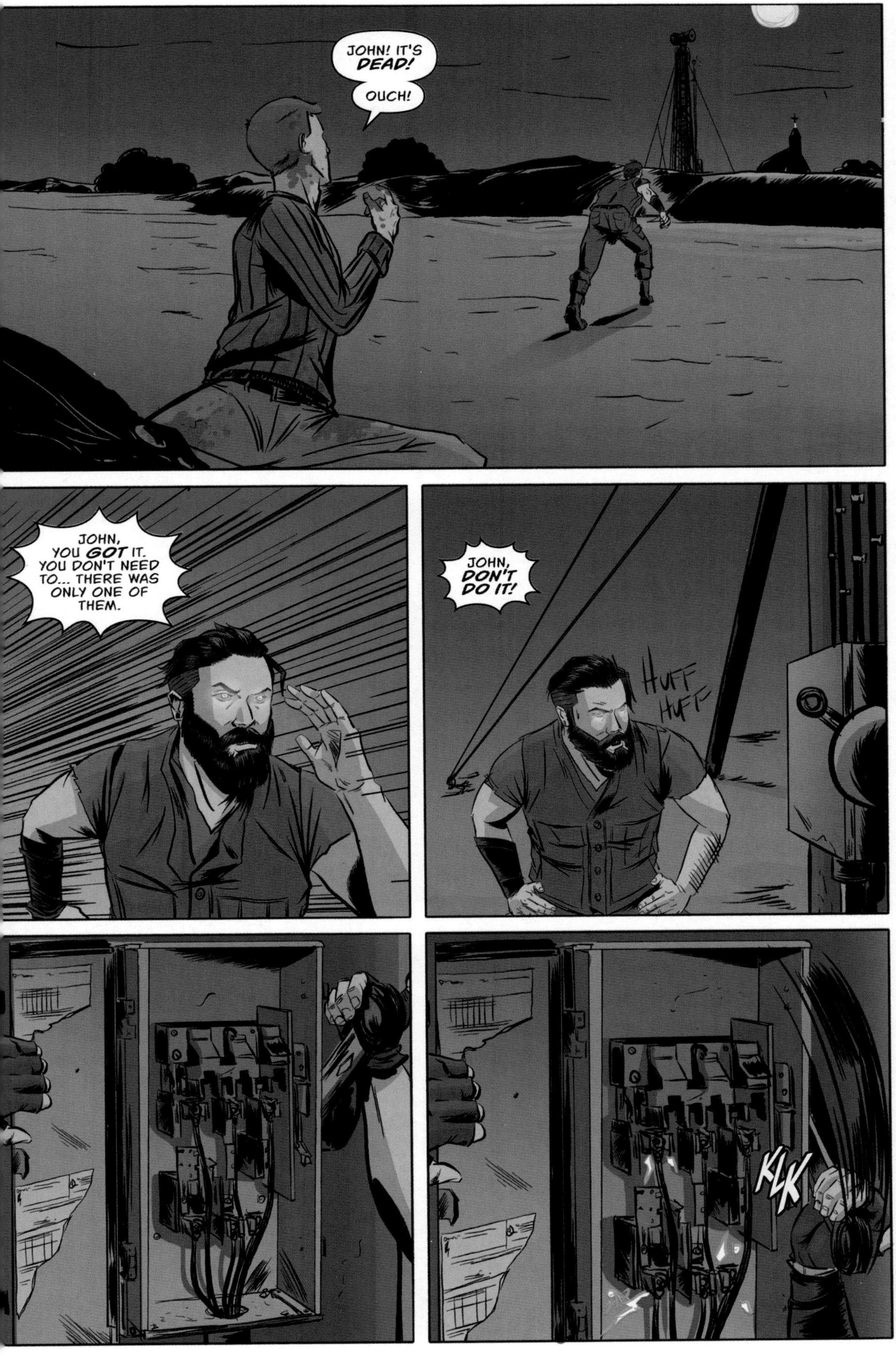

JOHN! IT'S DEAD!
OUCH!
JOHN, YOU GOT IT. YOU DON'T NEED TO... THERE WAS ONLY ONE OF THEM.
JOHN, DON'T DO IT!
HUFF HUFF
KLK

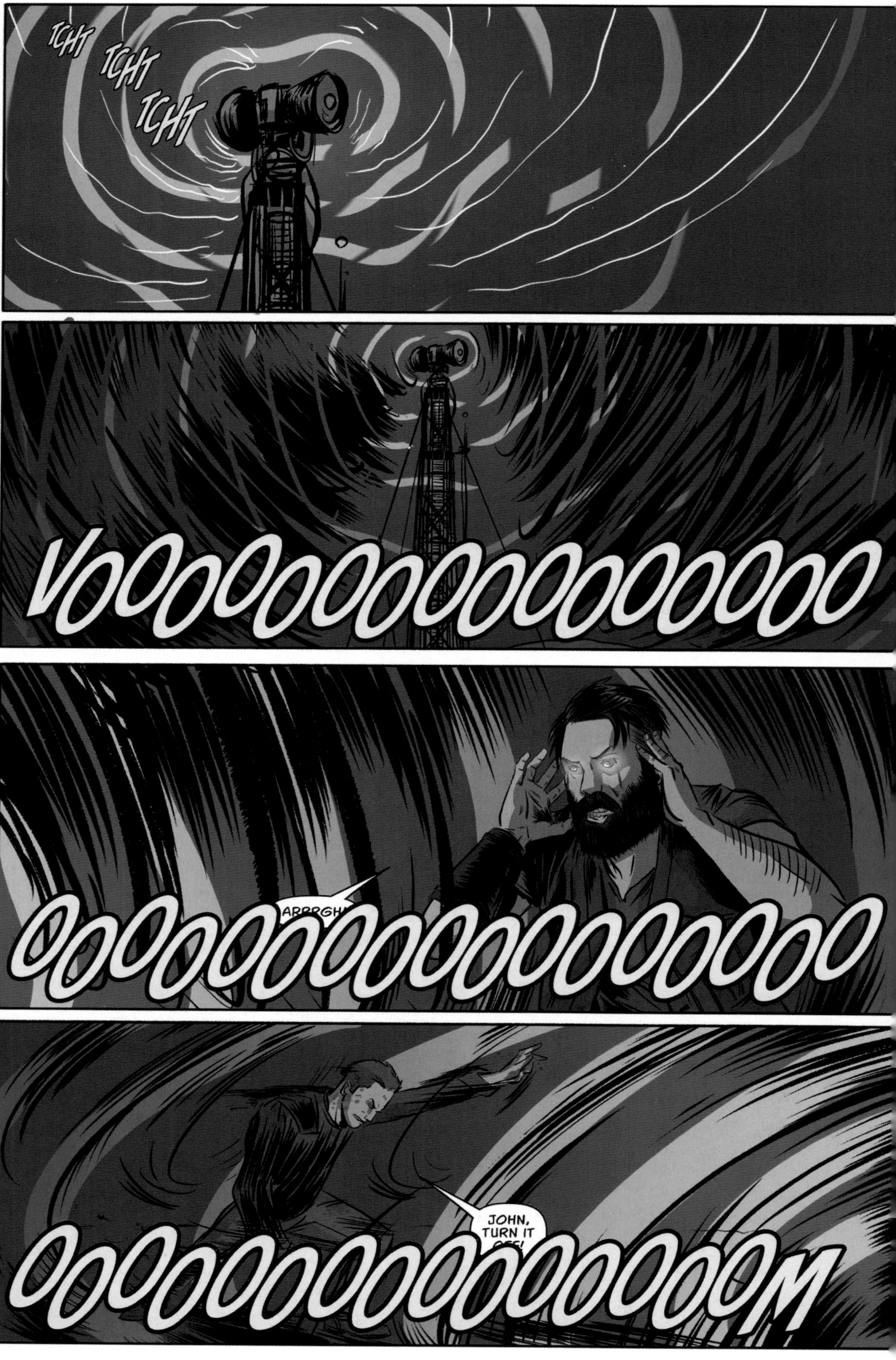
TCHT
TCHT
TCHT
VOOOOOOOOOOOOOOOOO
OOOOOOOOOOOOOOOOOO
ARRRGH
OOOOOOOOOOOOOOOOOM
JOHN, TURN IT

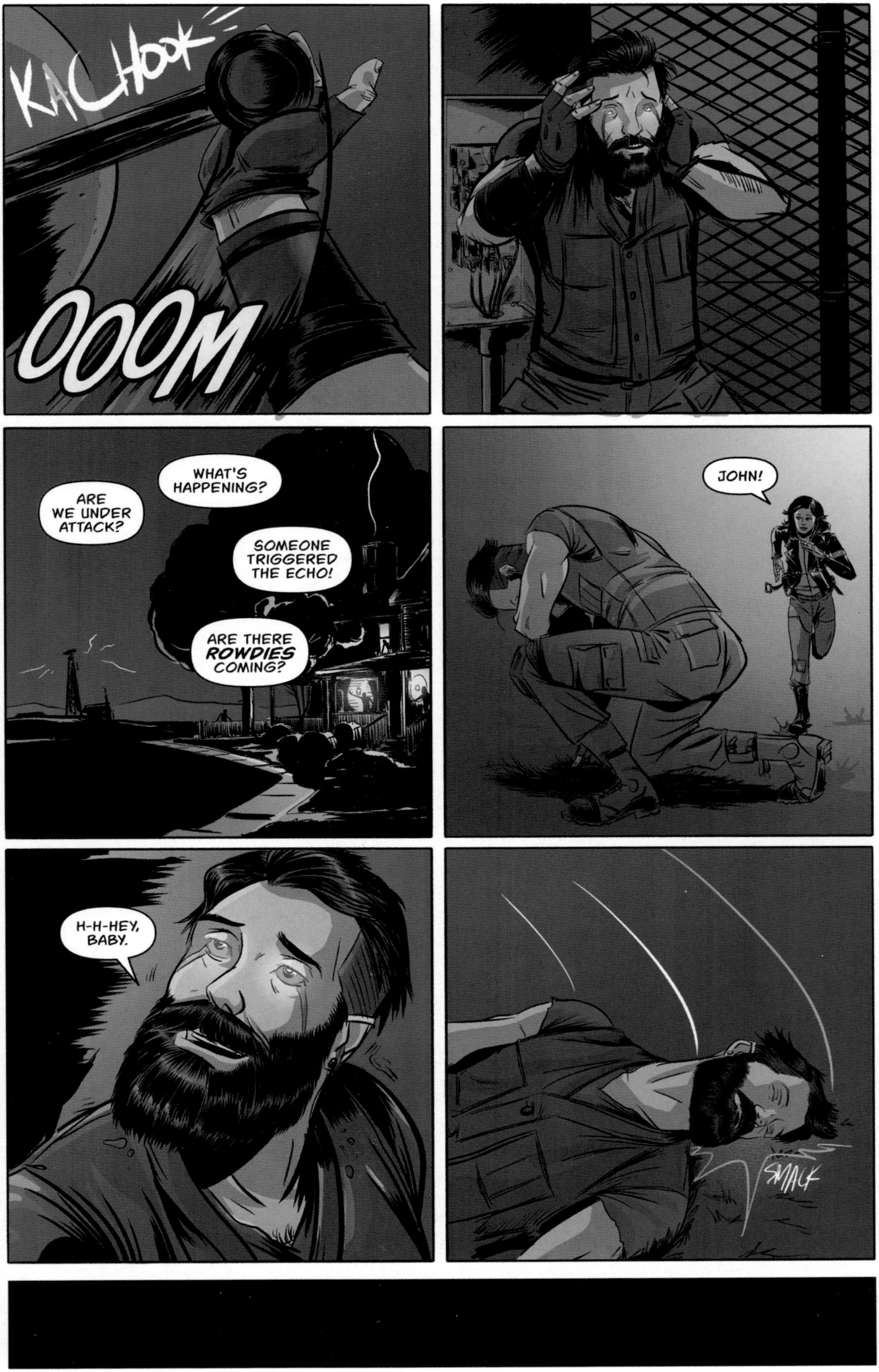
KACHOOK
OOOM
ARE WE UNDER ATTACK?
WHAT'S HAPPENING?
SOMEONE TRIGGERED THE ECHO!
ARE THERE *ROWDIES* COMING?
JOHN!
H-H-HEY, BABY.
SMACK

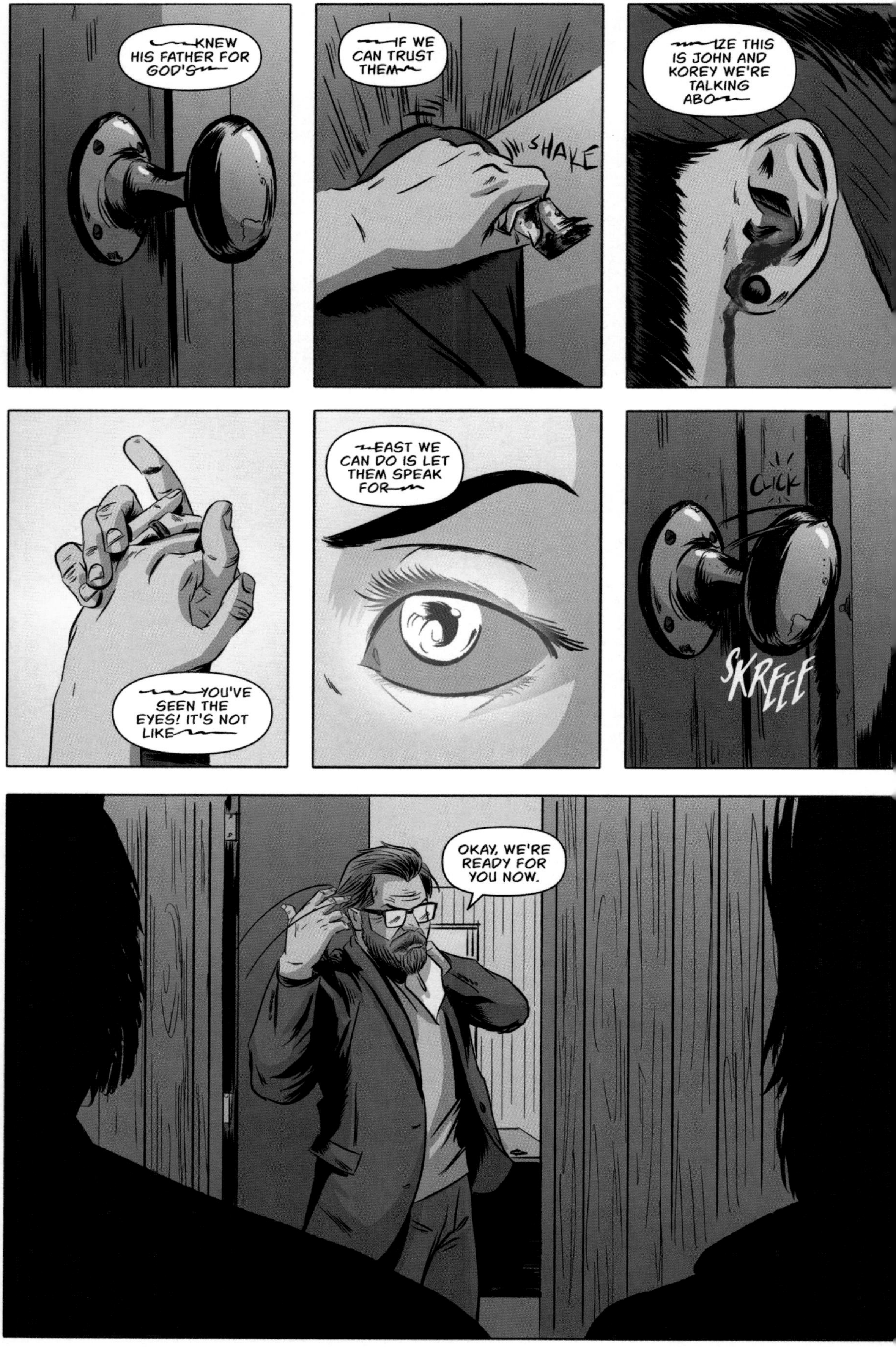
KNEW HIS FATHER FOR GOD'S
IF WE CAN TRUST THEM
SHAKE
IZE THIS IS JOHN AND KOREY WE'RE TALKING ABO
YOU'VE SEEN THE EYES! IT'S NOT LIKE
EAST WE CAN DO IS LET THEM SPEAK FOR
CLICK
SKREEE
OKAY, WE'RE READY FOR YOU NOW.

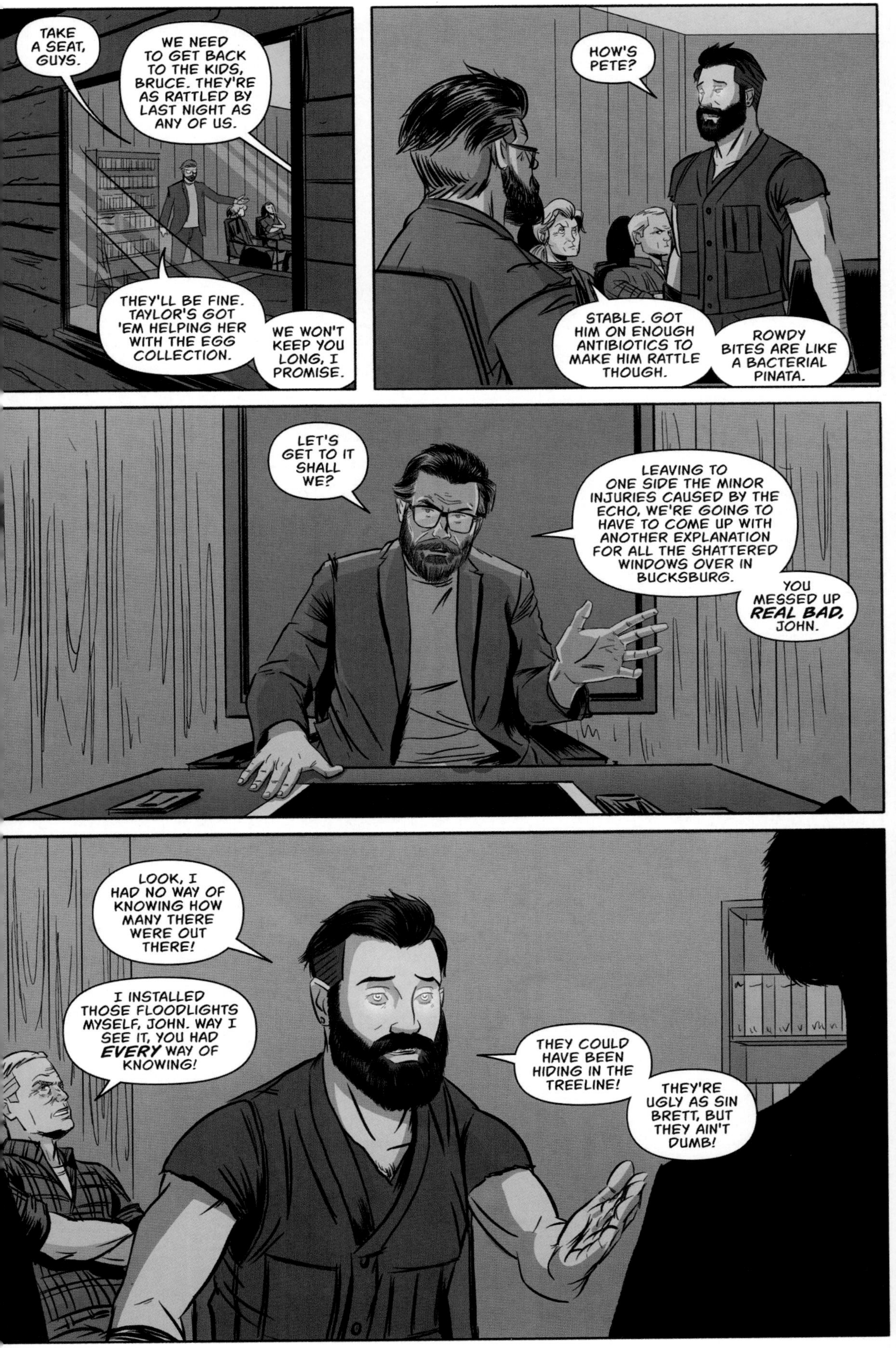
TAKE A SEAT, GUYS.
WE NEED TO GET BACK TO THE KIDS, BRUCE. THEY'RE AS RATTLED BY LAST NIGHT AS ANY OF US.
THEY'LL BE FINE. TAYLOR'S GOT 'EM HELPING HER WITH THE EGG COLLECTION.
WE WON'T KEEP YOU LONG, I PROMISE.
HOW'S PETE?
STABLE. GOT HIM ON ENOUGH ANTIBIOTICS TO MAKE HIM RATTLE THOUGH.
ROWDY BITES ARE LIKE A BACTERIAL PINATA.
LET'S GET TO IT SHALL WE?
LEAVING TO ONE SIDE THE MINOR INJURIES CAUSED BY THE ECHO, WE'RE GOING TO HAVE TO COME UP WITH ANOTHER EXPLANATION FOR ALL THE SHATTERED WINDOWS OVER IN BUCKSBURG.
YOU MESSED UP **REAL BAD,** JOHN.
LOOK, I HAD NO WAY OF KNOWING HOW MANY THERE WERE OUT THERE!
I INSTALLED THOSE FLOODLIGHTS MYSELF, JOHN. WAY I SEE IT, YOU HAD **EVERY** WAY OF KNOWING!
THEY COULD HAVE BEEN HIDING IN THE TREELINE!
THEY'RE UGLY AS SIN BRETT, BUT THEY AIN'T DUMB!

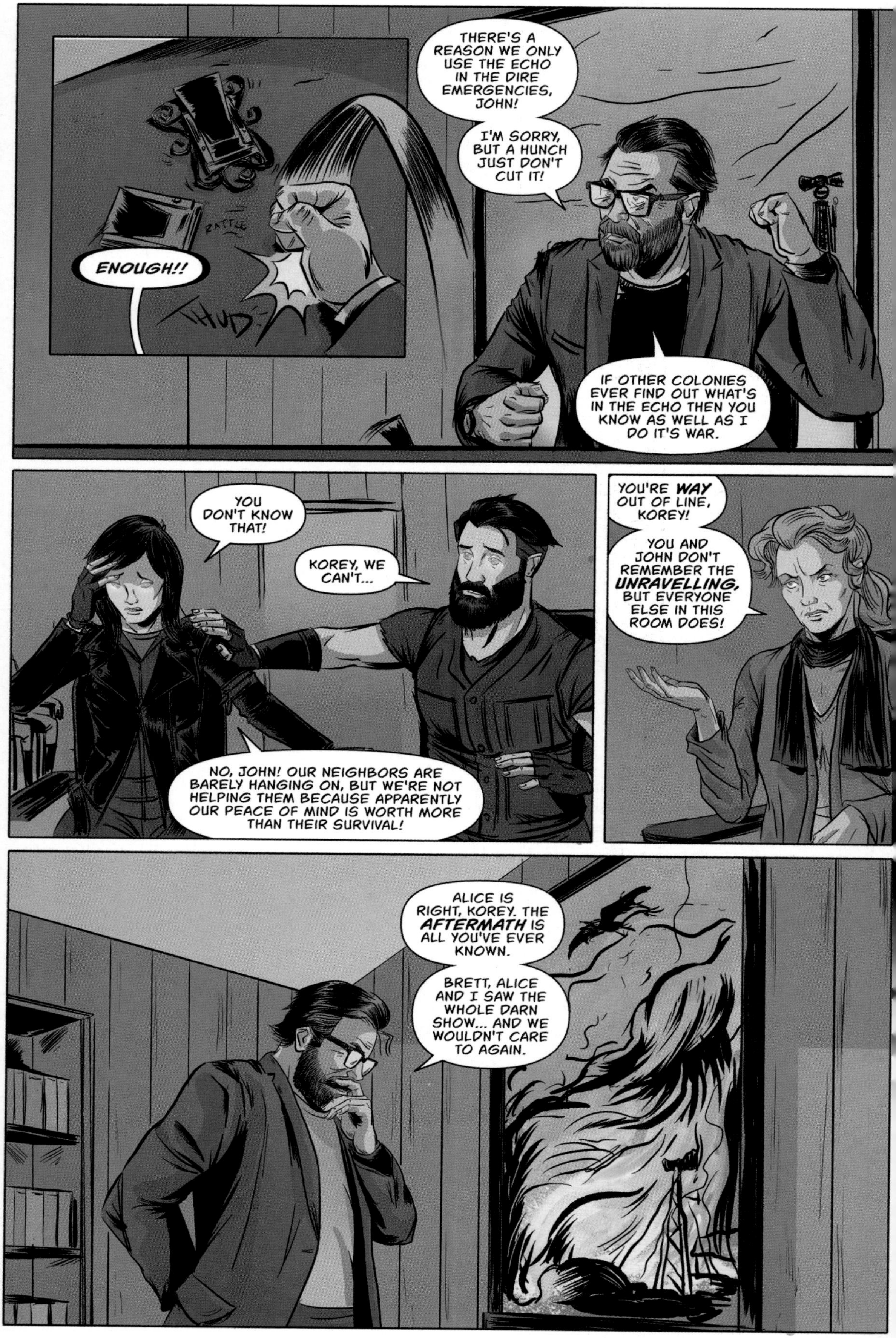

THERE'S A REASON WE ONLY USE THE ECHO IN THE DIRE EMERGENCIES, JOHN!
I'M SORRY, BUT A HUNCH JUST DON'T CUT IT!
RATTLE
ENOUGH!!
THUD
IF OTHER COLONIES EVER FIND OUT WHAT'S IN THE ECHO THEN YOU KNOW AS WELL AS I DO IT'S WAR.
YOU DON'T KNOW THAT!
KOREY, WE CAN'T...
NO, JOHN! OUR NEIGHBORS ARE BARELY HANGING ON, BUT WE'RE NOT HELPING THEM BECAUSE APPARENTLY OUR PEACE OF MIND IS WORTH MORE THAN THEIR SURVIVAL!
YOU'RE WAY OUT OF LINE, KOREY!
YOU AND JOHN DON'T REMEMBER THE UNRAVELLING, BUT EVERYONE ELSE IN THIS ROOM DOES!
ALICE IS RIGHT, KOREY. THE AFTERMATH IS ALL YOU'VE EVER KNOWN.
BRETT, ALICE AND I SAW THE WHOLE DARN SHOW... AND WE WOULDN'T CARE TO AGAIN.

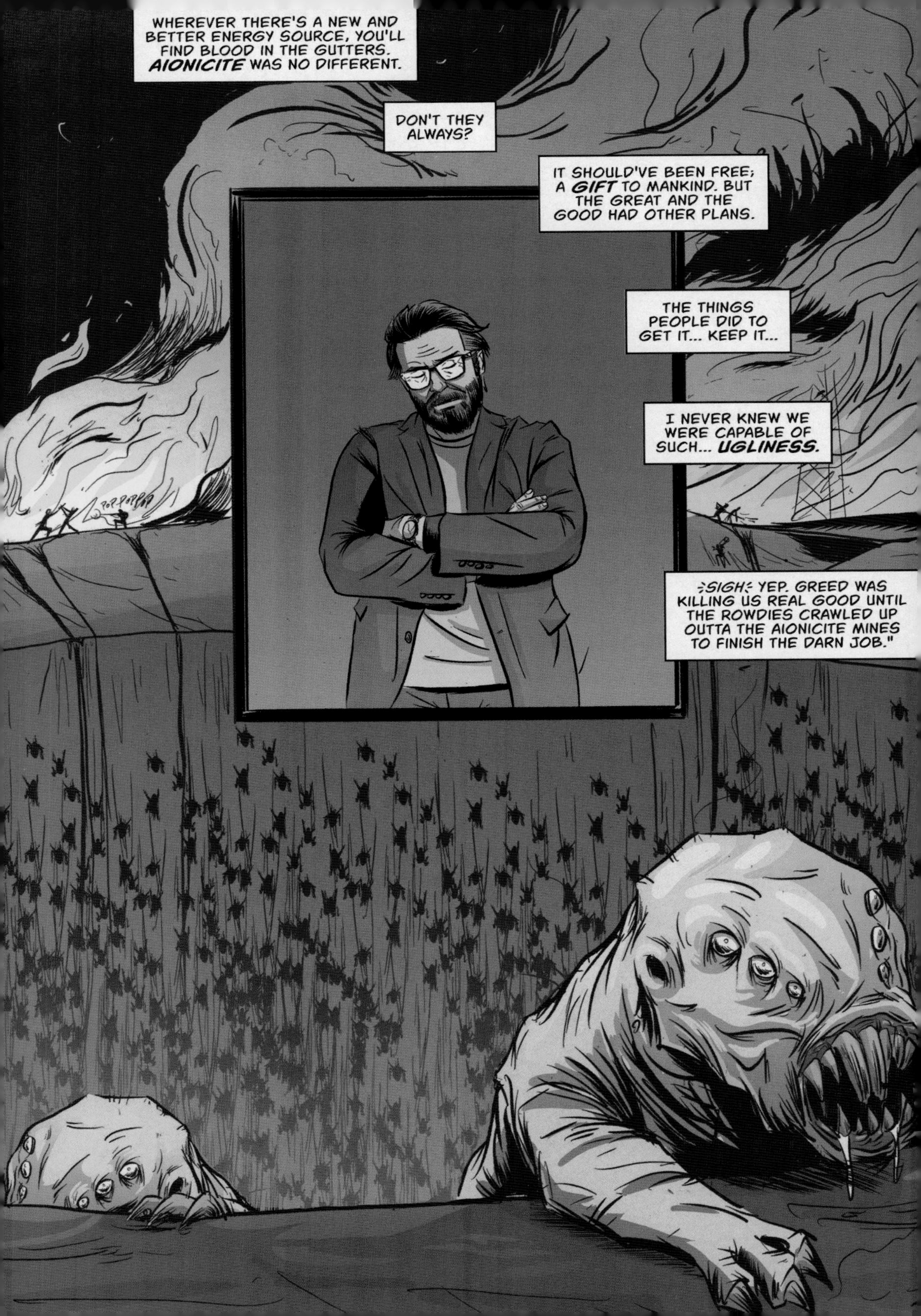
WHEREVER THERE'S A NEW AND BETTER ENERGY SOURCE, YOU'LL FIND BLOOD IN THE GUTTERS. AIONICITE WAS NO DIFFERENT.
DON'T THEY ALWAYS?
IT SHOULD'VE BEEN FREE; A GIFT TO MANKIND. BUT THE GREAT AND THE GOOD HAD OTHER PLANS.
THE THINGS PEOPLE DID TO GET IT... KEEP IT...
I NEVER KNEW WE WERE CAPABLE OF SUCH... UGLINESS.
SIGH YEP. GREED WAS KILLING US REAL GOOD UNTIL THE ROWDIES CRAWLED UP OUTTA THE AIONICITE MINES TO FINISH THE DARN JOB."

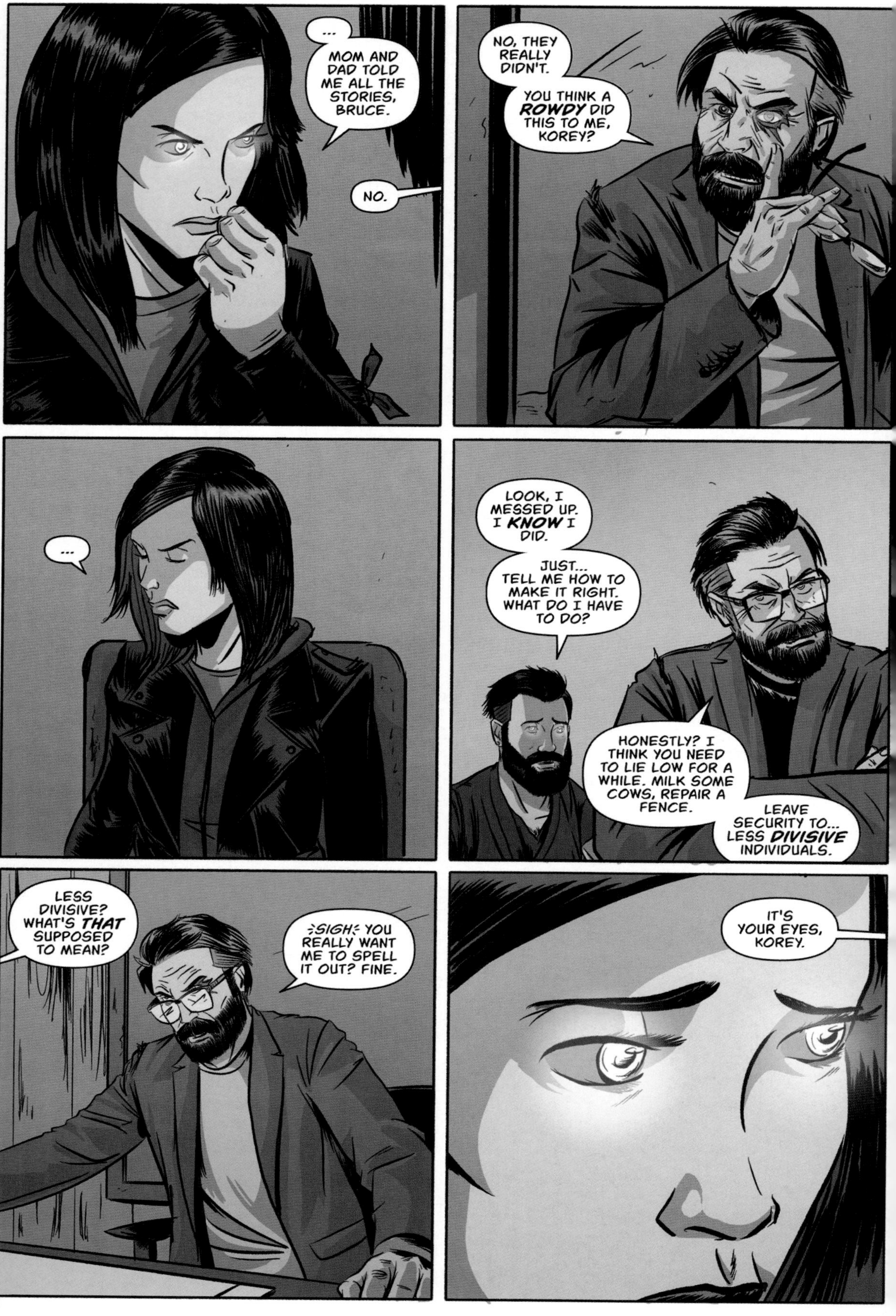
...
MOM AND DAD TOLD ME ALL THE STORIES, BRUCE.
NO.
NO, THEY REALLY DIDN'T.
YOU THINK A ROWDY DID THIS TO ME, KOREY?
...
LOOK, I MESSED UP. I KNOW I DID.
JUST... TELL ME HOW TO MAKE IT RIGHT. WHAT DO I HAVE TO DO?
HONESTLY? I THINK YOU NEED TO LIE LOW FOR A WHILE. MILK SOME COWS, REPAIR A FENCE.
LEAVE SECURITY TO... LESS DIVISIVE INDIVIDUALS.
LESS DIVISIVE? WHAT'S THAT SUPPOSED TO MEAN?
SIGH YOU REALLY WANT ME TO SPELL IT OUT? FINE.
IT'S YOUR EYES, KOREY.

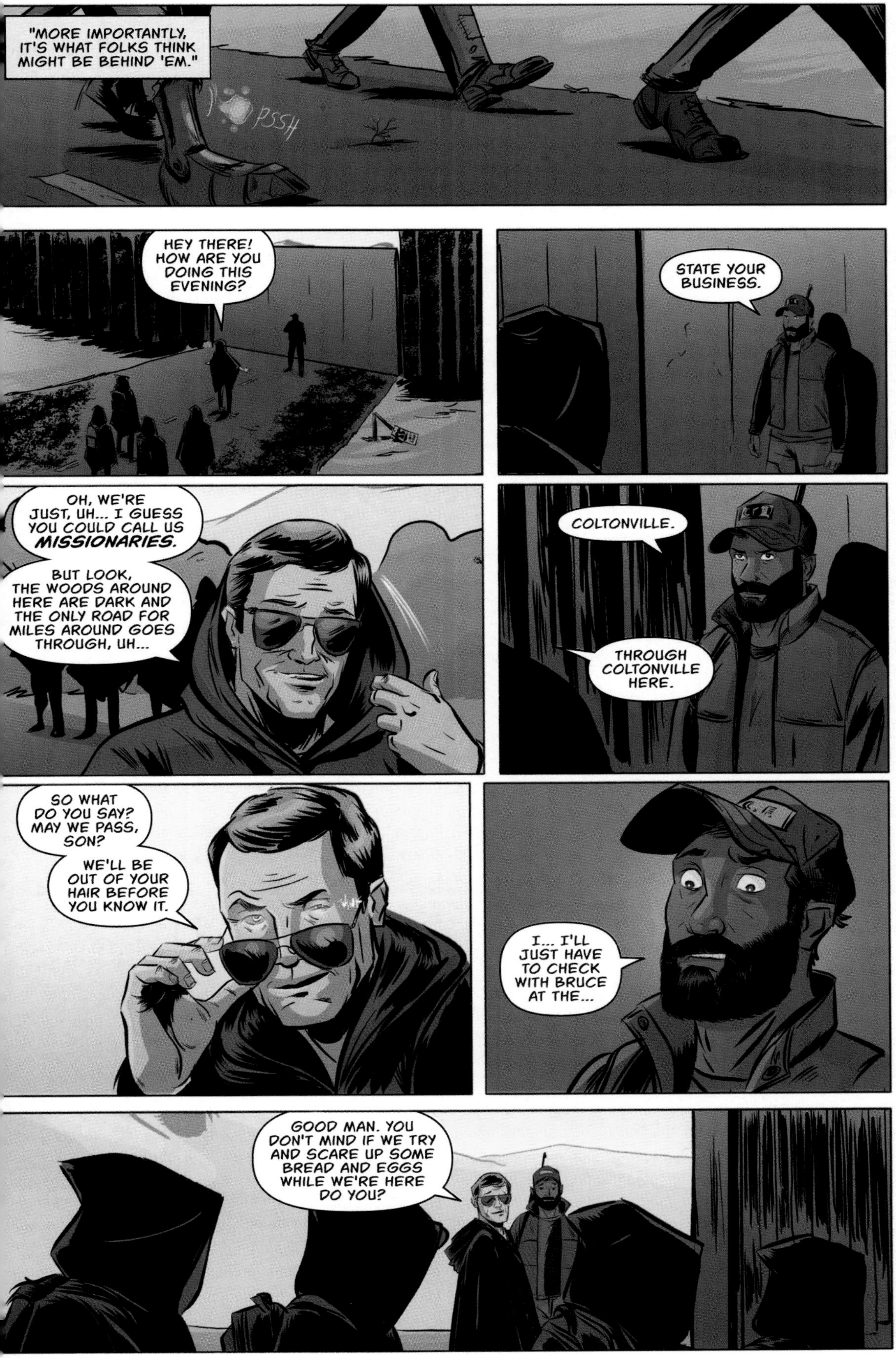
"MORE IMPORTANTLY, IT'S WHAT FOLKS THINK MIGHT BE BEHIND 'EM."
PSSH
HEY THERE! HOW ARE YOU DOING THIS EVENING?
STATE YOUR BUSINESS.
OH, WE'RE JUST, UH... I GUESS YOU COULD CALL US **MISSIONARIES**.
BUT LOOK, THE WOODS AROUND HERE ARE DARK AND THE ONLY ROAD FOR MILES AROUND GOES THROUGH, UH...
COLTONVILLE.
THROUGH COLTONVILLE HERE.
SO WHAT DO YOU SAY? MAY WE PASS, SON?
WE'LL BE OUT OF YOUR HAIR BEFORE YOU KNOW IT.
I... I'LL JUST HAVE TO CHECK WITH BRUCE AT THE...
GOOD MAN. YOU DON'T MIND IF WE TRY AND SCARE UP SOME BREAD AND EGGS WHILE WE'RE HERE DO YOU?

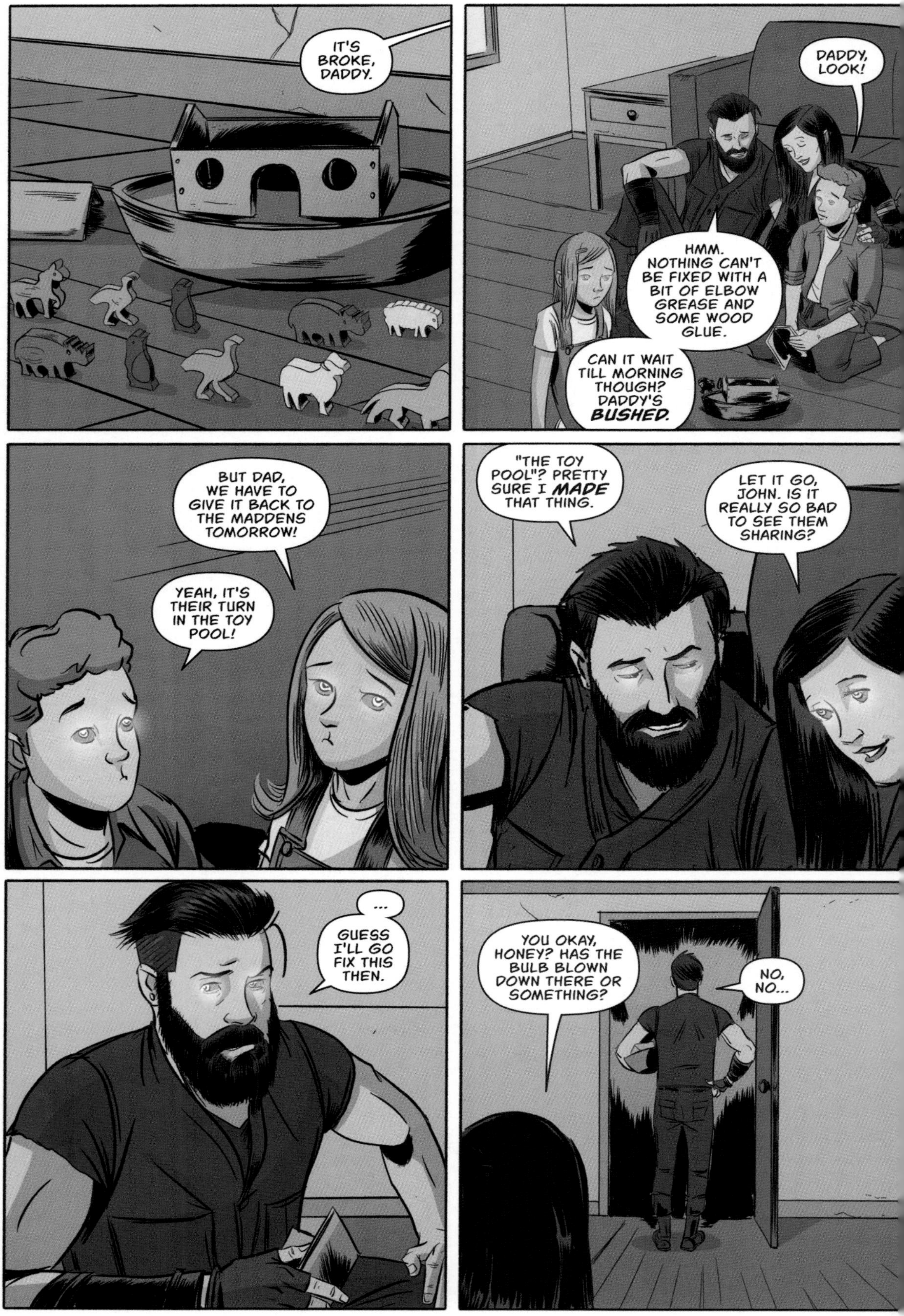
IT'S BROKE, DADDY.
DADDY, LOOK!
HMM. NOTHING CAN'T BE FIXED WITH A BIT OF ELBOW GREASE AND SOME WOOD GLUE.
CAN IT WAIT TILL MORNING THOUGH? DADDY'S *BUSHED.*
BUT DAD, WE HAVE TO GIVE IT BACK TO THE MADDENS TOMORROW!
YEAH, IT'S THEIR TURN IN THE TOY POOL!
"THE TOY POOL"? PRETTY SURE I *MADE* THAT THING.
LET IT GO, JOHN. IS IT REALLY SO BAD TO SEE THEM SHARING?
...
GUESS I'LL GO FIX THIS THEN.
YOU OKAY, HONEY? HAS THE BULB BLOWN DOWN THERE OR SOMETHING?
NO, NO...

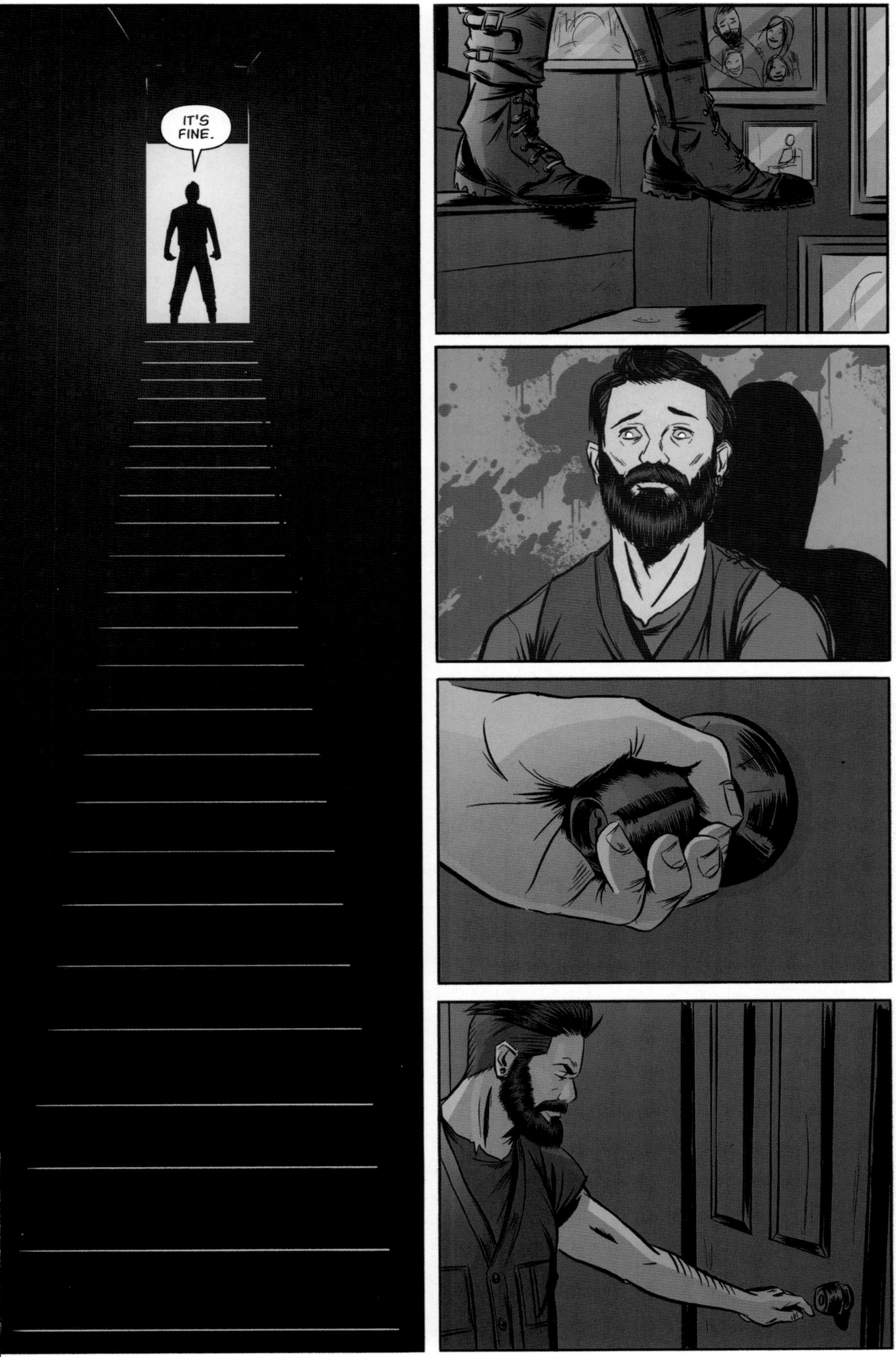
IT'S FINE.

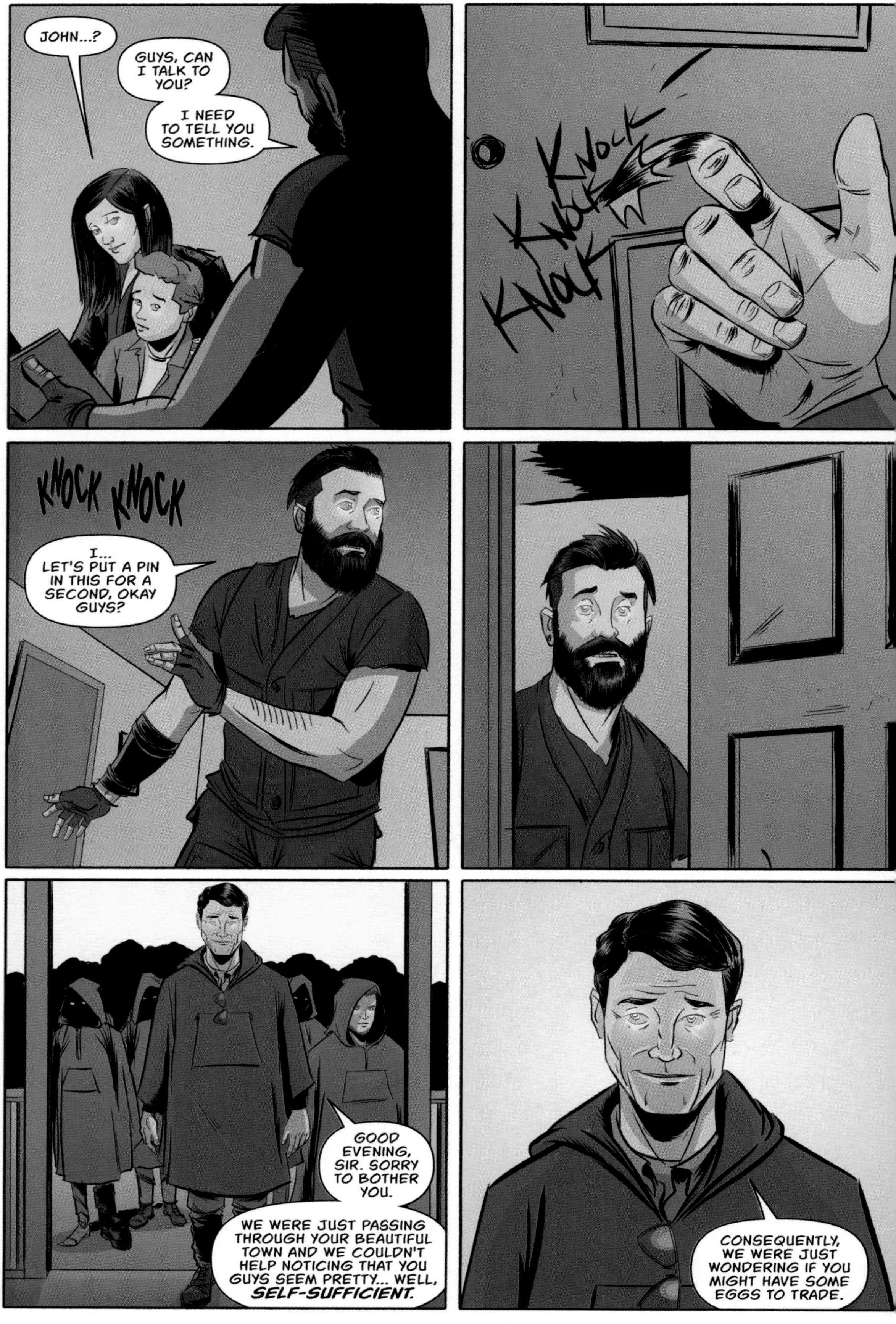
JOHN...?
GUYS, CAN I TALK TO YOU?
I NEED TO TELL YOU SOMETHING.
KNOCK KNOCK KNOCK
KNOCK KNOCK
I... LET'S PUT A PIN IN THIS FOR A SECOND, OKAY GUYS?
GOOD EVENING, SIR. SORRY TO BOTHER YOU.
WE WERE JUST PASSING THROUGH YOUR BEAUTIFUL TOWN AND WE COULDN'T HELP NOTICING THAT YOU GUYS SEEM PRETTY... WELL, SELF-SUFFICIENT.
CONSEQUENTLY, WE WERE JUST WONDERING IF YOU MIGHT HAVE SOME EGGS TO TRADE.

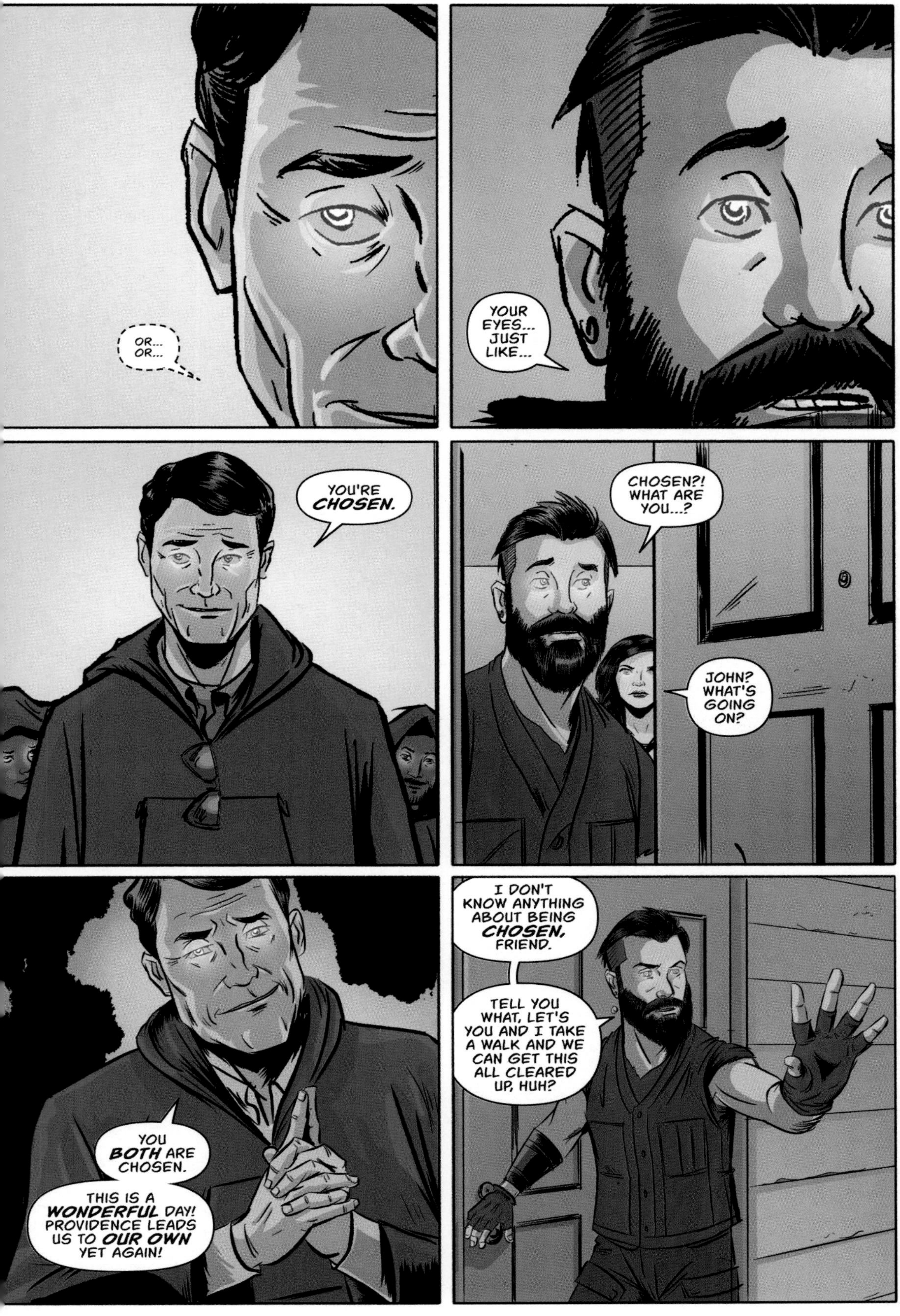
OR... OR...
YOUR EYES... JUST LIKE...
YOU'RE CHOSEN.
CHOSEN?! WHAT ARE YOU...?
JOHN? WHAT'S GOING ON?
YOU BOTH ARE CHOSEN.
THIS IS A WONDERFUL DAY! PROVIDENCE LEADS US TO OUR OWN YET AGAIN!
I DON'T KNOW ANYTHING ABOUT BEING CHOSEN, FRIEND.
TELL YOU WHAT, LET'S YOU AND I TAKE A WALK AND WE CAN GET THIS ALL CLEARED UP, HUH?

YOU HAVE NOTHING TO FEAR, JOHN. EITHER OF YOU. BEHIND YOU, THAT'S YOUR WIFE?

MY NAME'S HARRY... HARRY TRENCH. WE ARE THE LILAC LODGE.

SHOULD I KNOW WHAT THAT IS? I DON'T... WE DON'T GET OUT MUCH AROUND HERE.

HMM.

TELL ME, JOHN. HAS THE DOOR OPENED FOR YOU, YET?

WHAT?

THE DOOR YOU DREAM OF EACH NIGHT...

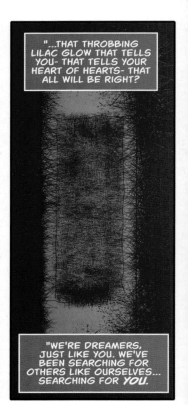

"...THAT THROBBING LILAC GLOW THAT TELLS YOU- THAT TELLS YOUR HEART OF HEARTS- THAT ALL WILL BE RIGHT?

"WE'RE DREAMERS, JUST LIKE YOU. WE'VE BEEN SEARCHING FOR OTHERS LIKE OURSELVES... SEARCHING FOR *YOU*.

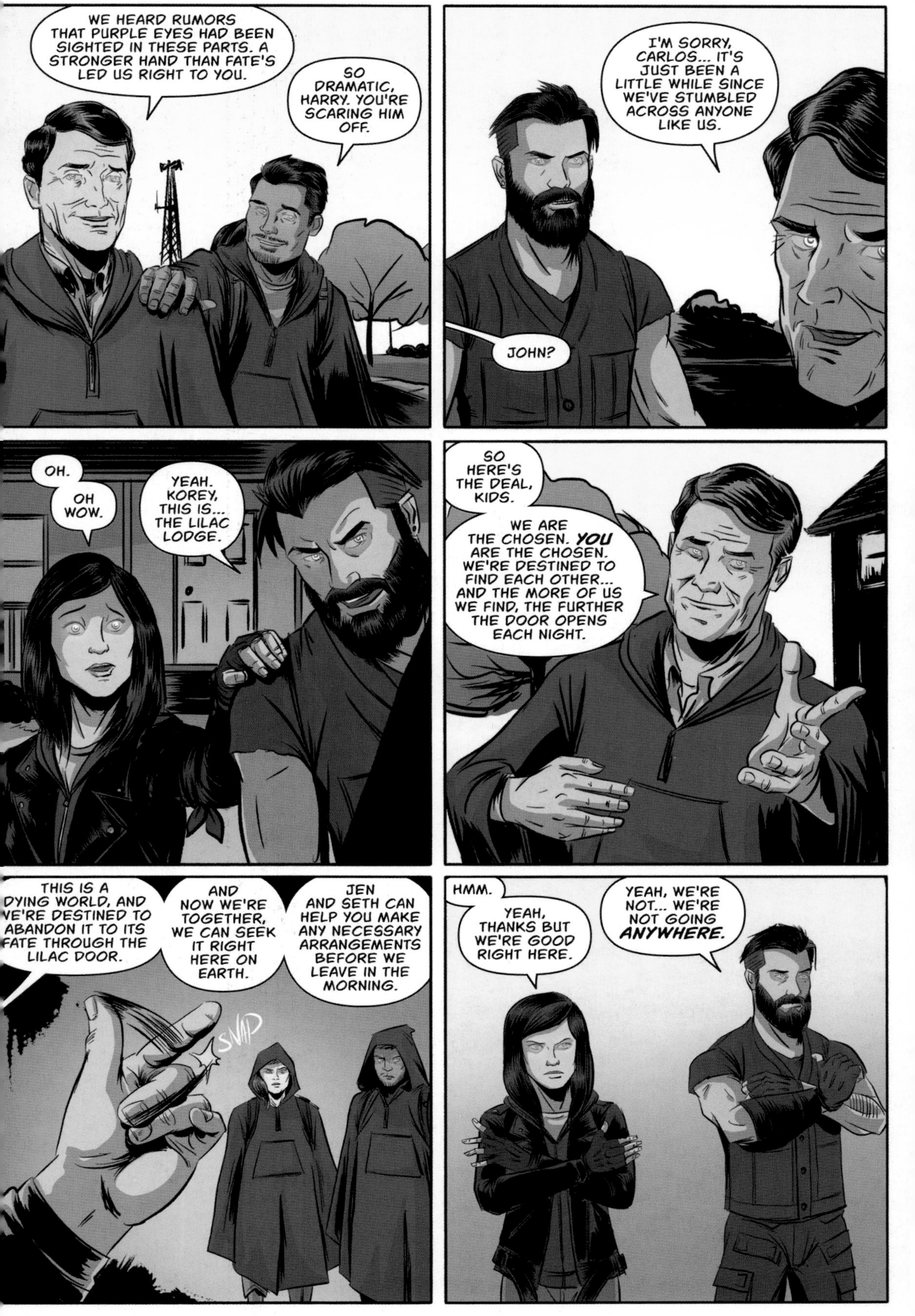
WE HEARD RUMORS THAT PURPLE EYES HAD BEEN SIGHTED IN THESE PARTS. A STRONGER HAND THAN FATE'S LED US RIGHT TO YOU.
SO DRAMATIC, HARRY. YOU'RE SCARING HIM OFF.
I'M SORRY, CARLOS... IT'S JUST BEEN A LITTLE WHILE SINCE WE'VE STUMBLED ACROSS ANYONE LIKE US.
JOHN?
OH.
OH WOW.
YEAH. KOREY, THIS IS... THE LILAC LODGE.
SO HERE'S THE DEAL, KIDS.
WE ARE THE CHOSEN. *YOU* ARE THE CHOSEN. WE'RE DESTINED TO FIND EACH OTHER... AND THE MORE OF US WE FIND, THE FURTHER THE DOOR OPENS EACH NIGHT.
THIS IS A DYING WORLD, AND WE'RE DESTINED TO ABANDON IT TO ITS FATE THROUGH THE LILAC DOOR.
AND NOW WE'RE TOGETHER, WE CAN SEEK IT RIGHT HERE ON EARTH.
JEN AND SETH CAN HELP YOU MAKE ANY NECESSARY ARRANGEMENTS BEFORE WE LEAVE IN THE MORNING.
SNAP
HMM.
YEAH, THANKS BUT WE'RE GOOD RIGHT HERE.
YEAH, WE'RE NOT... WE'RE NOT GOING ***ANYWHERE.***

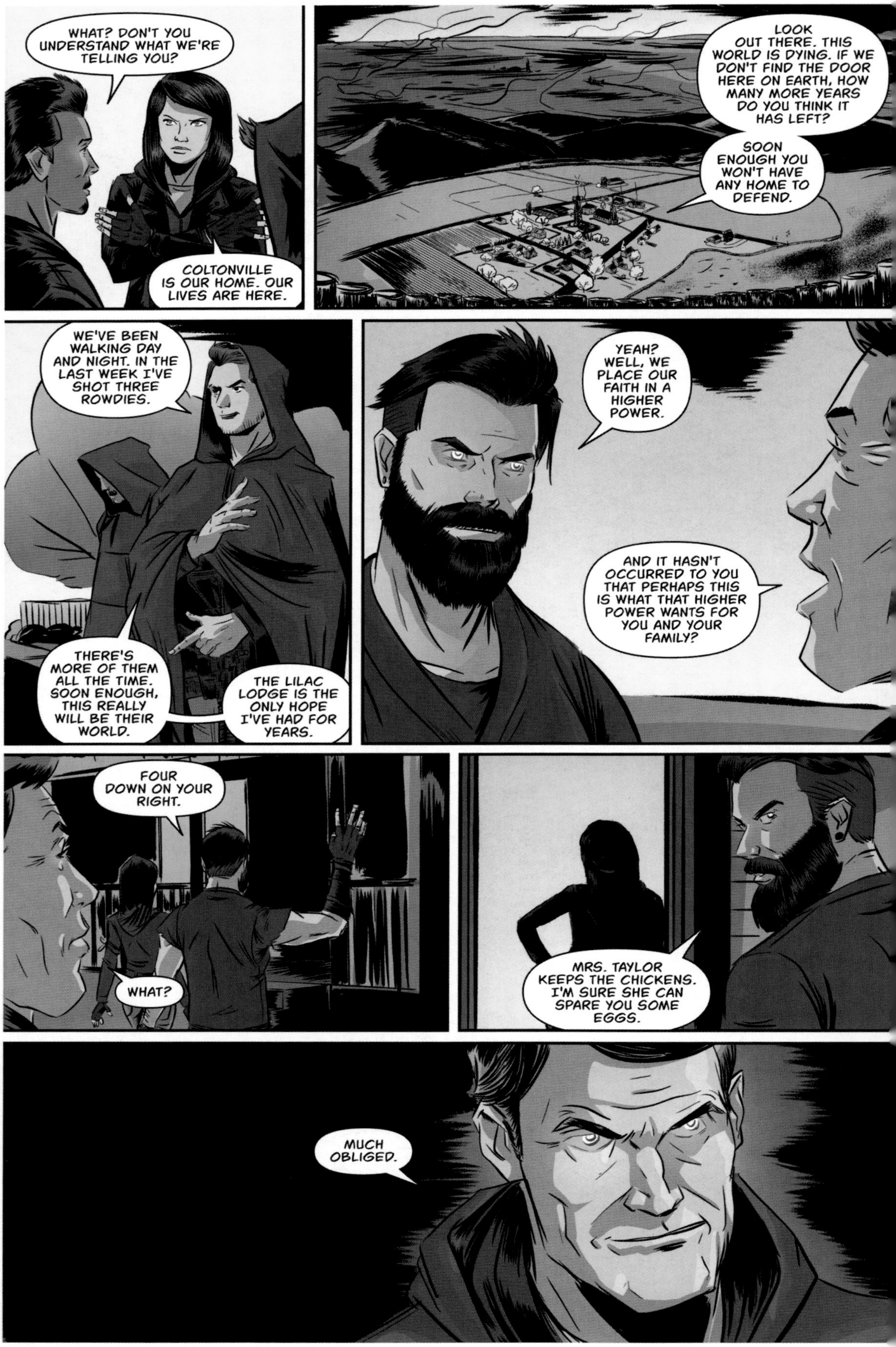
WHAT? DON'T YOU UNDERSTAND WHAT WE'RE TELLING YOU?
COLTONVILLE IS OUR HOME. OUR LIVES ARE HERE.
LOOK OUT THERE. THIS WORLD IS DYING. IF WE DON'T FIND THE DOOR HERE ON EARTH, HOW MANY MORE YEARS DO YOU THINK IT HAS LEFT?
SOON ENOUGH YOU WON'T HAVE ANY HOME TO DEFEND.
WE'VE BEEN WALKING DAY AND NIGHT. IN THE LAST WEEK I'VE SHOT THREE ROWDIES.
THERE'S MORE OF THEM ALL THE TIME. SOON ENOUGH, THIS REALLY WILL BE THEIR WORLD.
THE LILAC LODGE IS THE ONLY HOPE I'VE HAD FOR YEARS.
YEAH? WELL, WE PLACE OUR FAITH IN A HIGHER POWER.
AND IT HASN'T OCCURRED TO YOU THAT PERHAPS THIS IS WHAT THAT HIGHER POWER WANTS FOR YOU AND YOUR FAMILY?
FOUR DOWN ON YOUR RIGHT.
WHAT?
MRS. TAYLOR KEEPS THE CHICKENS. I'M SURE SHE CAN SPARE YOU SOME EGGS.
MUCH OBLIGED.

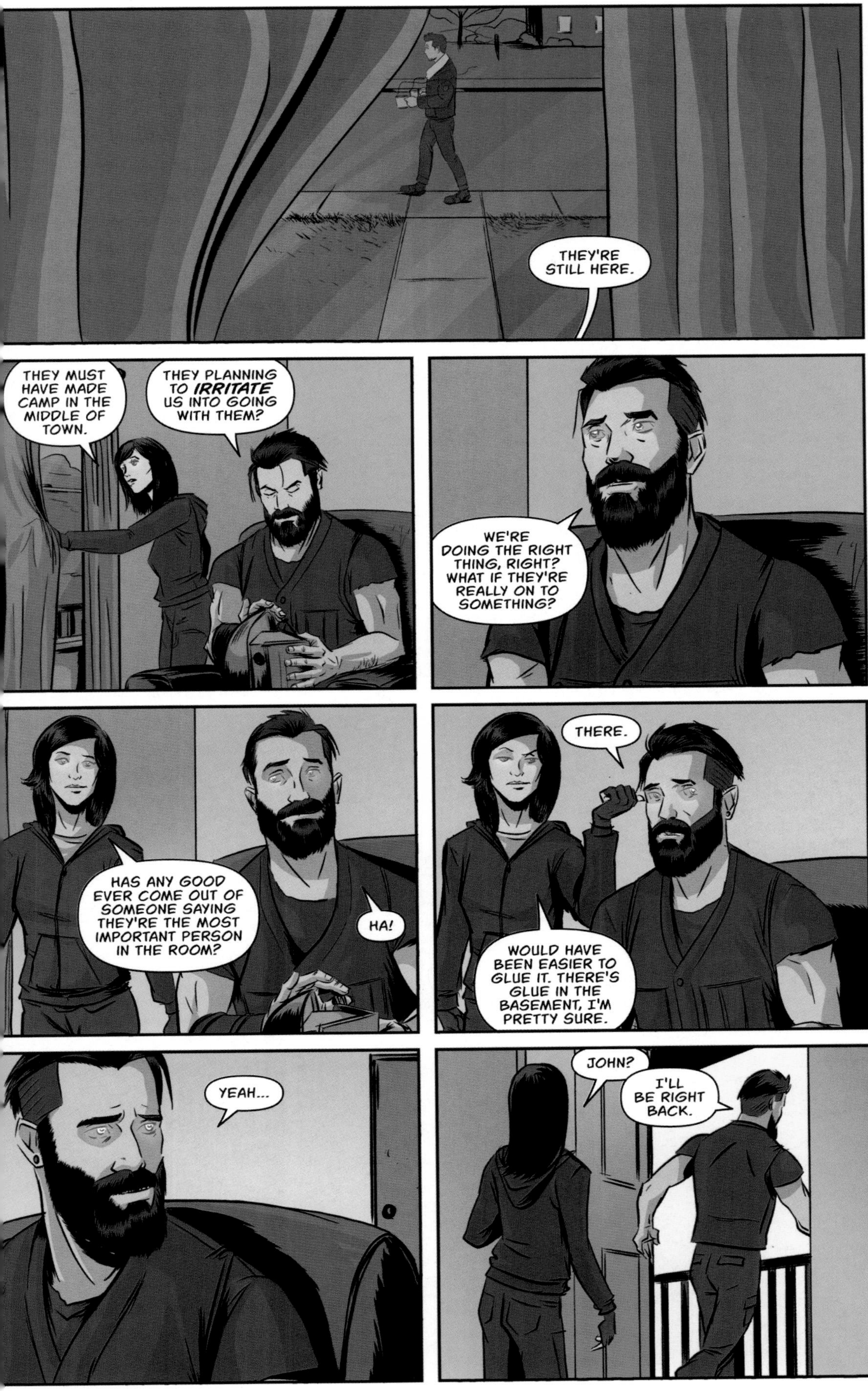
THEY'RE STILL HERE.
THEY MUST HAVE MADE CAMP IN THE MIDDLE OF TOWN.
THEY PLANNING TO *IRRITATE* US INTO GOING WITH THEM?
WE'RE DOING THE RIGHT THING, RIGHT? WHAT IF THEY'RE REALLY ON TO SOMETHING?
HAS ANY GOOD EVER COME OUT OF SOMEONE SAYING THEY'RE THE MOST IMPORTANT PERSON IN THE ROOM?
HA!
THERE.
WOULD HAVE BEEN EASIER TO GLUE IT. THERE'S GLUE IN THE BASEMENT, I'M PRETTY SURE.
YEAH...
JOHN?
I'LL BE RIGHT BACK.

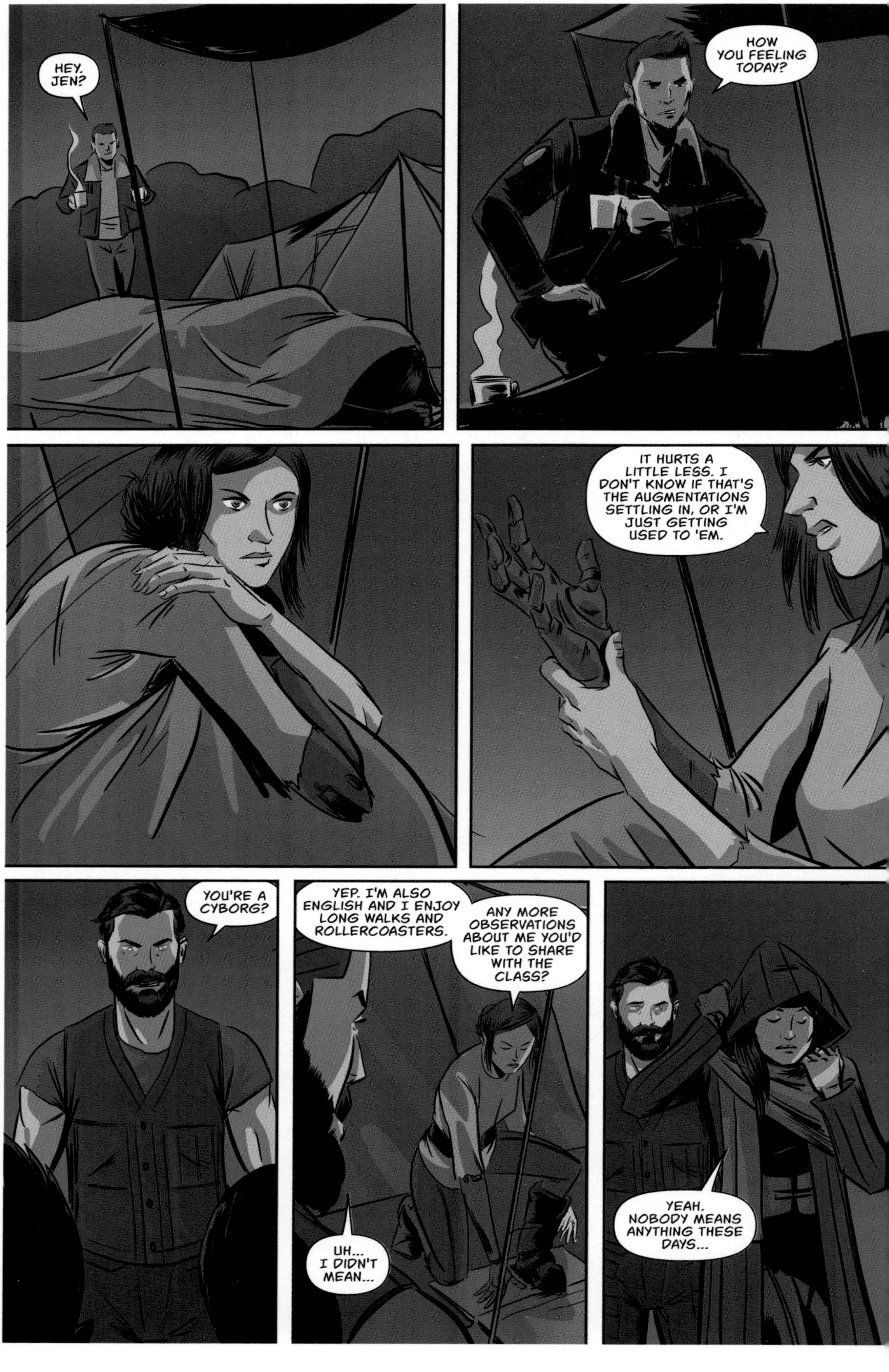
HEY. JEN?
HOW YOU FEELING TODAY?
IT HURTS A LITTLE LESS. I DON'T KNOW IF THAT'S THE AUGMENTATIONS SETTLING IN, OR I'M JUST GETTING USED TO 'EM.
YOU'RE A CYBORG?
YEP. I'M ALSO ENGLISH AND I ENJOY LONG WALKS AND ROLLERCOASTERS.
ANY MORE OBSERVATIONS ABOUT ME YOU'D LIKE TO SHARE WITH THE CLASS?
UH... I DIDN'T MEAN...
YEAH. NOBODY MEANS ANYTHING THESE DAYS...

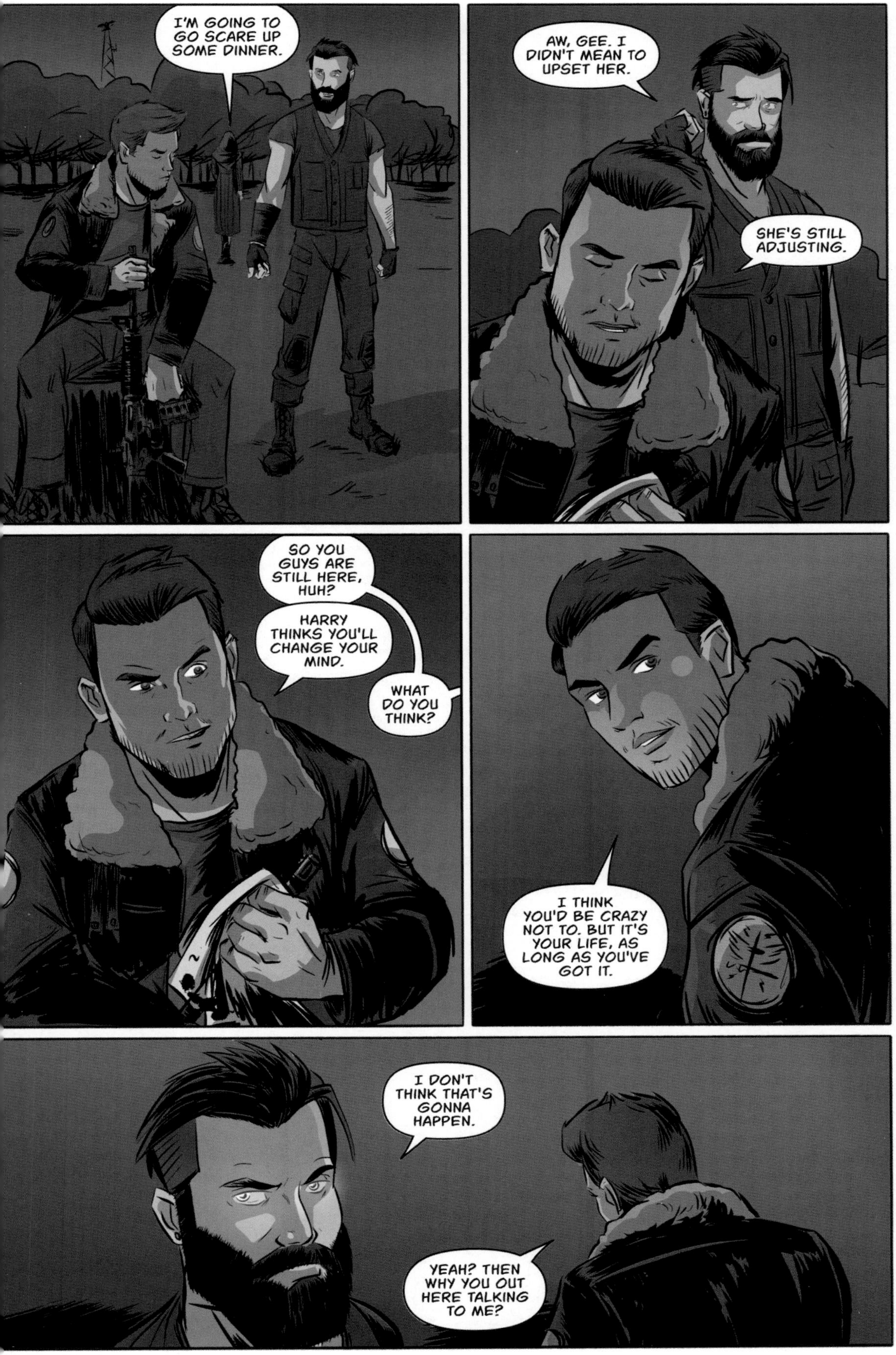
I'M GOING TO GO SCARE UP SOME DINNER.
AW, GEE. I DIDN'T MEAN TO UPSET HER.
SHE'S STILL ADJUSTING.
SO YOU GUYS ARE STILL HERE, HUH?
HARRY THINKS YOU'LL CHANGE YOUR MIND.
WHAT DO YOU THINK?
I THINK YOU'D BE CRAZY NOT TO. BUT IT'S YOUR LIFE, AS LONG AS YOU'VE GOT IT.
I DON'T THINK THAT'S GONNA HAPPEN.
YEAH? THEN WHY YOU OUT HERE TALKING TO ME?

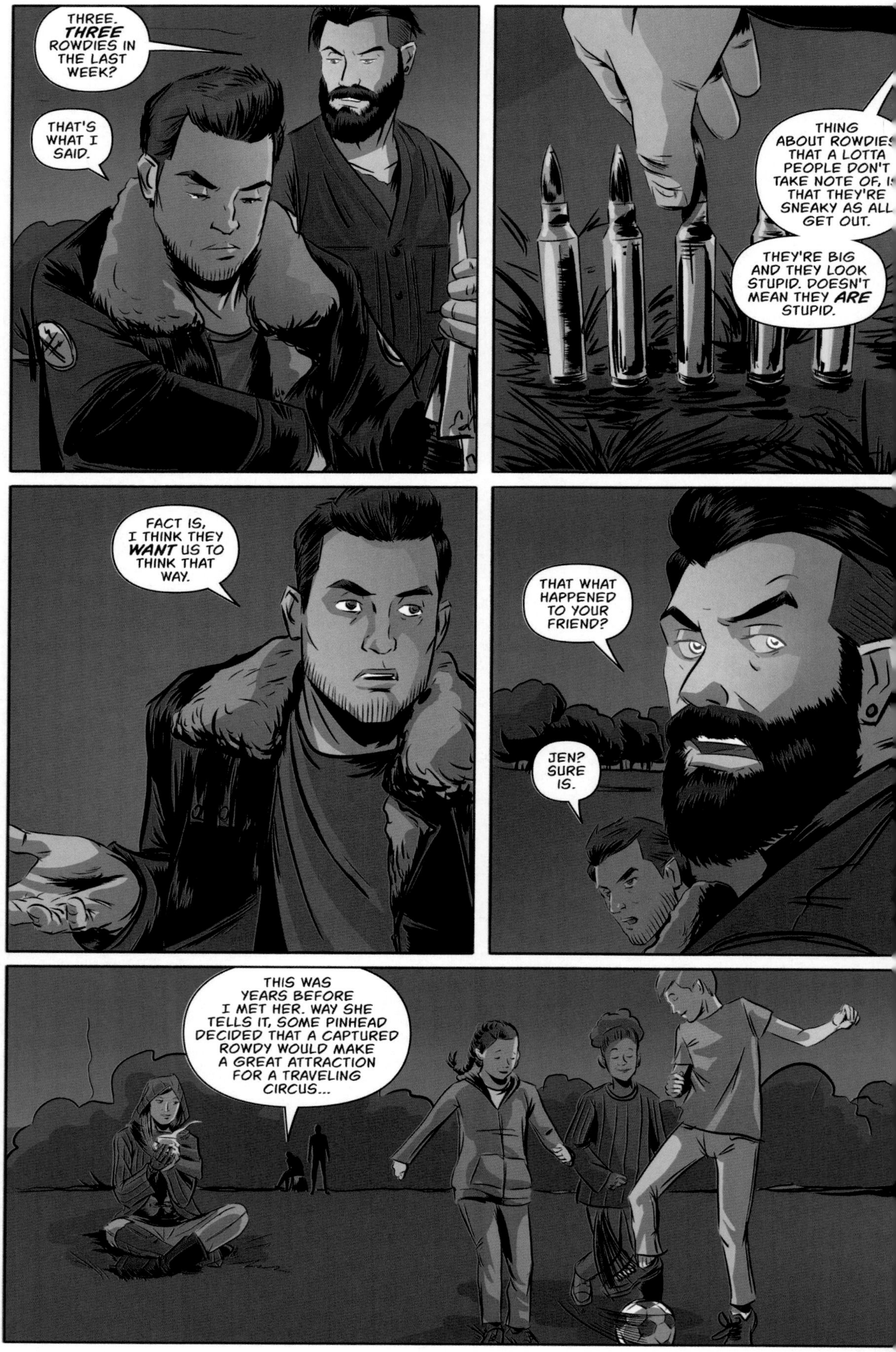
THREE. *THREE* ROWDIES IN THE LAST WEEK?
THAT'S WHAT I SAID.
THING ABOUT ROWDIES THAT A LOTTA PEOPLE DON'T TAKE NOTE OF, IS THAT THEY'RE SNEAKY AS ALL GET OUT.
THEY'RE BIG AND THEY LOOK STUPID. DOESN'T MEAN THEY *ARE* STUPID.
FACT IS, I THINK THEY *WANT* US TO THINK THAT WAY.
THAT WHAT HAPPENED TO YOUR FRIEND?
JEN? SURE IS.
THIS WAS YEARS BEFORE I MET HER. WAY SHE TELLS IT, SOME PINHEAD DECIDED THAT A CAPTURED ROWDY WOULD MAKE A GREAT ATTRACTION FOR A TRAVELING CIRCUS...

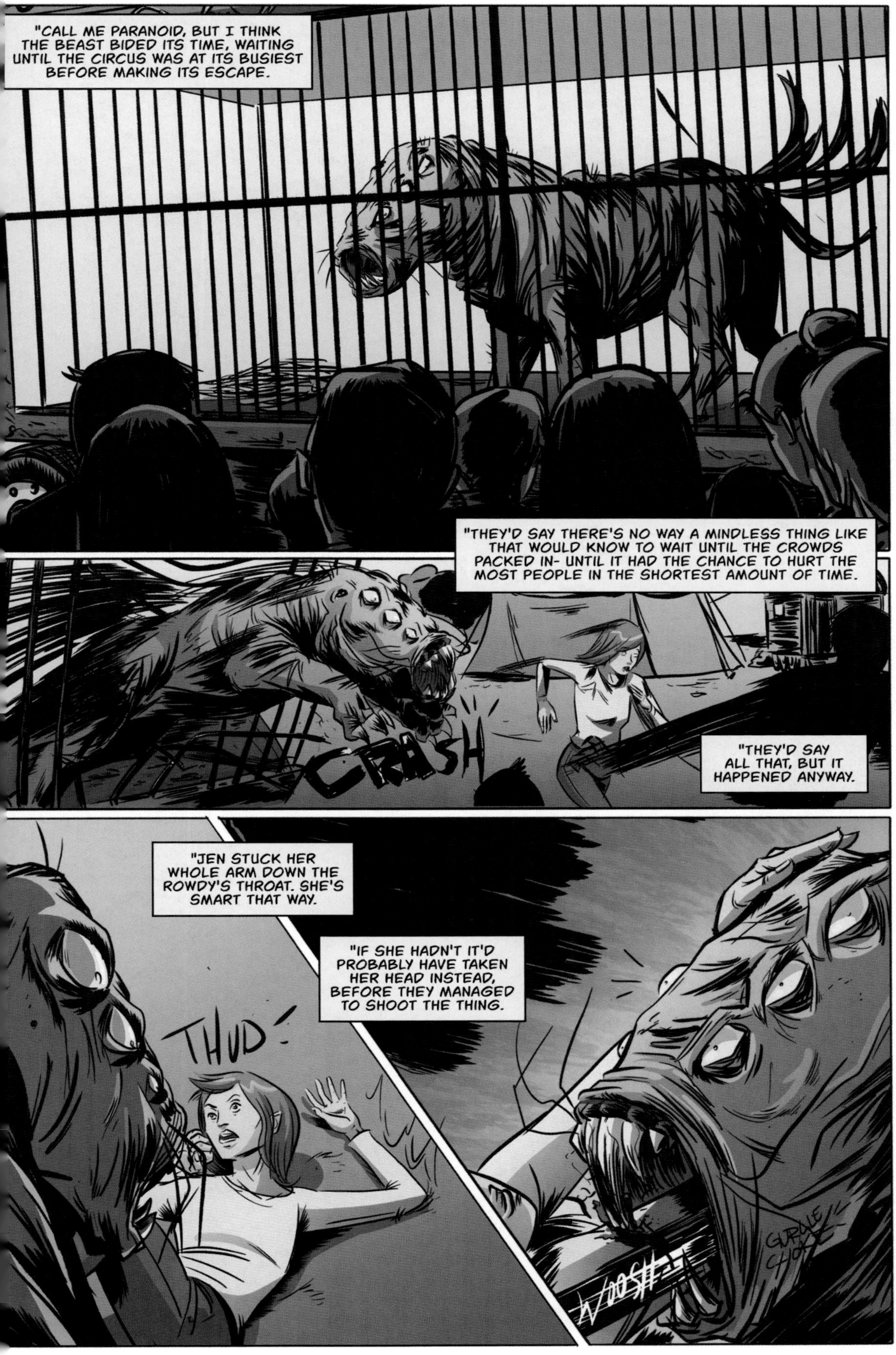
"CALL ME PARANOID, BUT I THINK THE BEAST BIDED ITS TIME, WAITING UNTIL THE CIRCUS WAS AT ITS BUSIEST BEFORE MAKING ITS ESCAPE.
"THEY'D SAY THERE'S NO WAY A MINDLESS THING LIKE THAT WOULD KNOW TO WAIT UNTIL THE CROWDS PACKED IN- UNTIL IT HAD THE CHANCE TO HURT THE MOST PEOPLE IN THE SHORTEST AMOUNT OF TIME.
CRASH
"THEY'D SAY ALL THAT, BUT IT HAPPENED ANYWAY.
"JEN STUCK HER WHOLE ARM DOWN THE ROWDY'S THROAT. SHE'S SMART THAT WAY.
"IF SHE HADN'T IT'D PROBABLY HAVE TAKEN HER HEAD INSTEAD, BEFORE THEY MANAGED TO SHOOT THE THING.
THUD!
GURGLE CHOKE
WOOSH

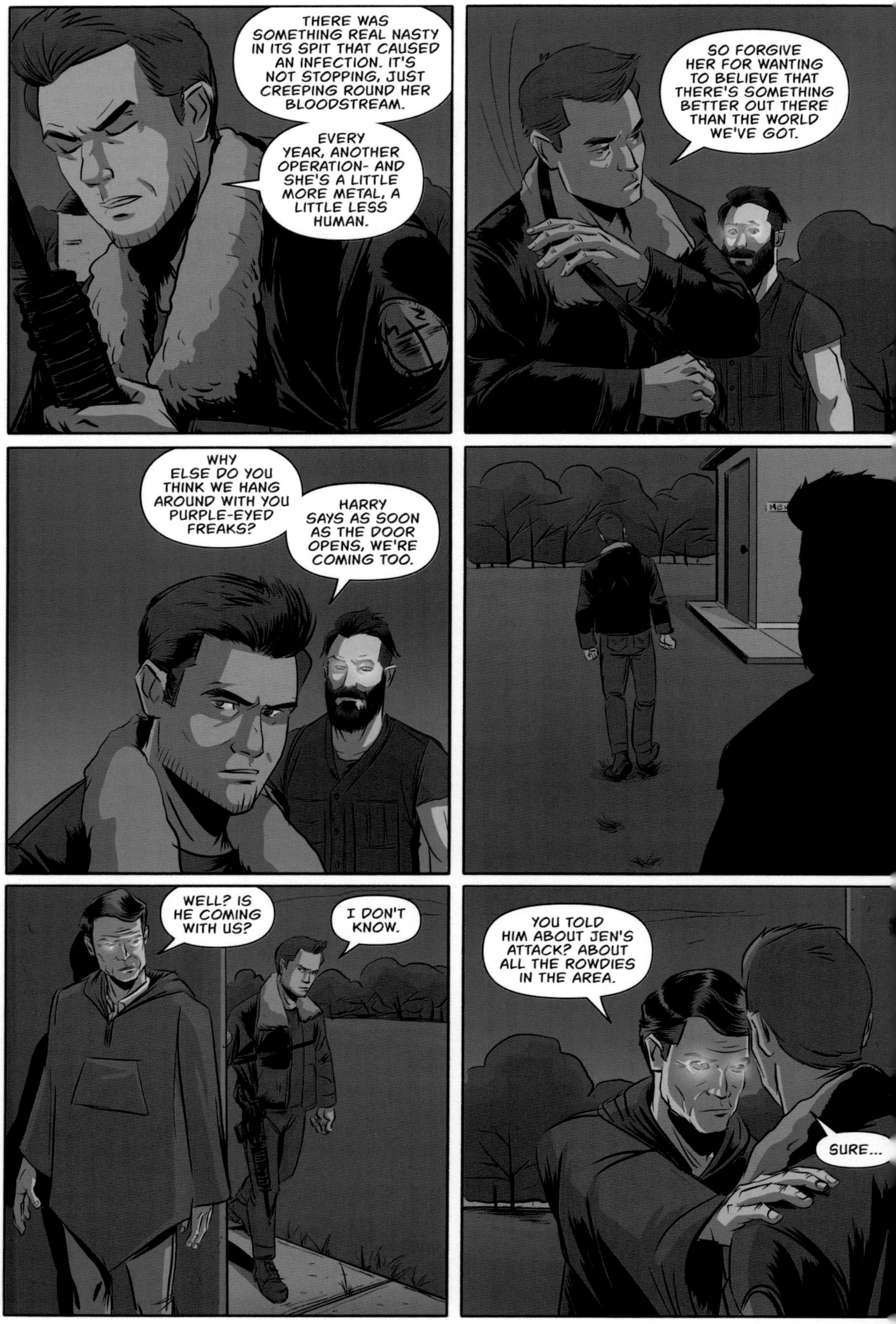

THERE WAS SOMETHING REAL NASTY IN ITS SPIT THAT CAUSED AN INFECTION. IT'S NOT STOPPING, JUST CREEPING ROUND HER BLOODSTREAM.
EVERY YEAR, ANOTHER OPERATION- AND SHE'S A LITTLE MORE METAL, A LITTLE LESS HUMAN.
SO FORGIVE HER FOR WANTING TO BELIEVE THAT THERE'S SOMETHING BETTER OUT THERE THAN THE WORLD WE'VE GOT.
WHY ELSE DO YOU THINK WE HANG AROUND WITH YOU PURPLE-EYED FREAKS?
HARRY SAYS AS SOON AS THE DOOR OPENS, WE'RE COMING TOO.
WELL? IS HE COMING WITH US?
I DON'T KNOW.
YOU TOLD HIM ABOUT JEN'S ATTACK? ABOUT ALL THE ROWDIES IN THE AREA.
SURE...

THEY DON'T SEEM OVERLY CONCERNED ABOUT ATTACKS HERE. IT'S SO WEIRD.

THEY DON'T LOOK LIKE THEY'RE PROTECTED FROM ON HIGH, UNLESS...

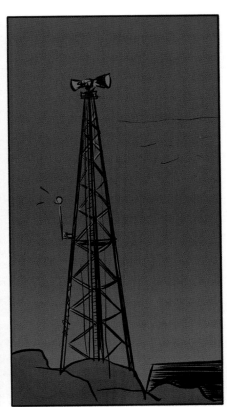

SETH, MY BOY. I KNEW THERE WAS A REASON WE KEEP YOU AROUND.

COME ON, IT'S PROBABLY JUST A RADIO TOWER. WE SEE 'EM ALL THE TIME.

NO, YOU'RE ONTO SOMETHING. CLEARLY I TRUST YOUR INSTINCTS MORE THAN YOU DO, SETH.

SECRETS ARE THICKER ON THE GROUND THAN CRABGRASS IN THIS TOWN. YOU CAN *FEEL* IT.

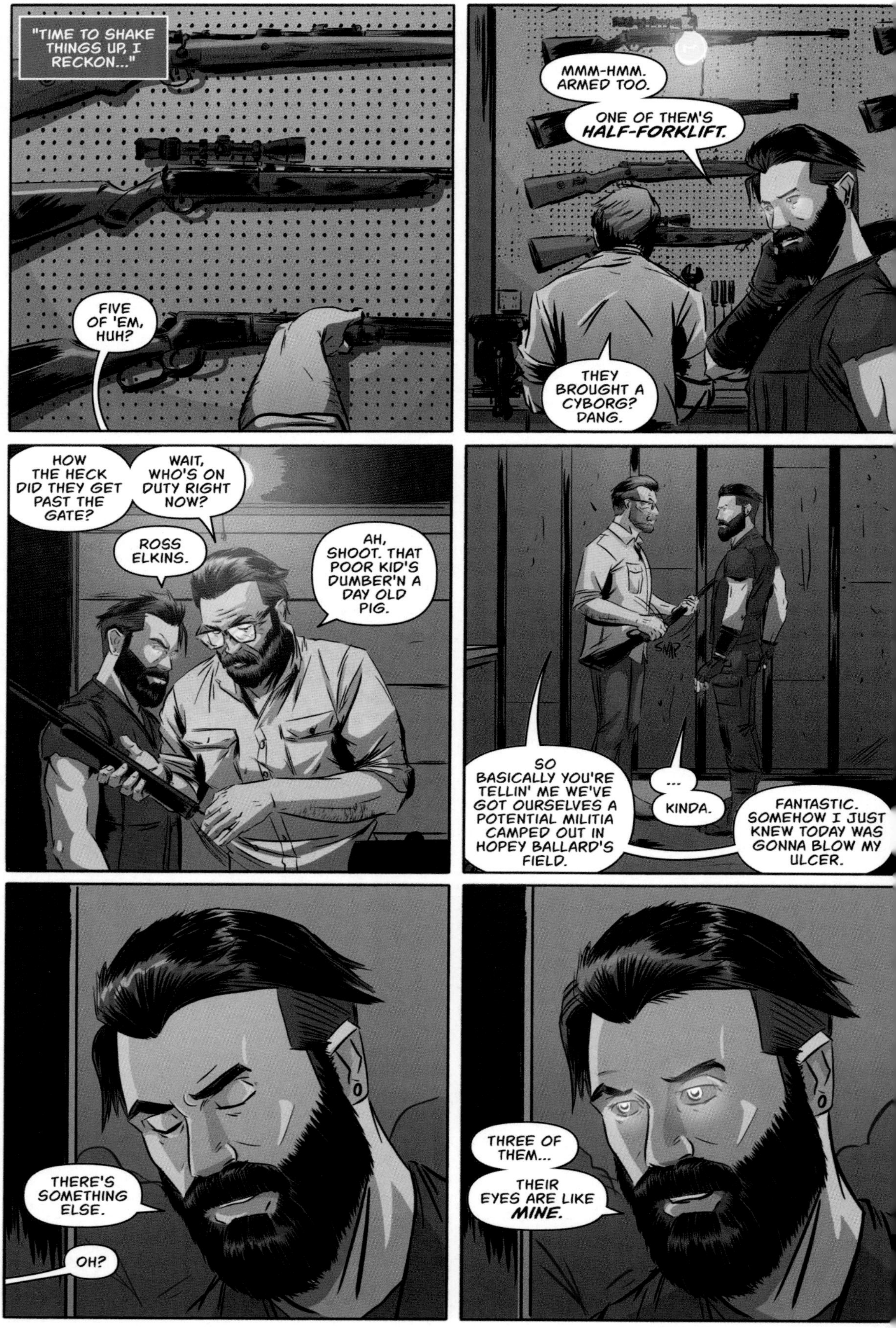

"TIME TO SHAKE THINGS UP, I RECKON..."
FIVE OF 'EM, HUH?
MMM-HMM. ARMED TOO.
ONE OF THEM'S *HALF-FORKLIFT.*
THEY BROUGHT A CYBORG? DANG.
HOW THE HECK DID THEY GET PAST THE GATE?
WAIT, WHO'S ON DUTY RIGHT NOW?
ROSS ELKINS.
AH, SHOOT. THAT POOR KID'S DUMBER'N A DAY OLD PIG.
SNAP
SO BASICALLY YOU'RE TELLIN' ME WE'VE GOT OURSELVES A POTENTIAL MILITIA CAMPED OUT IN HOPEY BALLARD'S FIELD.
... KINDA.
FANTASTIC. SOMEHOW I JUST KNEW TODAY WAS GONNA BLOW MY ULCER.
THERE'S SOMETHING ELSE.
OH?
THREE OF THEM...
THEIR EYES ARE LIKE *MINE.*

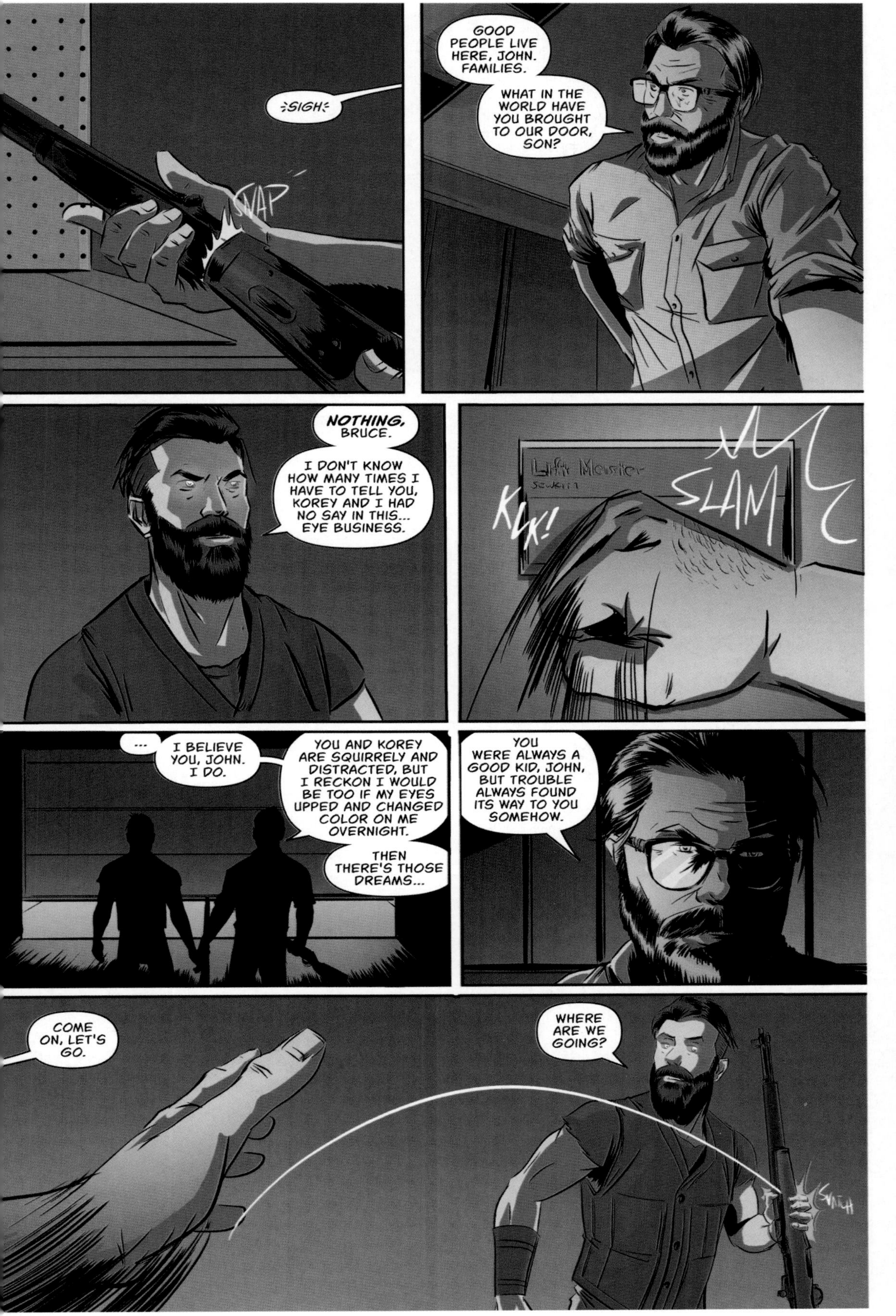

SIGH
SWAP
GOOD PEOPLE LIVE HERE, JOHN. FAMILIES.
WHAT IN THE WORLD HAVE YOU BROUGHT TO OUR DOOR, SON?
NOTHING, BRUCE.
I DON'T KNOW HOW MANY TIMES I HAVE TO TELL YOU, KOREY AND I HAD NO SAY IN THIS... EYE BUSINESS.
Lift Master
KLK!
SLAM
...
I BELIEVE YOU, JOHN. I DO.
YOU AND KOREY ARE SQUIRRELY AND DISTRACTED, BUT I RECKON I WOULD BE TOO IF MY EYES UPPED AND CHANGED COLOR ON ME OVERNIGHT.
THEN THERE'S THOSE DREAMS...
YOU WERE ALWAYS A GOOD KID, JOHN, BUT TROUBLE ALWAYS FOUND ITS WAY TO YOU SOMEHOW.
COME ON, LET'S GO.
WHERE ARE WE GOING?
SNATCH

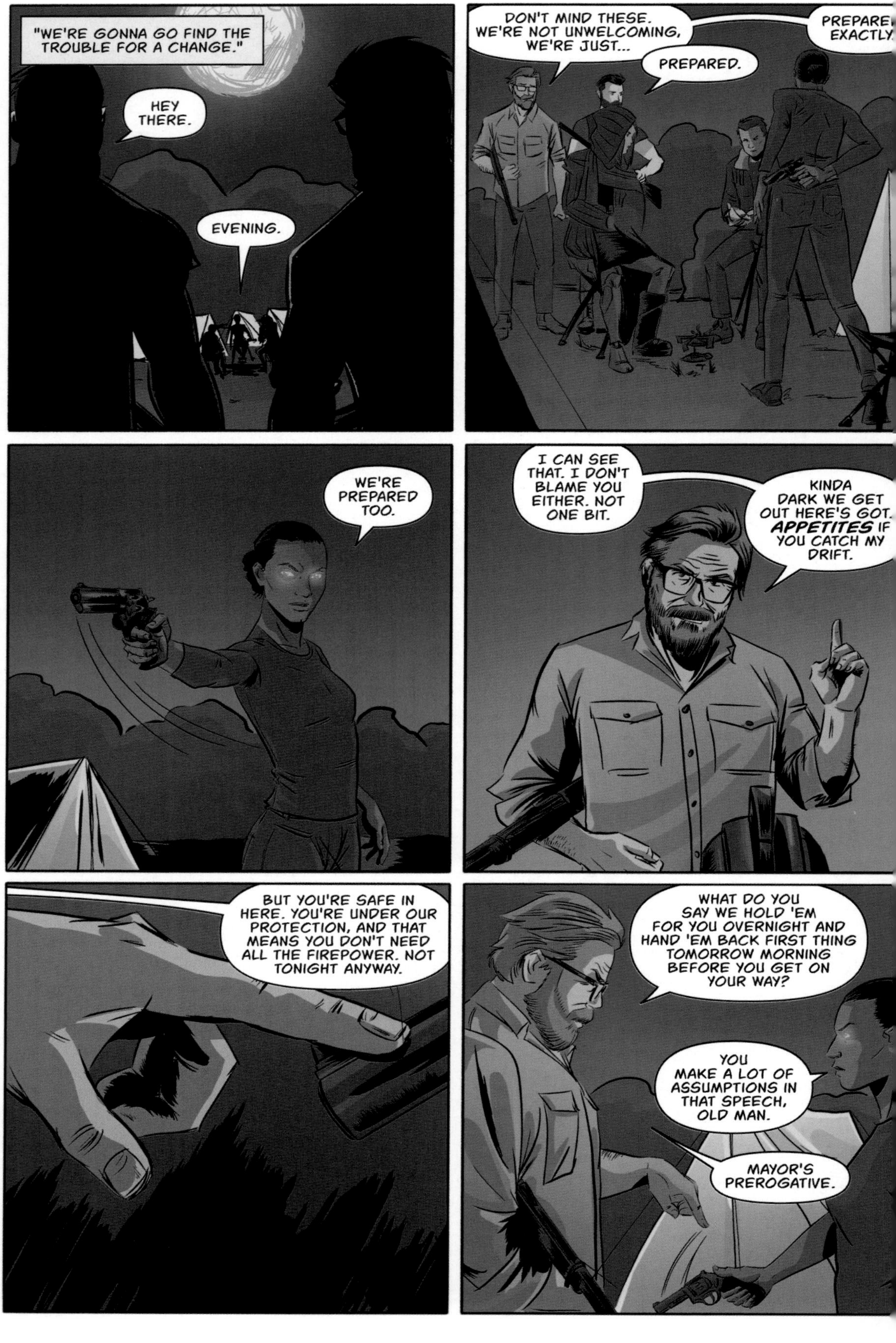
"WE'RE GONNA GO FIND THE TROUBLE FOR A CHANGE."
HEY THERE.
EVENING.
DON'T MIND THESE. WE'RE NOT UNWELCOMING, WE'RE JUST...
PREPARED.
PREPARE EXACTLY
WE'RE PREPARED TOO.
I CAN SEE THAT. I DON'T BLAME YOU EITHER. NOT ONE BIT.
KINDA DARK WE GET OUT HERE'S GOT. APPETITES IF YOU CATCH MY DRIFT.
BUT YOU'RE SAFE IN HERE. YOU'RE UNDER OUR PROTECTION, AND THAT MEANS YOU DON'T NEED ALL THE FIREPOWER. NOT TONIGHT ANYWAY.
WHAT DO YOU SAY WE HOLD 'EM FOR YOU OVERNIGHT AND HAND 'EM BACK FIRST THING TOMORROW MORNING BEFORE YOU GET ON YOUR WAY?
YOU MAKE A LOT OF ASSUMPTIONS IN THAT SPEECH, OLD MAN.
MAYOR'S PREROGATIVE.

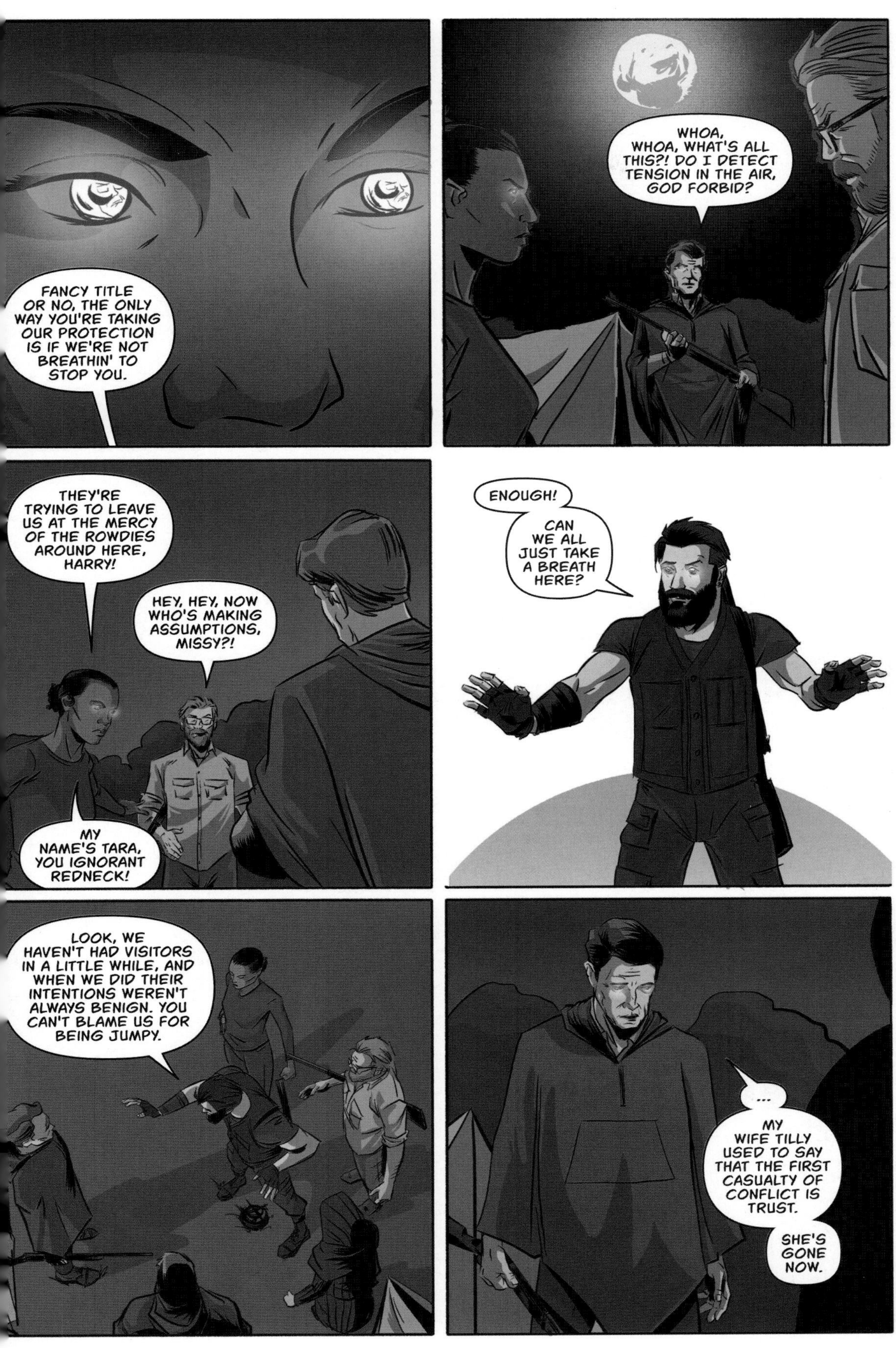
FANCY TITLE OR NO, THE ONLY WAY YOU'RE TAKING OUR PROTECTION IS IF WE'RE NOT BREATHIN' TO STOP YOU.
WHOA, WHOA, WHAT'S ALL THIS?! DO I DETECT TENSION IN THE AIR, GOD FORBID?
THEY'RE TRYING TO LEAVE US AT THE MERCY OF THE ROWDIES AROUND HERE, HARRY!
HEY, HEY, NOW WHO'S MAKING ASSUMPTIONS, MISSY?!
MY NAME'S TARA, YOU IGNORANT REDNECK!
ENOUGH!
CAN WE ALL JUST TAKE A BREATH HERE?
LOOK, WE HAVEN'T HAD VISITORS IN A LITTLE WHILE, AND WHEN WE DID THEIR INTENTIONS WEREN'T ALWAYS BENIGN. YOU CAN'T BLAME US FOR BEING JUMPY.
...
MY WIFE TILLY USED TO SAY THAT THE FIRST CASUALTY OF CONFLICT IS TRUST.
SHE'S GONE NOW.

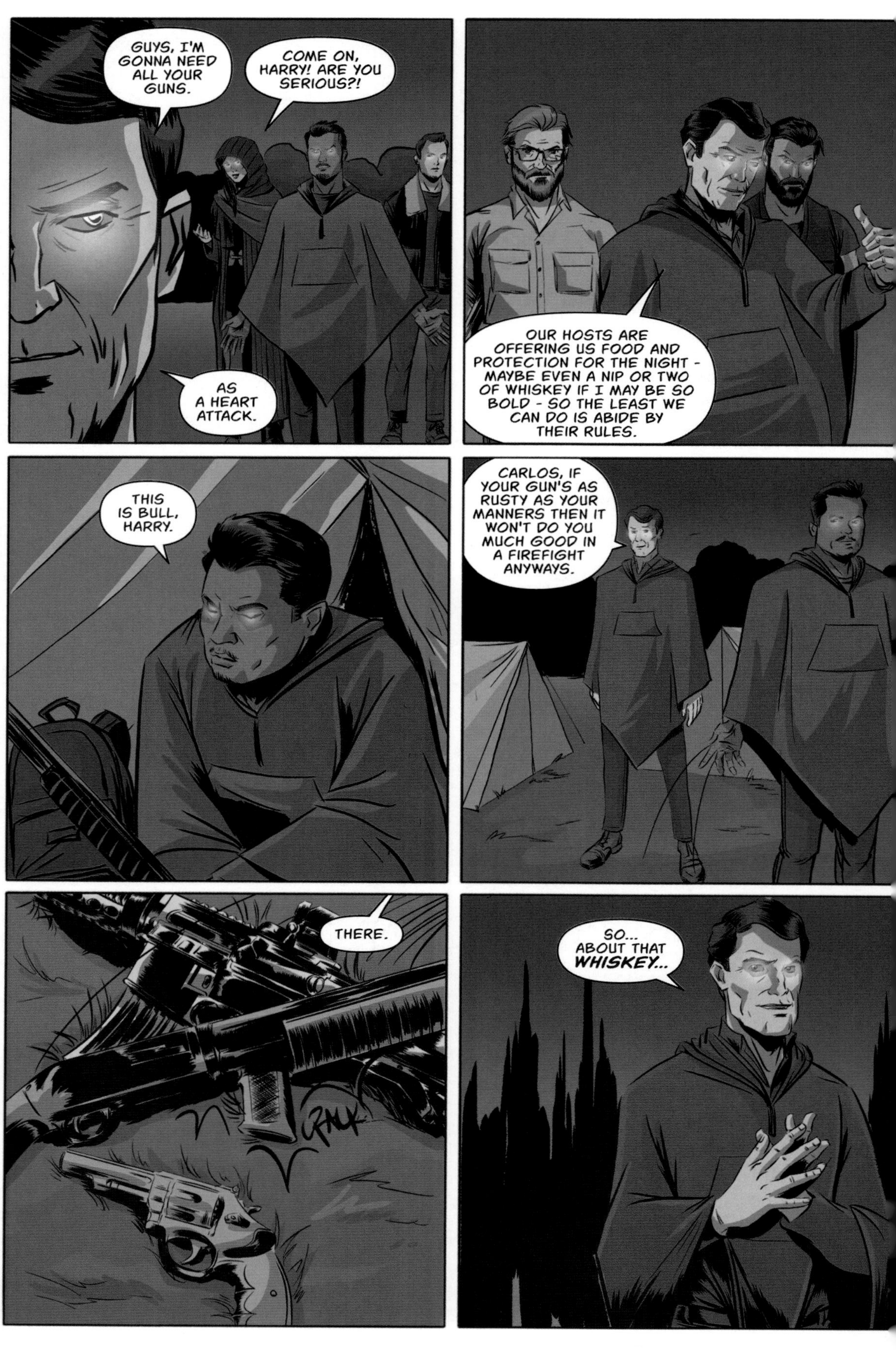
GUYS, I'M GONNA NEED ALL YOUR GUNS.
COME ON, HARRY! ARE YOU SERIOUS?!
AS A HEART ATTACK.
OUR HOSTS ARE OFFERING US FOOD AND PROTECTION FOR THE NIGHT - MAYBE EVEN A NIP OR TWO OF WHISKEY IF I MAY BE SO BOLD - SO THE LEAST WE CAN DO IS ABIDE BY THEIR RULES.
THIS IS BULL, HARRY.
CARLOS, IF YOUR GUN'S AS RUSTY AS YOUR MANNERS THEN IT WON'T DO YOU MUCH GOOD IN A FIREFIGHT ANYWAYS.
THERE.
SO... ABOUT THAT *WHISKEY...*

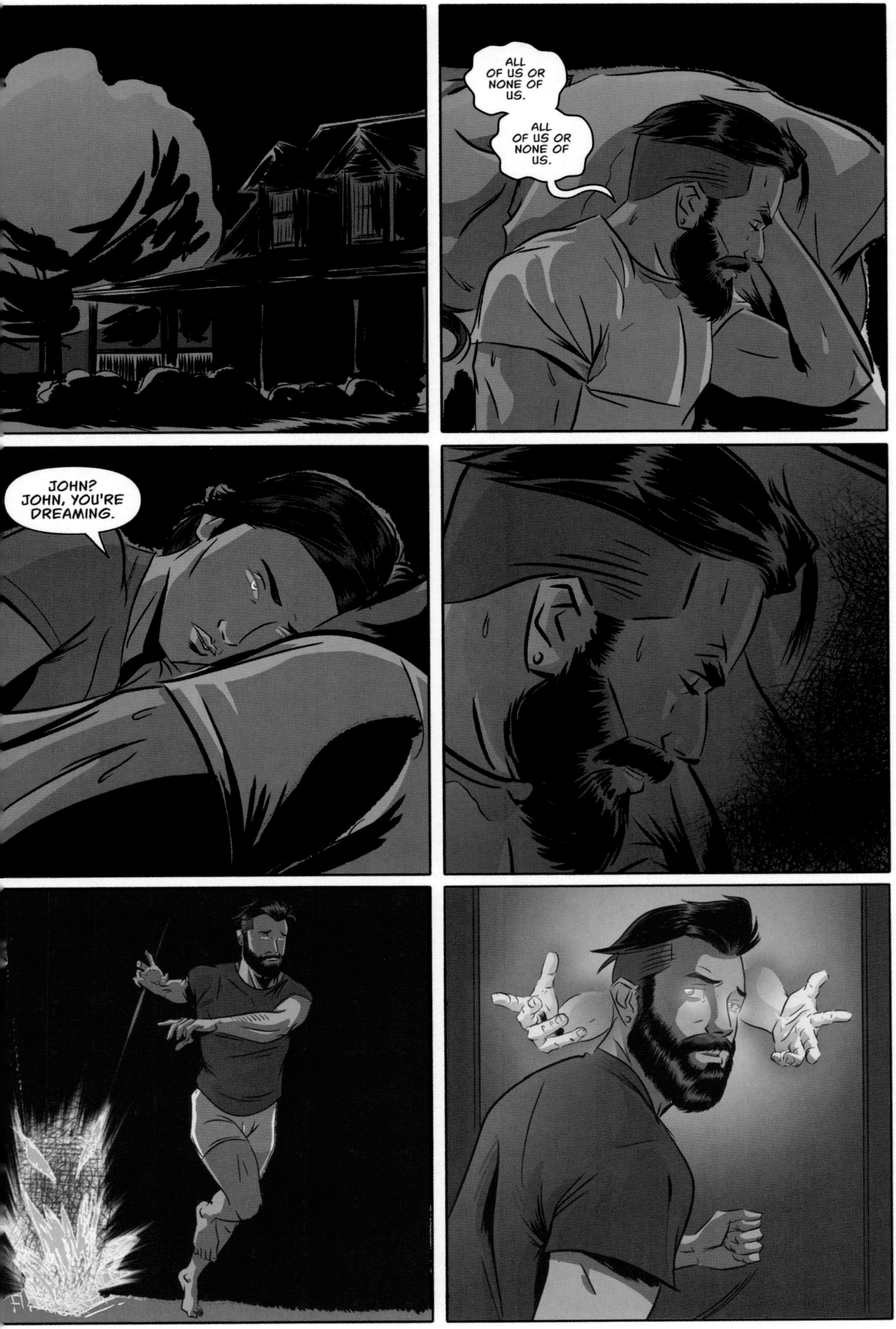
ALL OF US OR NONE OF US.
ALL OF US OR NONE OF US.
JOHN? JOHN, YOU'RE DREAMING.

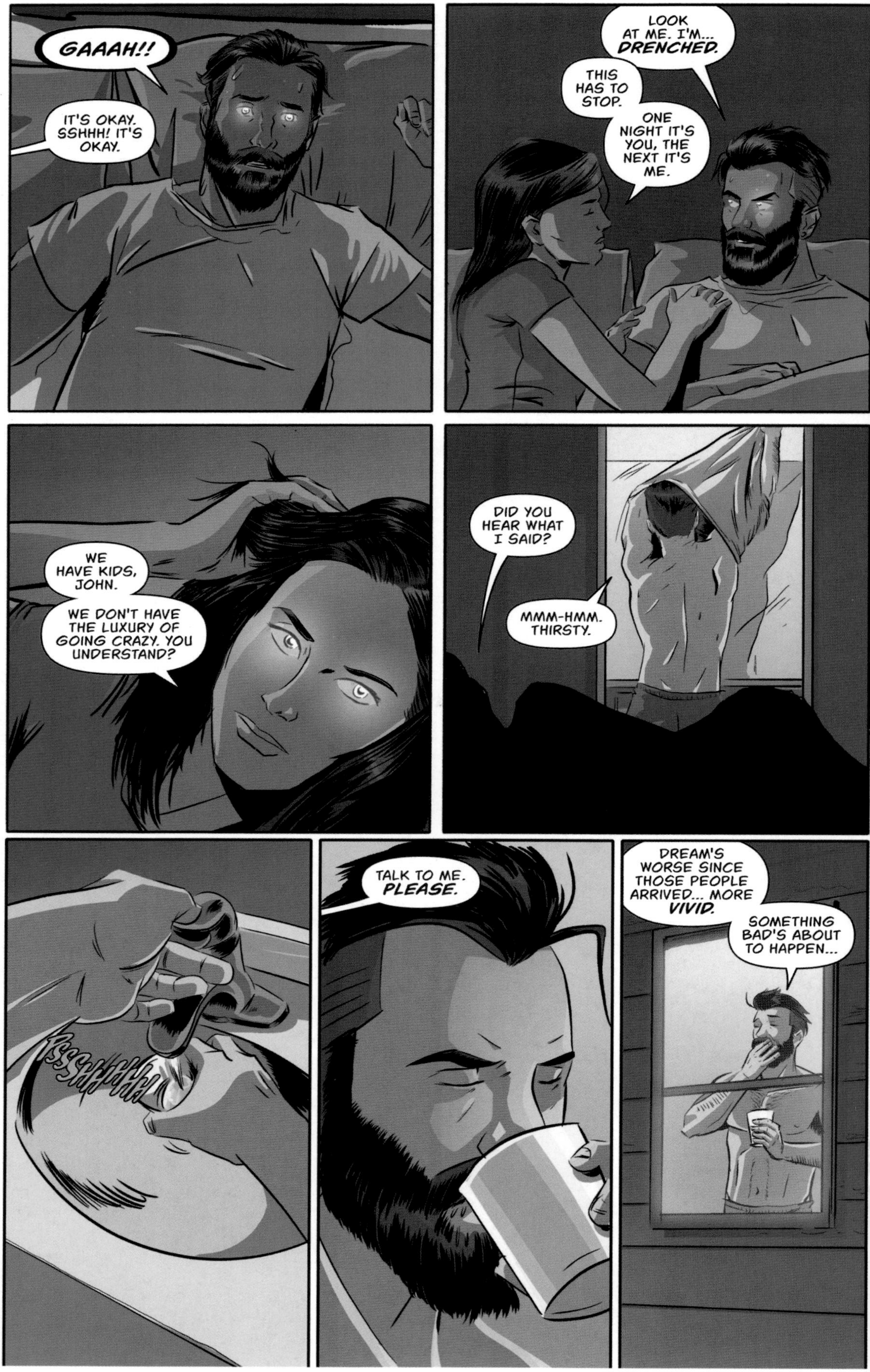
GAAAH!!
IT'S OKAY. SSHHH! IT'S OKAY.
LOOK AT ME. I'M... DRENCHED.
THIS HAS TO STOP.
ONE NIGHT IT'S YOU, THE NEXT IT'S ME.
WE HAVE KIDS, JOHN.
WE DON'T HAVE THE LUXURY OF GOING CRAZY. YOU UNDERSTAND?
DID YOU HEAR WHAT I SAID?
MMM-HMM. THIRSTY.
PSSSHHHHH
TALK TO ME. PLEASE.
DREAM'S WORSE SINCE THOSE PEOPLE ARRIVED... MORE VIVID.
SOMETHING BAD'S ABOUT TO HAPPEN...

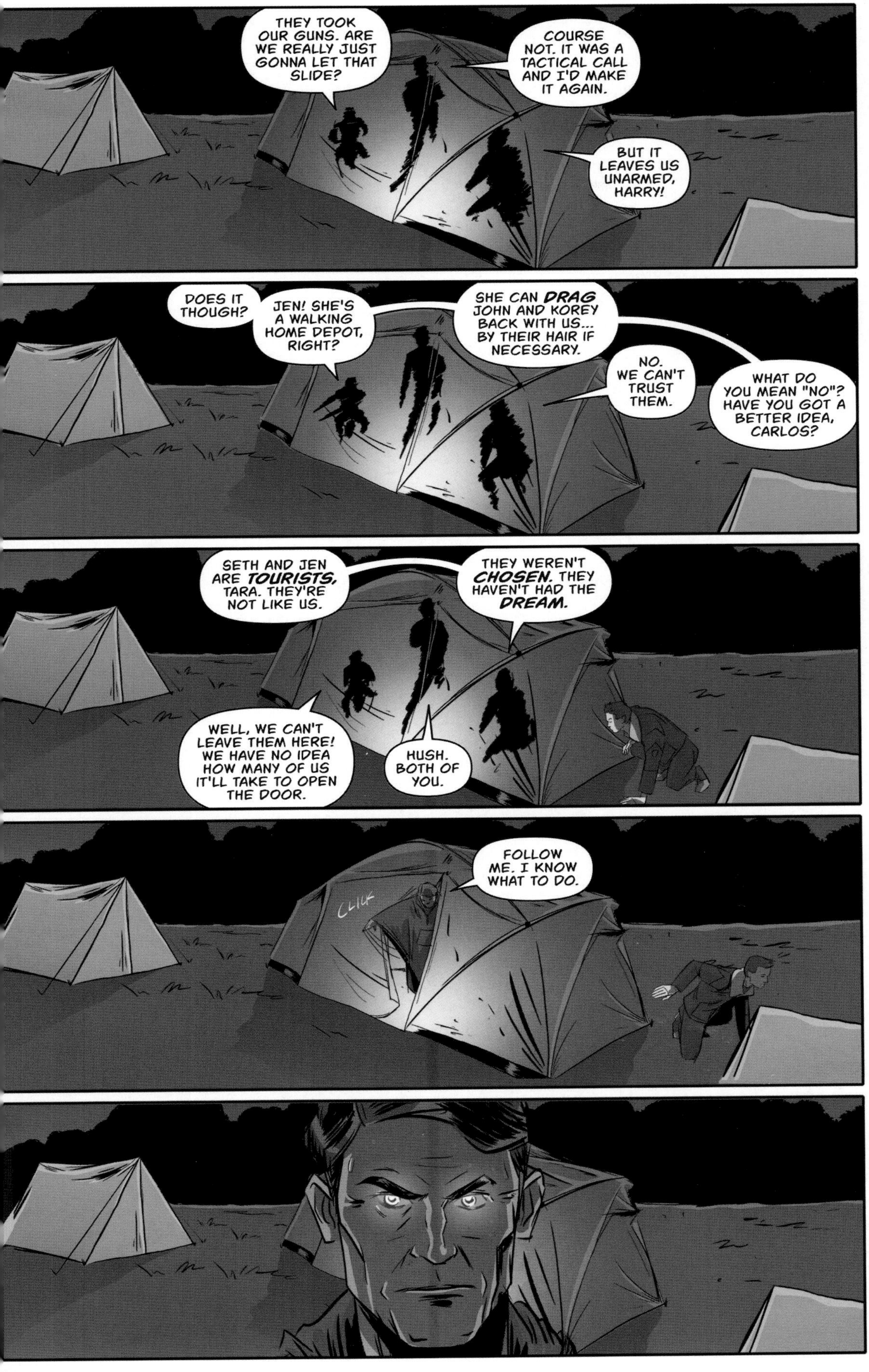

THEY TOOK OUR GUNS. ARE WE REALLY JUST GONNA LET THAT SLIDE?
COURSE NOT. IT WAS A TACTICAL CALL AND I'D MAKE IT AGAIN.
BUT IT LEAVES US UNARMED, HARRY!
DOES IT THOUGH?
JEN! SHE'S A WALKING HOME DEPOT, RIGHT?
SHE CAN DRAG JOHN AND KOREY BACK WITH US... BY THEIR HAIR IF NECESSARY.
NO. WE CAN'T TRUST THEM.
WHAT DO YOU MEAN "NO"? HAVE YOU GOT A BETTER IDEA, CARLOS?
SETH AND JEN ARE TOURISTS, TARA. THEY'RE NOT LIKE US.
THEY WEREN'T CHOSEN. THEY HAVEN'T HAD THE DREAM.
WELL, WE CAN'T LEAVE THEM HERE! WE HAVE NO IDEA HOW MANY OF US IT'LL TAKE TO OPEN THE DOOR.
HUSH. BOTH OF YOU.
FOLLOW ME. I KNOW WHAT TO DO.
CLICK

WHERE ARE THEY GOING?

JEN, YOU GOTTA STAY BACK!

VRT! VRT!

WHAT? WHY?

BECAUSE... AW, DANGIT!

BECAUSE YOUR IMPLANTS GIVE YOU THE STEALTH CAPABILITY OF A JACKHAMMER, ALRIGHT?!

YOU'RE MEAN. YOU'RE A MEAN PERSON.

♪♫

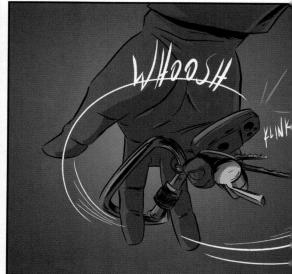

WHOOSH

KLINK

HI!

WHOA!

SHHH! SHHH!

MMMFFF!!!

SLASH

GUKK! GUKK!

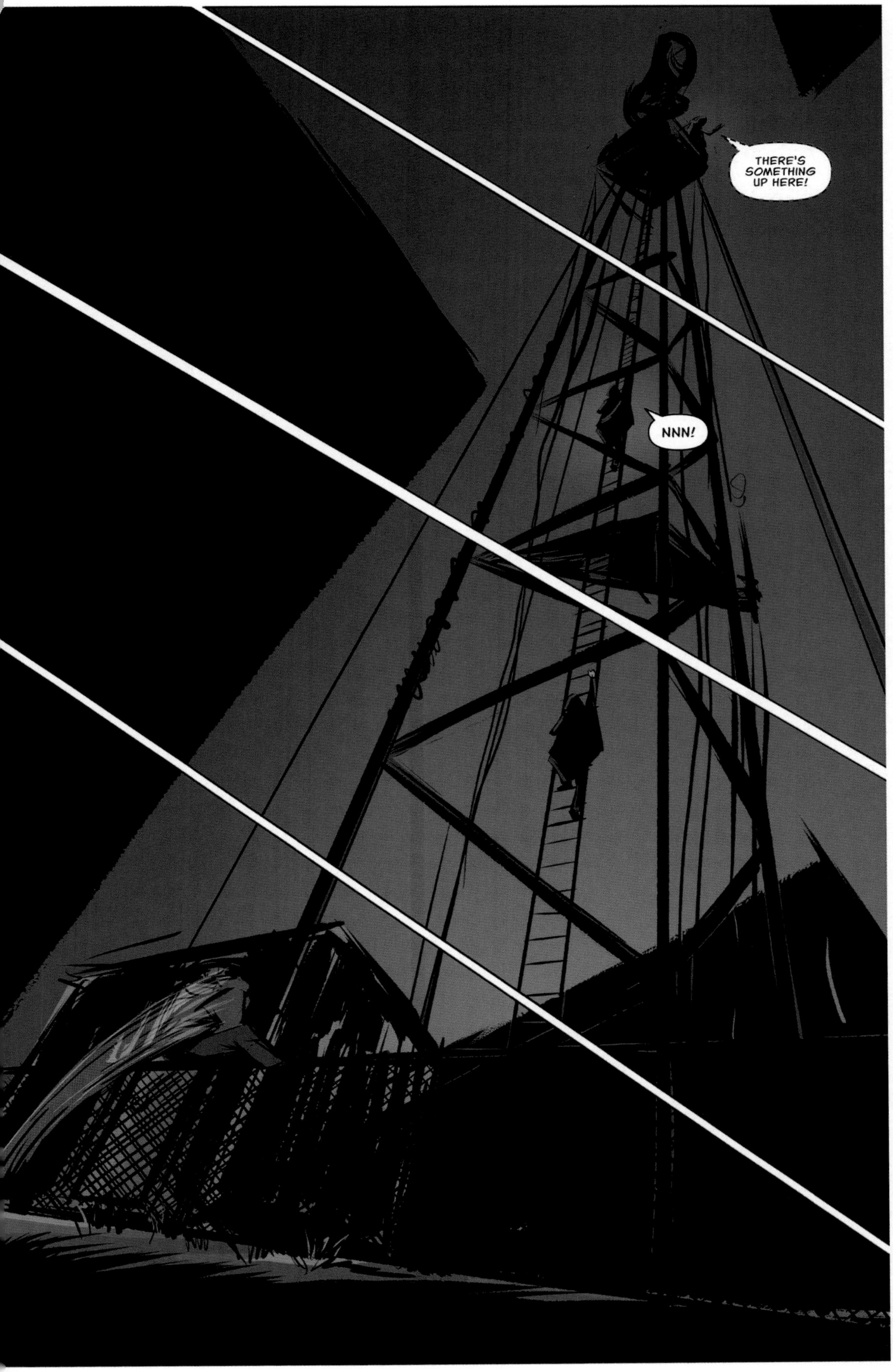
THERE'S SOMETHING UP HERE!
NNN!

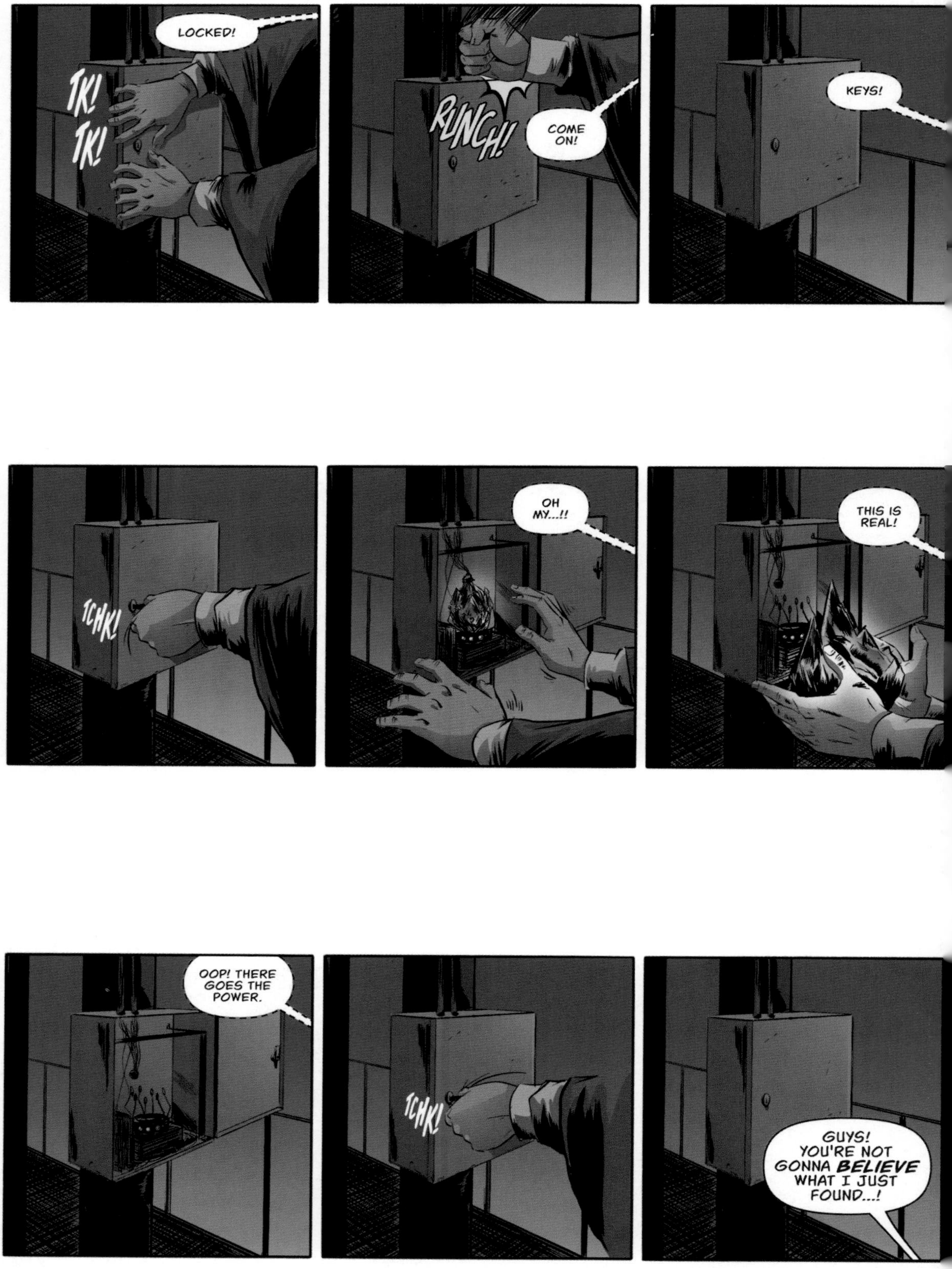
LOCKED!
TK! TK!
RUNCH!
COME ON!
KEYS!
TCHK!
OH MY...!!
THIS IS REAL!
OOP! THERE GOES THE POWER.
TCHK!
GUYS! YOU'RE NOT GONNA **BELIEVE** WHAT I JUST FOUND...!

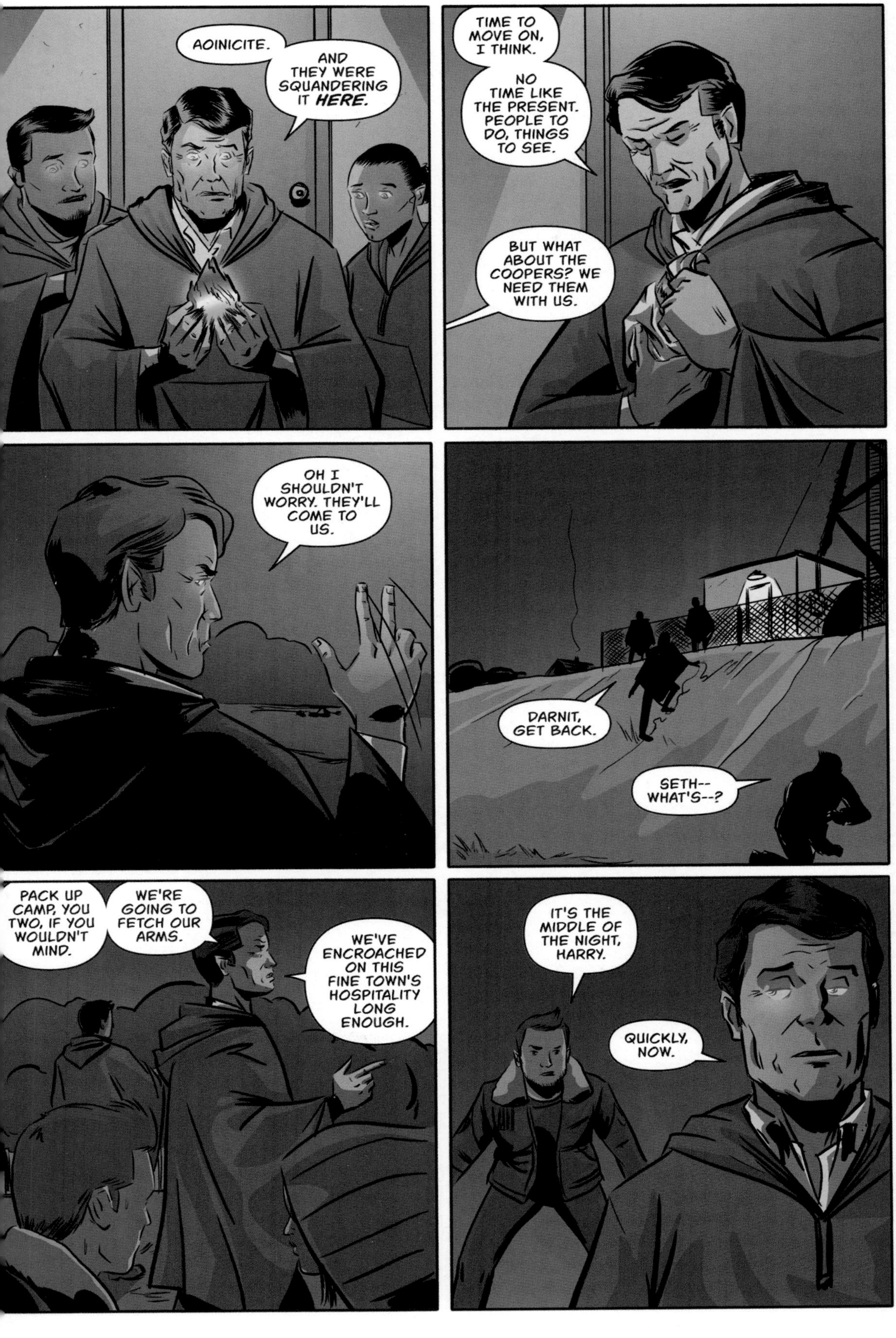
AOINICITE.
AND THEY WERE SQUANDERING IT **HERE.**
TIME TO MOVE ON, I THINK.
NO TIME LIKE THE PRESENT. PEOPLE TO DO, THINGS TO SEE.
BUT WHAT ABOUT THE COOPERS? WE NEED THEM WITH US.
OH I SHOULDN'T WORRY. THEY'LL COME TO US.
DARNIT, GET BACK.
SETH-- WHAT'S--?
PACK UP CAMP, YOU TWO, IF YOU WOULDN'T MIND.
WE'RE GOING TO FETCH OUR ARMS.
WE'VE ENCROACHED ON THIS FINE TOWN'S HOSPITALITY LONG ENOUGH.
IT'S THE MIDDLE OF THE NIGHT, HARRY.
QUICKLY, NOW.

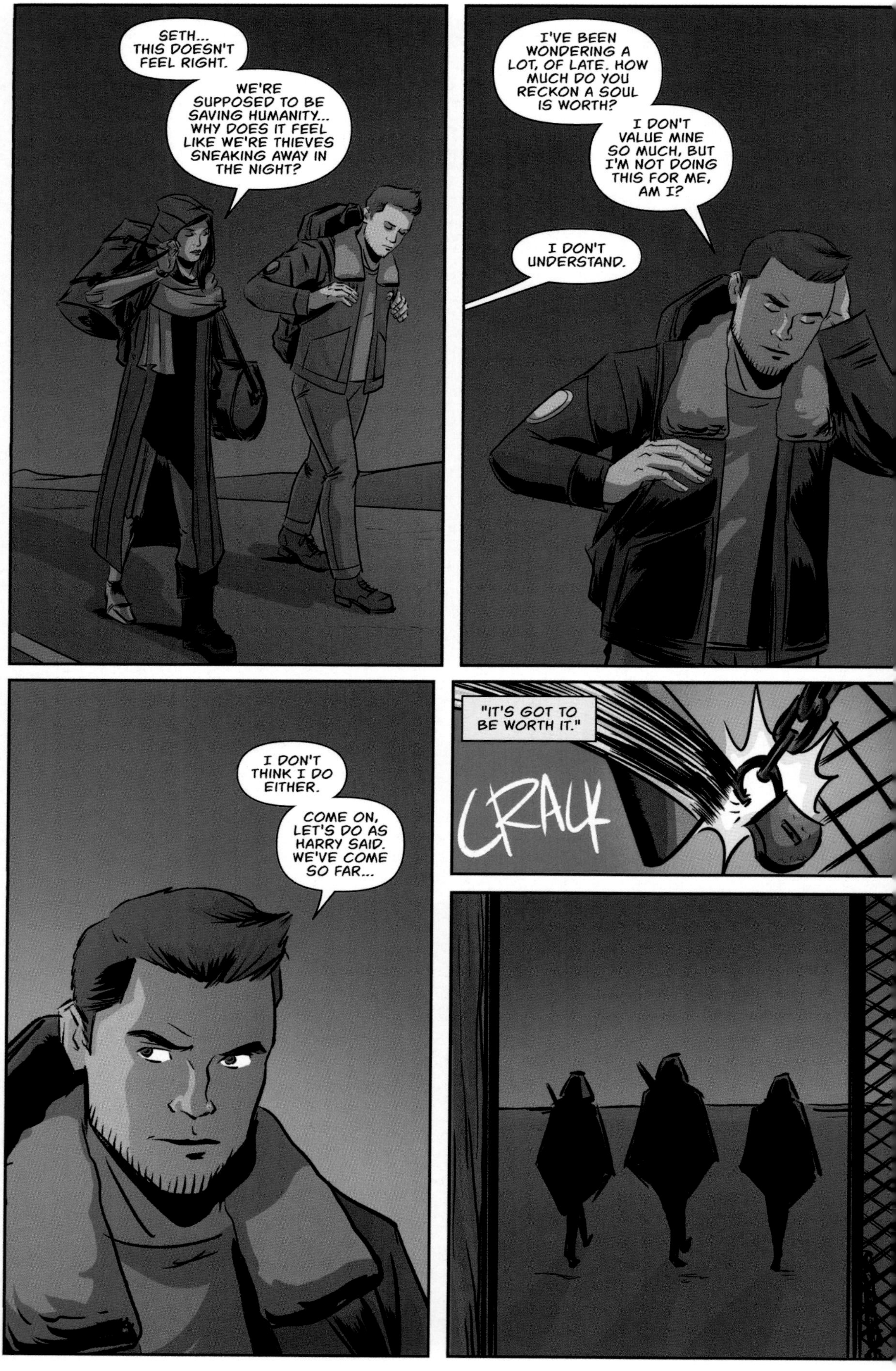
SETH... THIS DOESN'T FEEL RIGHT.
WE'RE SUPPOSED TO BE SAVING HUMANITY... WHY DOES IT FEEL LIKE WE'RE THIEVES SNEAKING AWAY IN THE NIGHT?
I'VE BEEN WONDERING A LOT, OF LATE. HOW MUCH DO YOU RECKON A SOUL IS WORTH?
I DON'T VALUE MINE SO MUCH, BUT I'M NOT DOING THIS FOR ME, AM I?
I DON'T UNDERSTAND.
I DON'T THINK I DO EITHER.
COME ON, LET'S DO AS HARRY SAID. WE'VE COME SO FAR...
"IT'S GOT TO BE WORTH IT."
CRACK

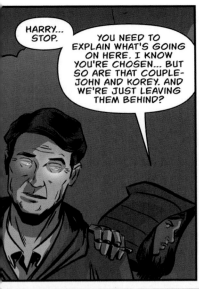

HARRY... STOP.

YOU NEED TO EXPLAIN WHAT'S GOING ON HERE. I KNOW YOU'RE CHOSEN... BUT SO ARE THAT COUPLE—JOHN AND KOREY. AND WE'RE JUST LEAVING THEM BEHIND?

OH, NO. NO WE'RE NOT. THEY'LL FOLLOW BEHIND IN THEIR OWN TIME.

WHY WOULD THEY?

A DEFENSE MECHANISM THAT BIG HAD TO BE POWERED BY AOICINITE.

HOW MUCH OF IT DID YOU LEAVE THEM, HARRY?

HOW MUCH TO DEFEND THEMSELVES WITH?

OH NO. OH NO NO. YOU'VE DOOMED THEM ALL. WE NEED TO GO BACK. THIS IS WRONG.

THEY HAVE TO LEARN. THIS IS THE END OF THE WORLD. NO PLACE FOR SOFT HEARTS OR STOMACHS.

I WASN'T ASKING.

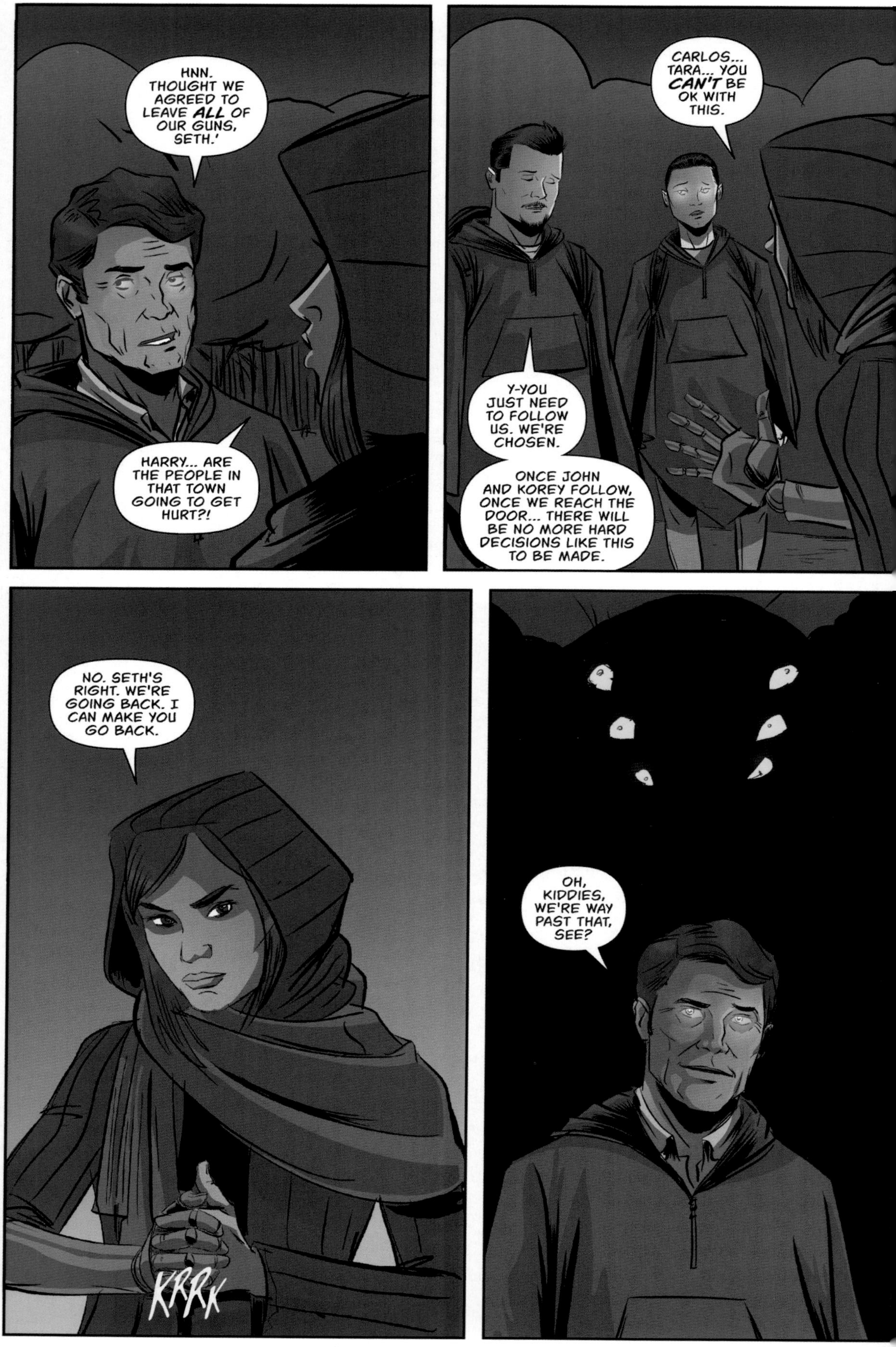
HNN. THOUGHT WE AGREED TO LEAVE ALL OF OUR GUNS, SETH.'
HARRY... ARE THE PEOPLE IN THAT TOWN GOING TO GET HURT?!
CARLOS... TARA... YOU CAN'T BE OK WITH THIS.
Y-YOU JUST NEED TO FOLLOW US. WE'RE CHOSEN.
ONCE JOHN AND KOREY FOLLOW, ONCE WE REACH THE DOOR... THERE WILL BE NO MORE HARD DECISIONS LIKE THIS TO BE MADE.
NO. SETH'S RIGHT. WE'RE GOING BACK. I CAN MAKE YOU GO BACK.
KRRK
OH, KIDDIES, WE'RE WAY PAST THAT, SEE?

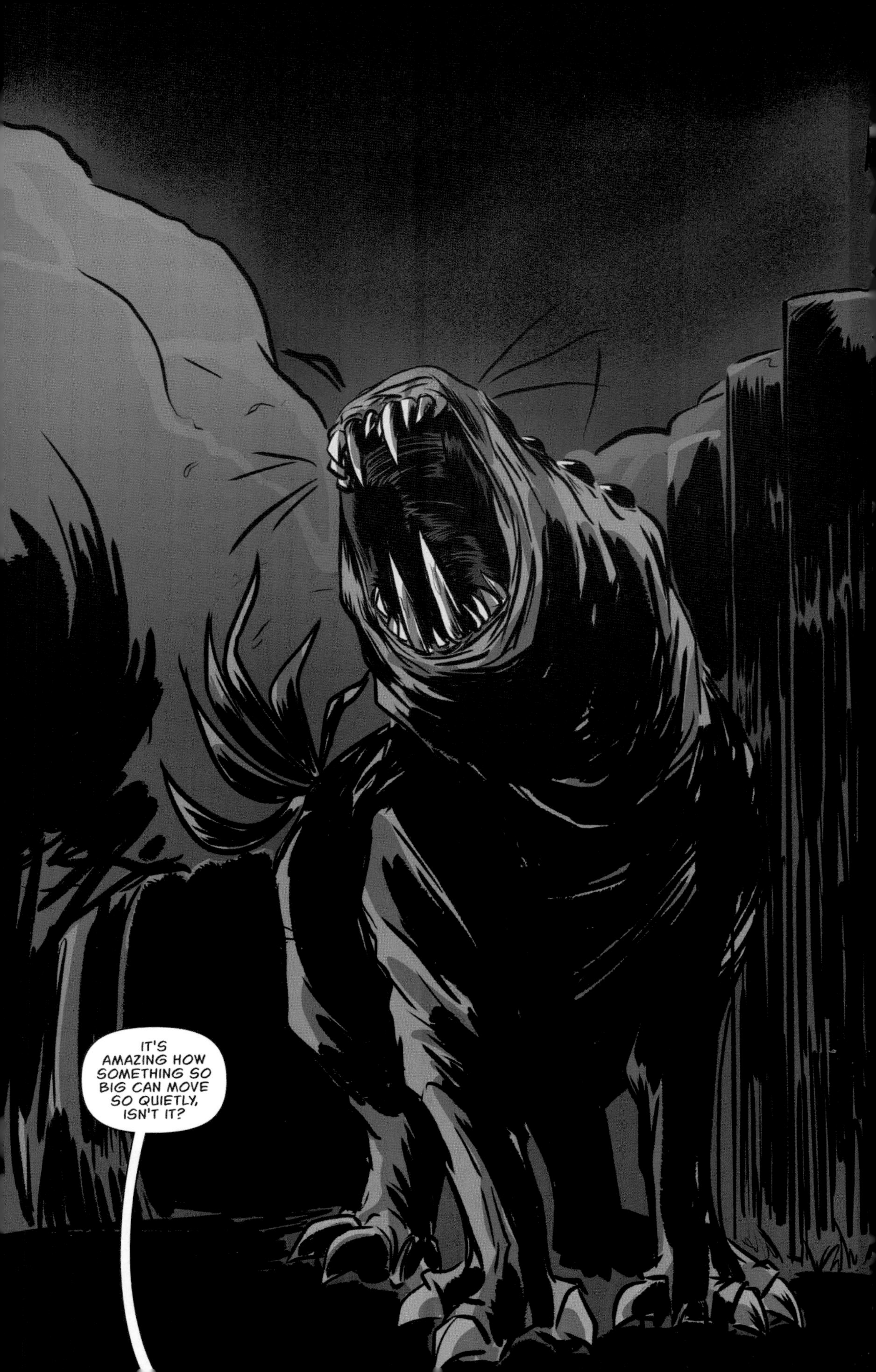
IT'S AMAZING HOW SOMETHING SO BIG CAN MOVE SO QUIETLY, ISN'T IT?

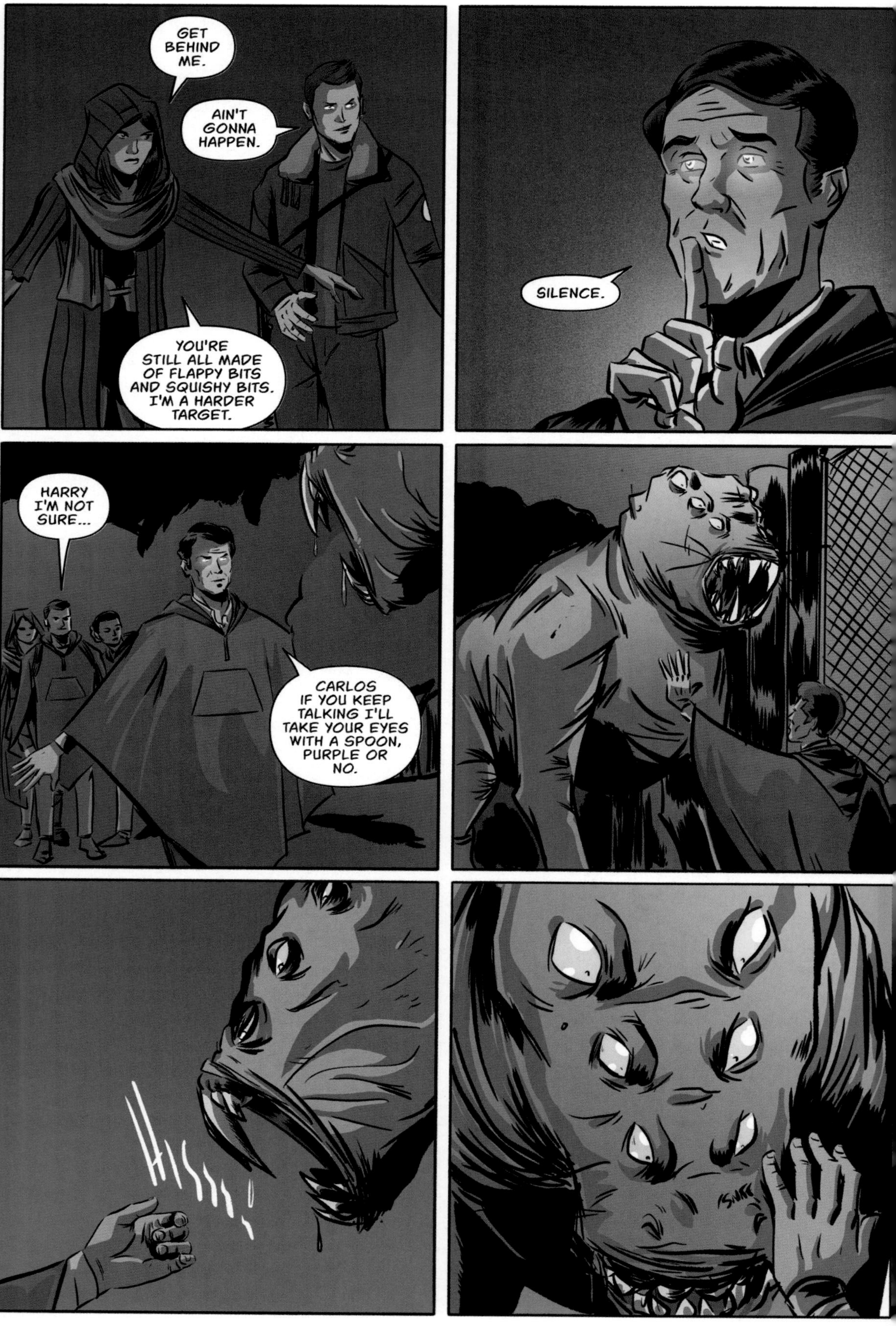
GET BEHIND ME.
AIN'T GONNA HAPPEN.
YOU'RE STILL ALL MADE OF FLAPPY BITS AND SQUISHY BITS. I'M A HARDER TARGET.
SILENCE.
HARRY I'M NOT SURE...
CARLOS IF YOU KEEP TALKING I'LL TAKE YOUR EYES WITH A SPOON, PURPLE OR NO.
HISSSS!
SNIFF

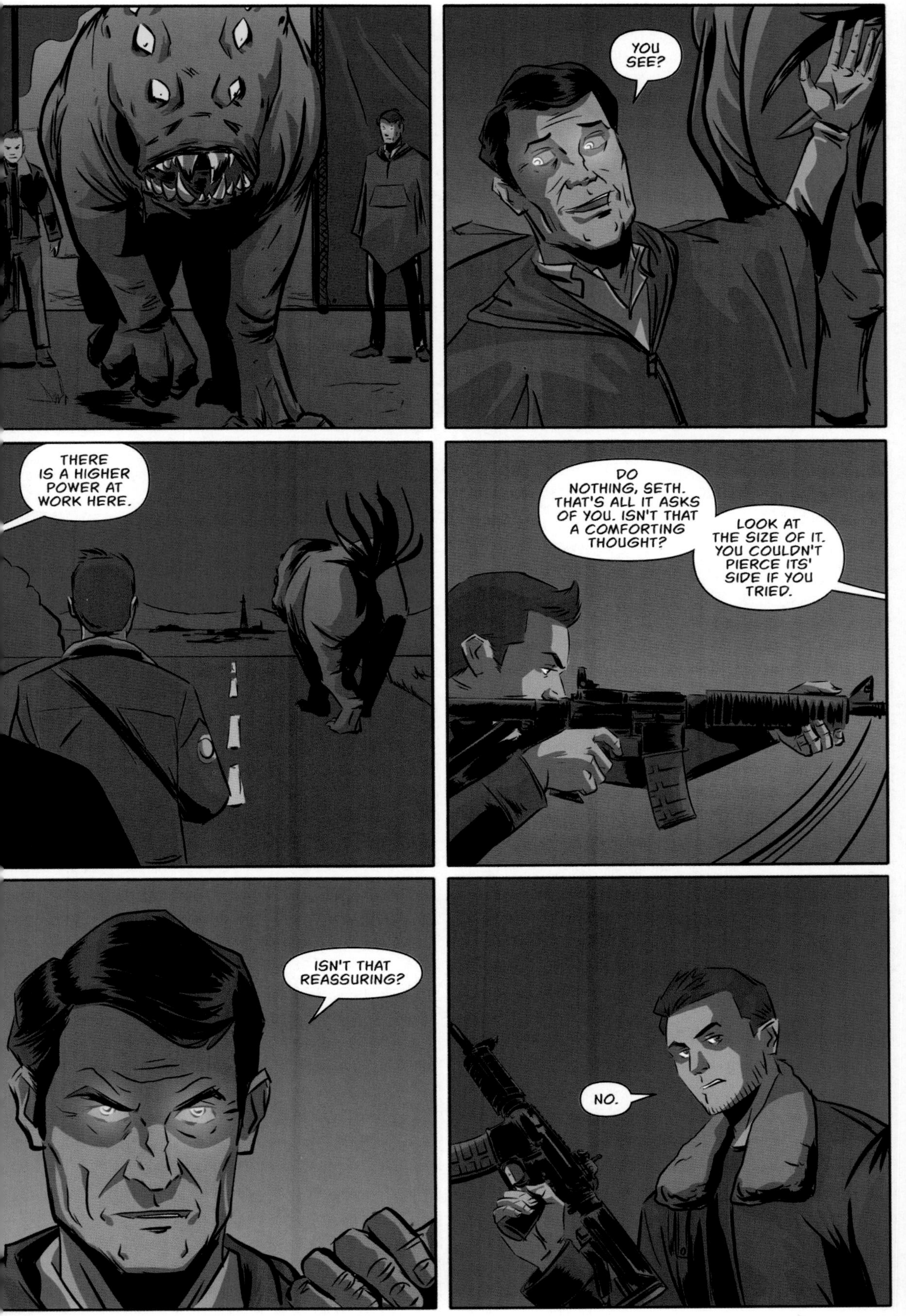

YOU SEE?
THERE IS A HIGHER POWER AT WORK HERE.
DO NOTHING, SETH. THAT'S ALL IT ASKS OF YOU. ISN'T THAT A COMFORTING THOUGHT?
LOOK AT THE SIZE OF IT. YOU COULDN'T PIERCE ITS' SIDE IF YOU TRIED.
ISN'T THAT REASSURING?
NO.

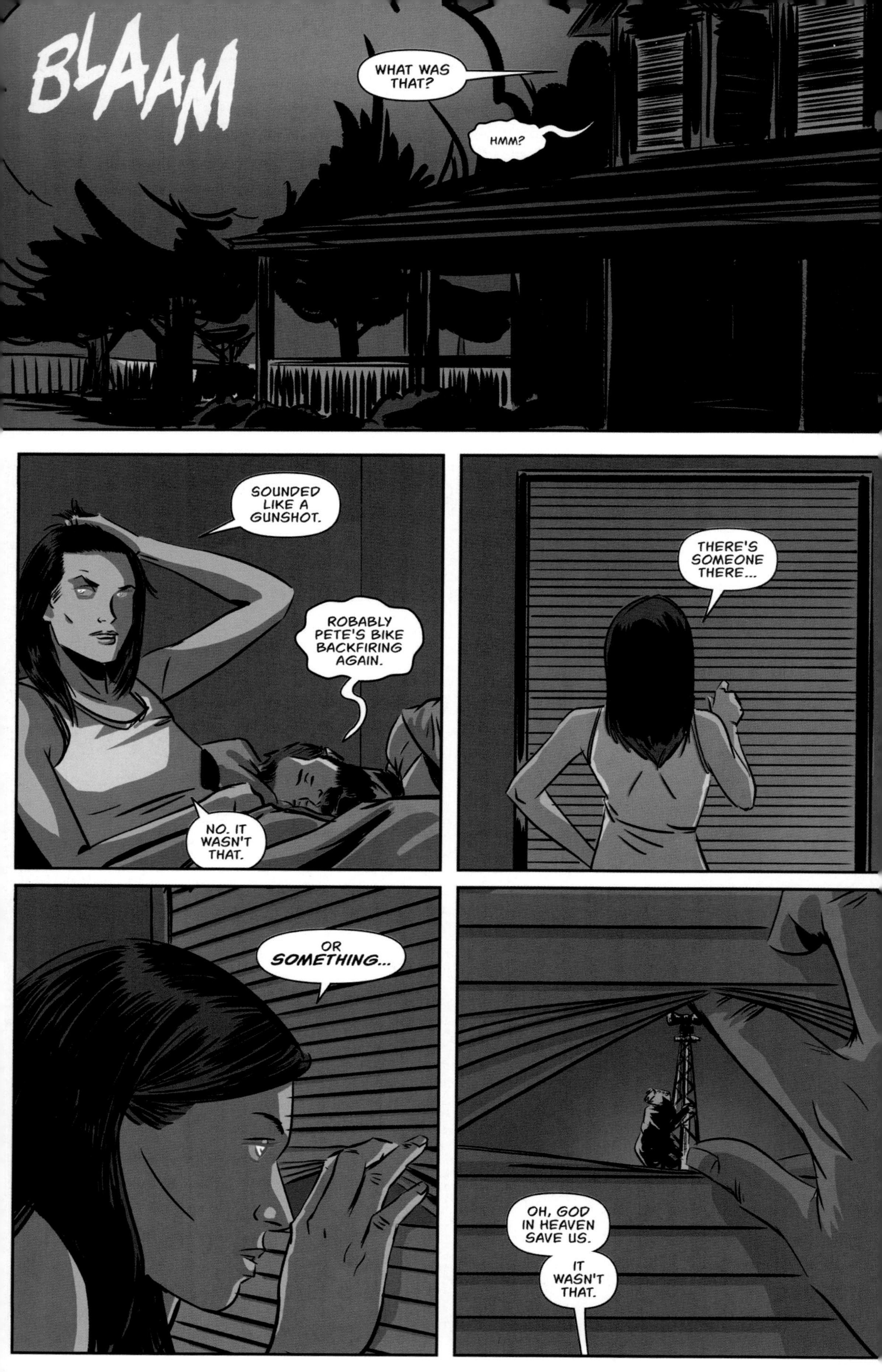
BLAAM
WHAT WAS THAT?
HMM?
SOUNDED LIKE A GUNSHOT.
ROBABLY PETE'S BIKE BACKFIRING AGAIN.
NO. IT WASN'T THAT.
THERE'S SOMEONE THERE...
OR *SOMETHING*...
OH, GOD IN HEAVEN SAVE US.
IT WASN'T THAT.

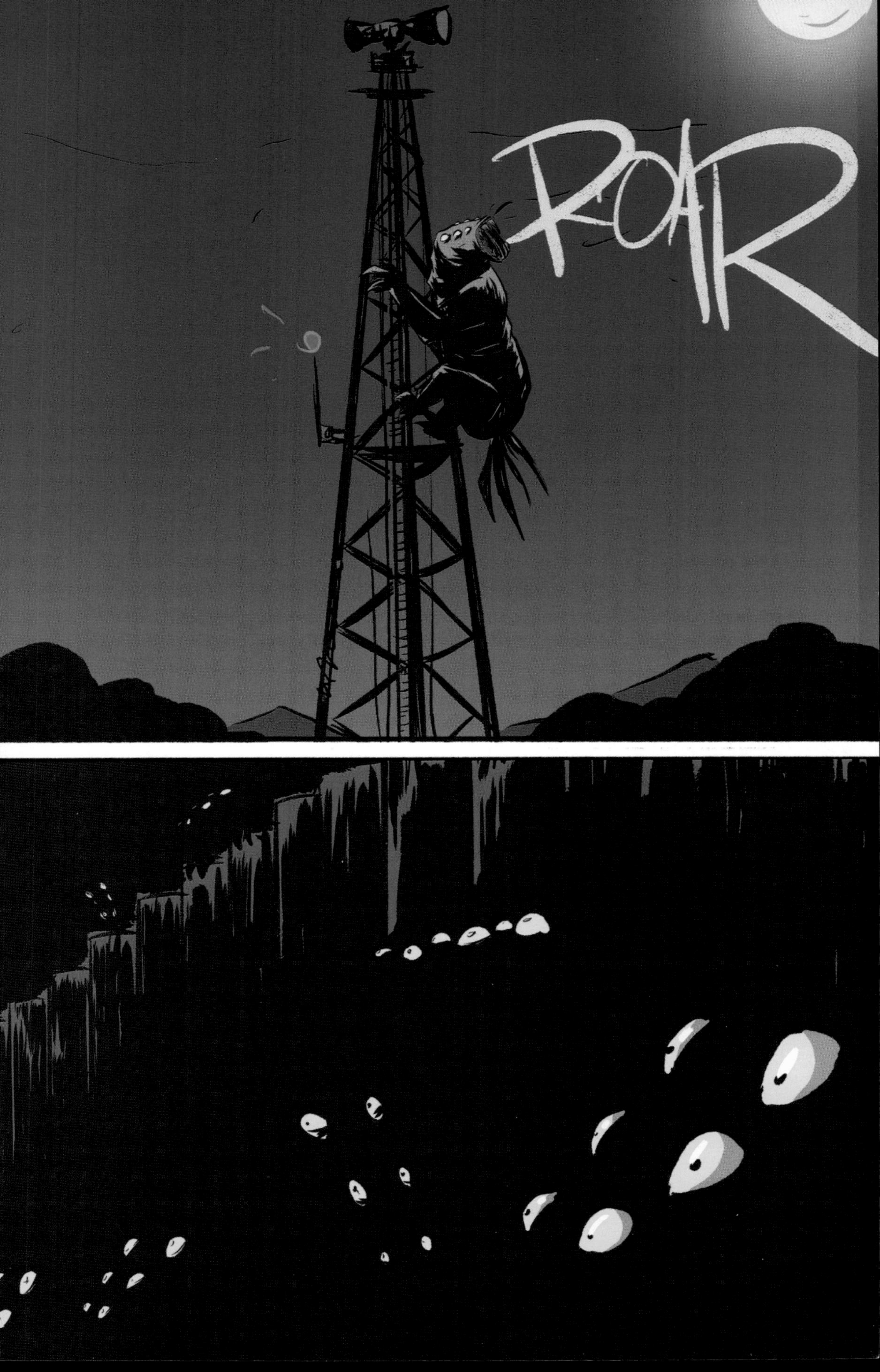
ROAR

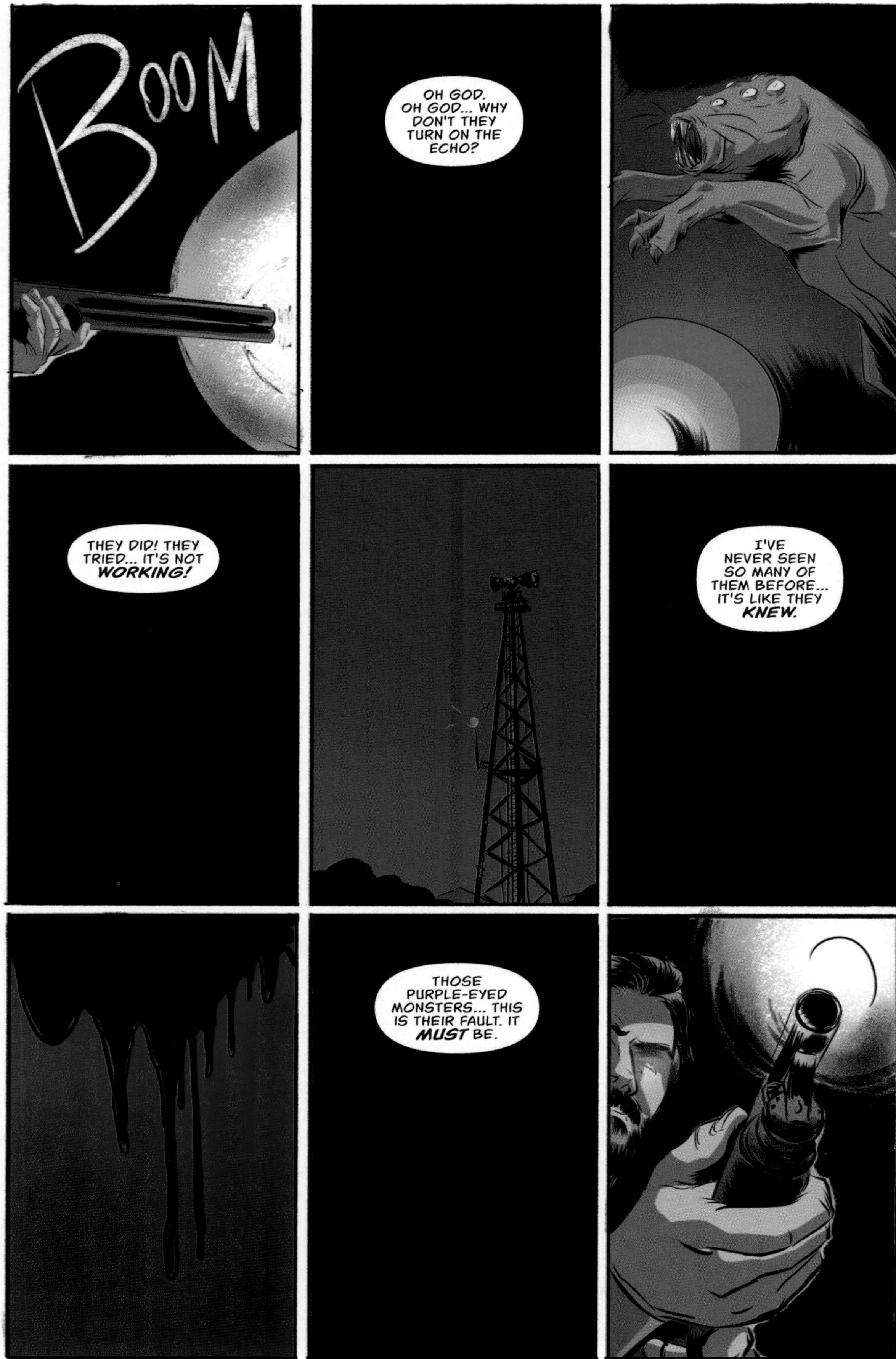
BOOM
OH GOD. OH GOD... WHY DON'T THEY TURN ON THE ECHO?
THEY DID! THEY TRIED... IT'S NOT WORKING!
I'VE NEVER SEEN SO MANY OF THEM BEFORE... IT'S LIKE THEY KNEW.
THOSE PURPLE-EYED MONSTERS... THIS IS THEIR FAULT. IT MUST BE.

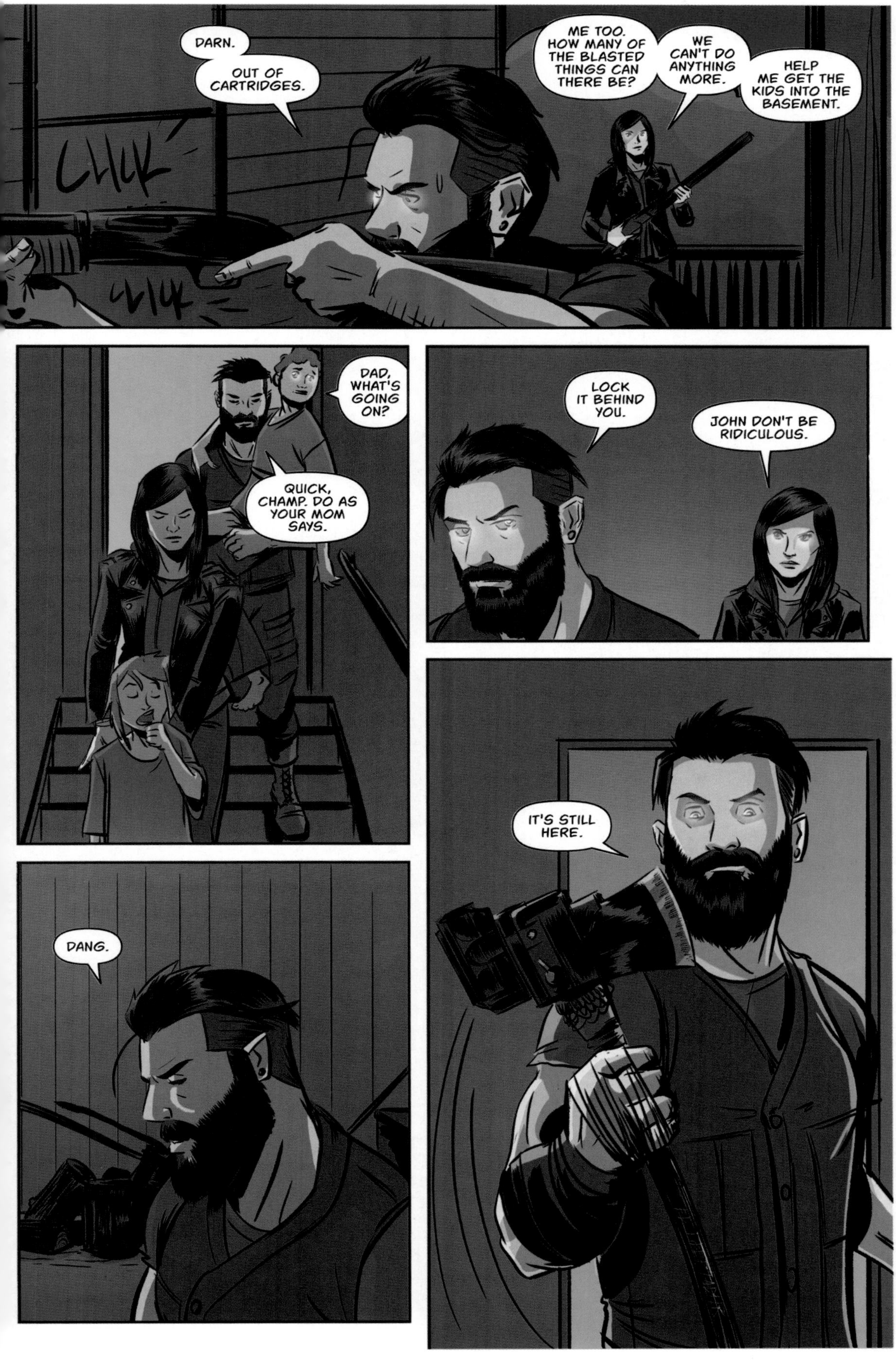
DARN.
OUT OF CARTRIDGES.
CLICK
CLICK
ME TOO. HOW MANY OF THE BLASTED THINGS CAN THERE BE?
WE CAN'T DO ANYTHING MORE.
HELP ME GET THE KIDS INTO THE BASEMENT.
DAD, WHAT'S GOING ON?
QUICK, CHAMP. DO AS YOUR MOM SAYS.
LOCK IT BEHIND YOU.
JOHN DON'T BE RIDICULOUS.
DANG.
IT'S STILL HERE.

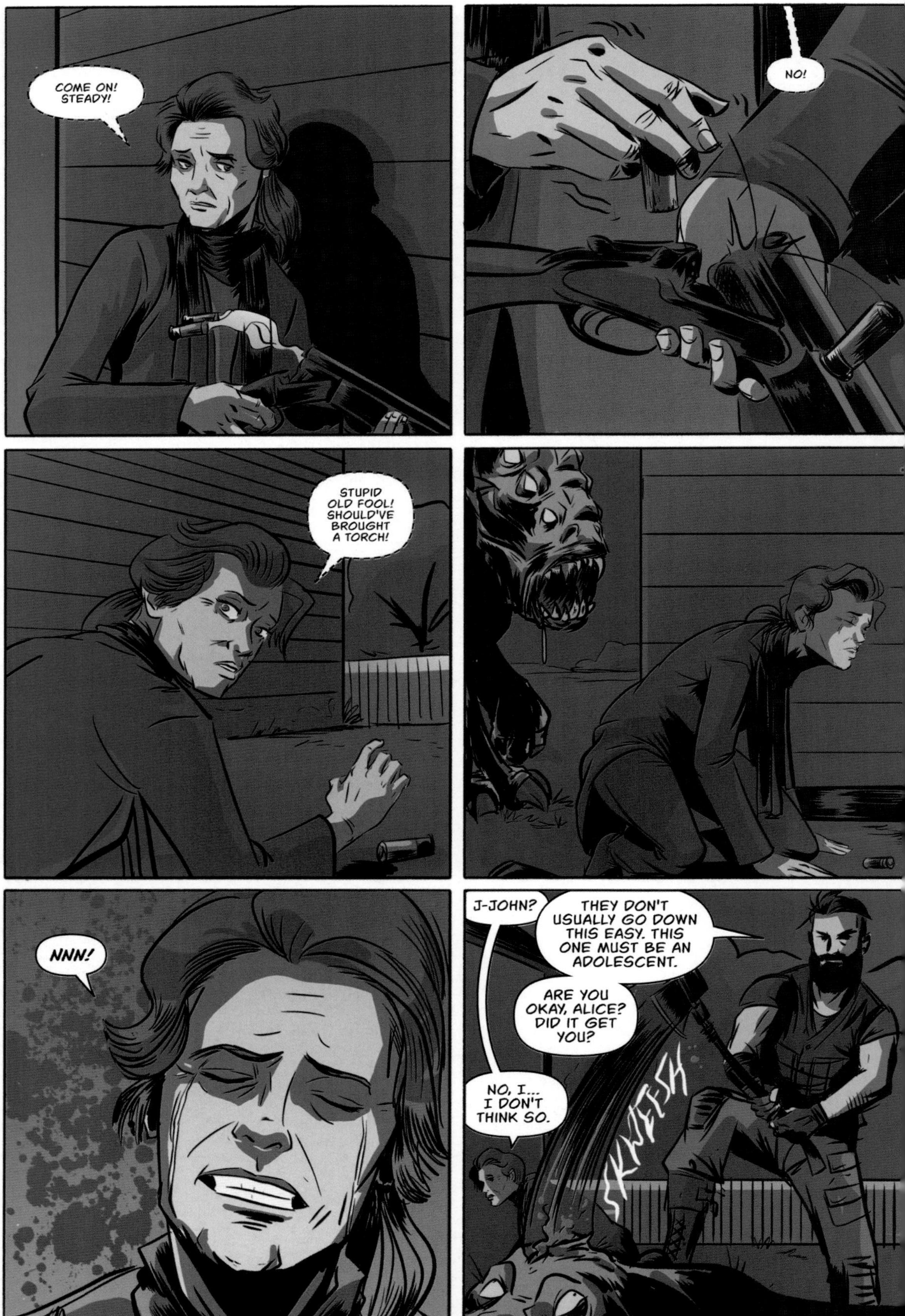
COME ON! STEADY!
NO!
STUPID OLD FOOL! SHOULD'VE BROUGHT A TORCH!
NNN!
J-JOHN?
THEY DON'T USUALLY GO DOWN THIS EASY. THIS ONE MUST BE AN ADOLESCENT.
ARE YOU OKAY, ALICE? DID IT GET YOU?
NO, I... I DON'T THINK SO.
SKWEESH

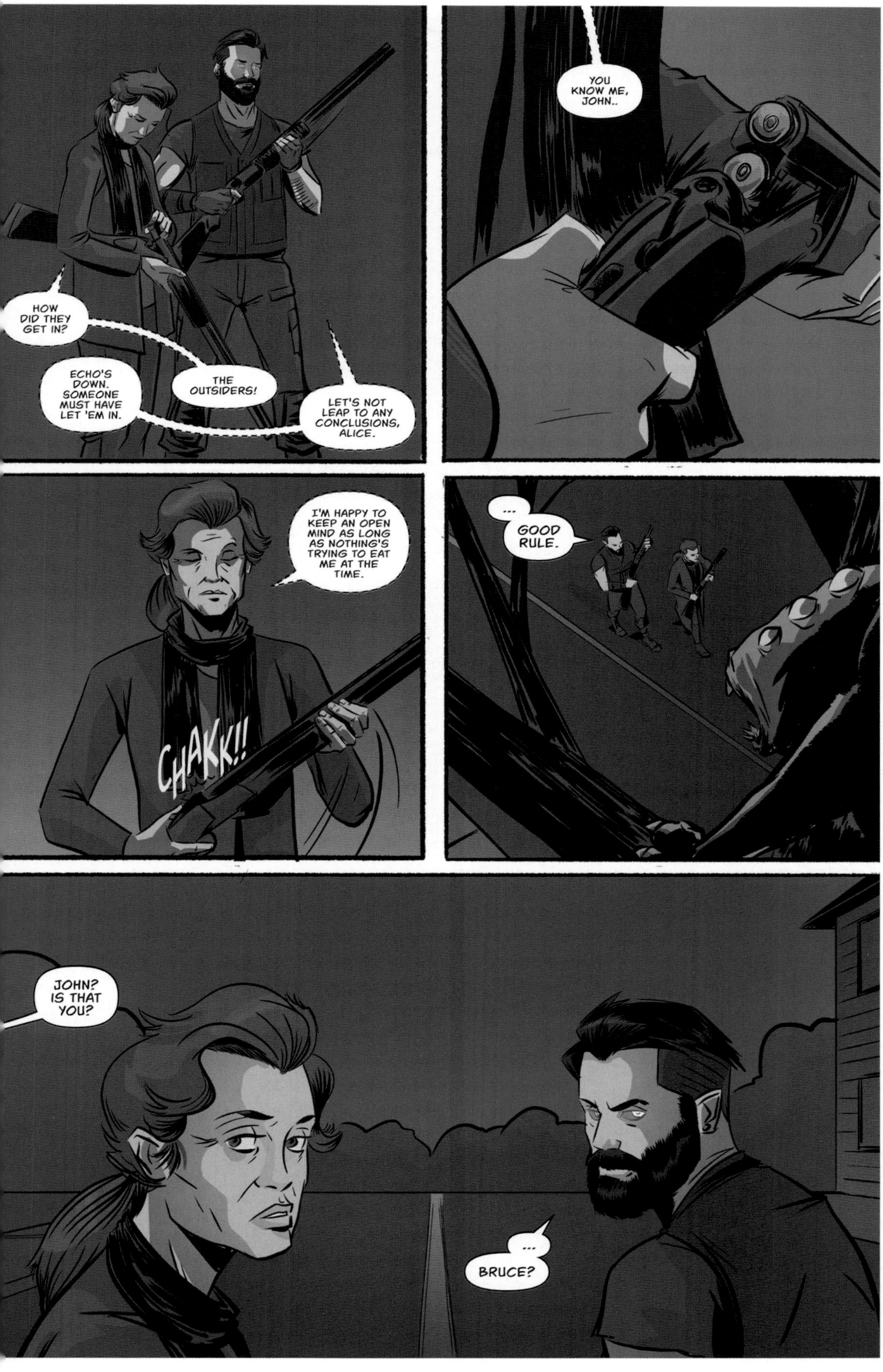
HOW DID THEY GET IN?
THE OUTSIDERS!
ECHO'S DOWN. SOMEONE MUST HAVE LET 'EM IN.
LET'S NOT LEAP TO ANY CONCLUSIONS, ALICE.
YOU KNOW ME, JOHN..
I'M HAPPY TO KEEP AN OPEN MIND AS LONG AS NOTHING'S TRYING TO EAT ME AT THE TIME.
CHAKK!!
... GOOD RULE.
JOHN? IS THAT YOU?
... BRUCE?

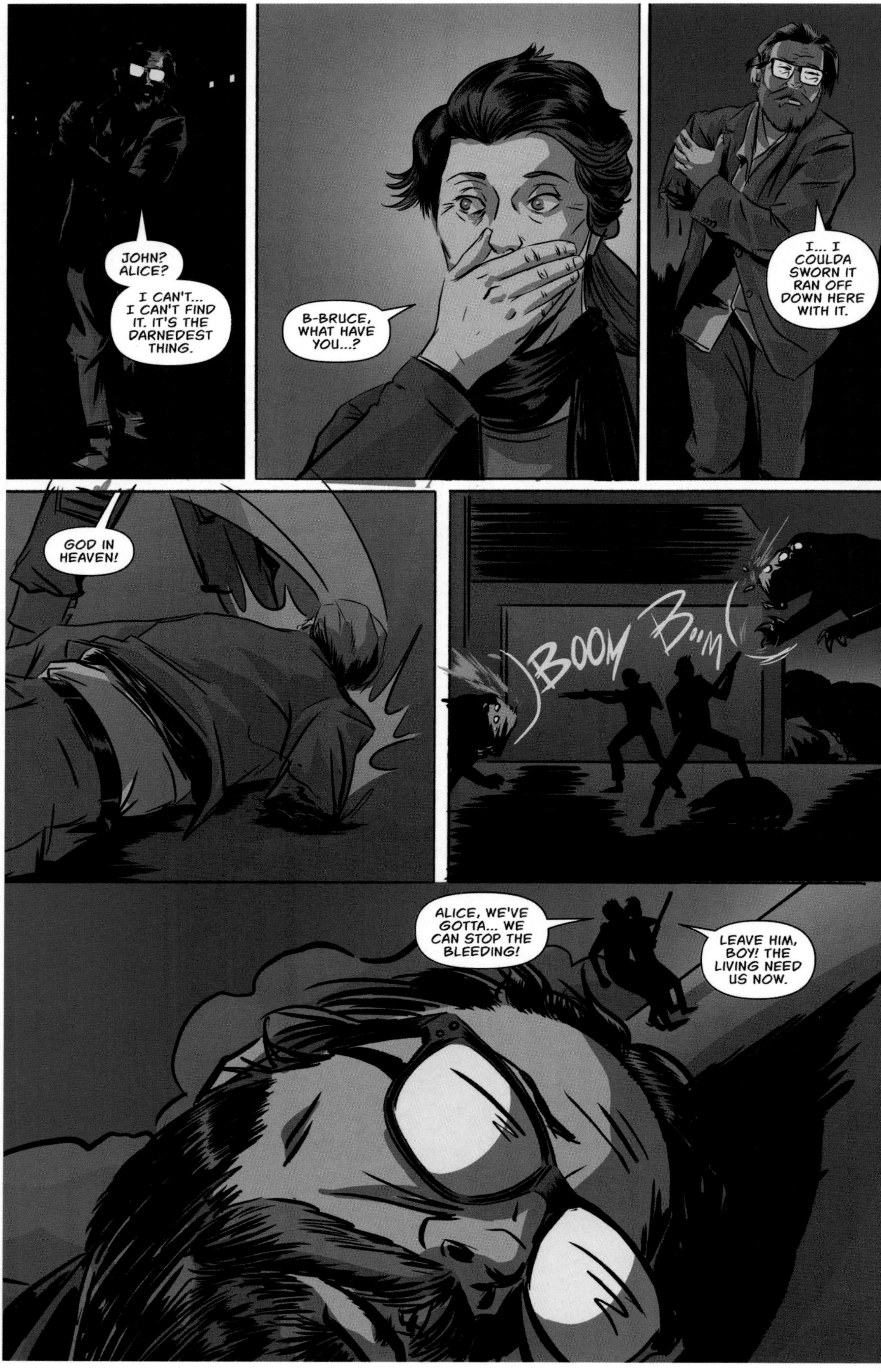

JOHN? ALICE?
I CAN'T... I CAN'T FIND IT. IT'S THE DARNEDEST THING.
B-BRUCE, WHAT HAVE YOU...?
I... I COULDA SWORN IT RAN OFF DOWN HERE WITH IT.
GOD IN HEAVEN!
BOOM BOOM
ALICE, WE'VE GOTTA... WE CAN STOP THE BLEEDING!
LEAVE HIM, BOY! THE LIVING NEED US NOW.

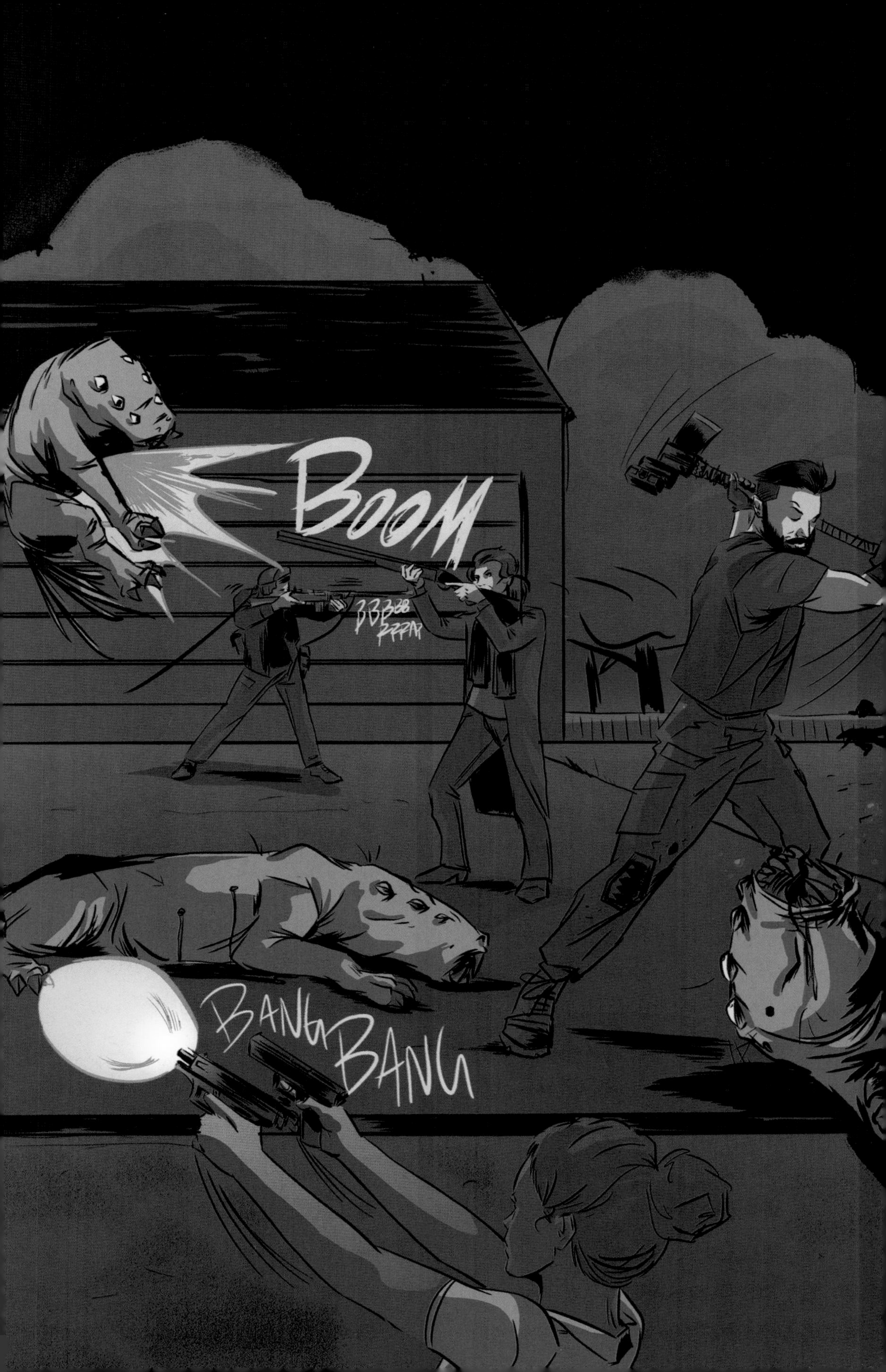
BOOM
BBBBB
RRRAR
BANG BANG

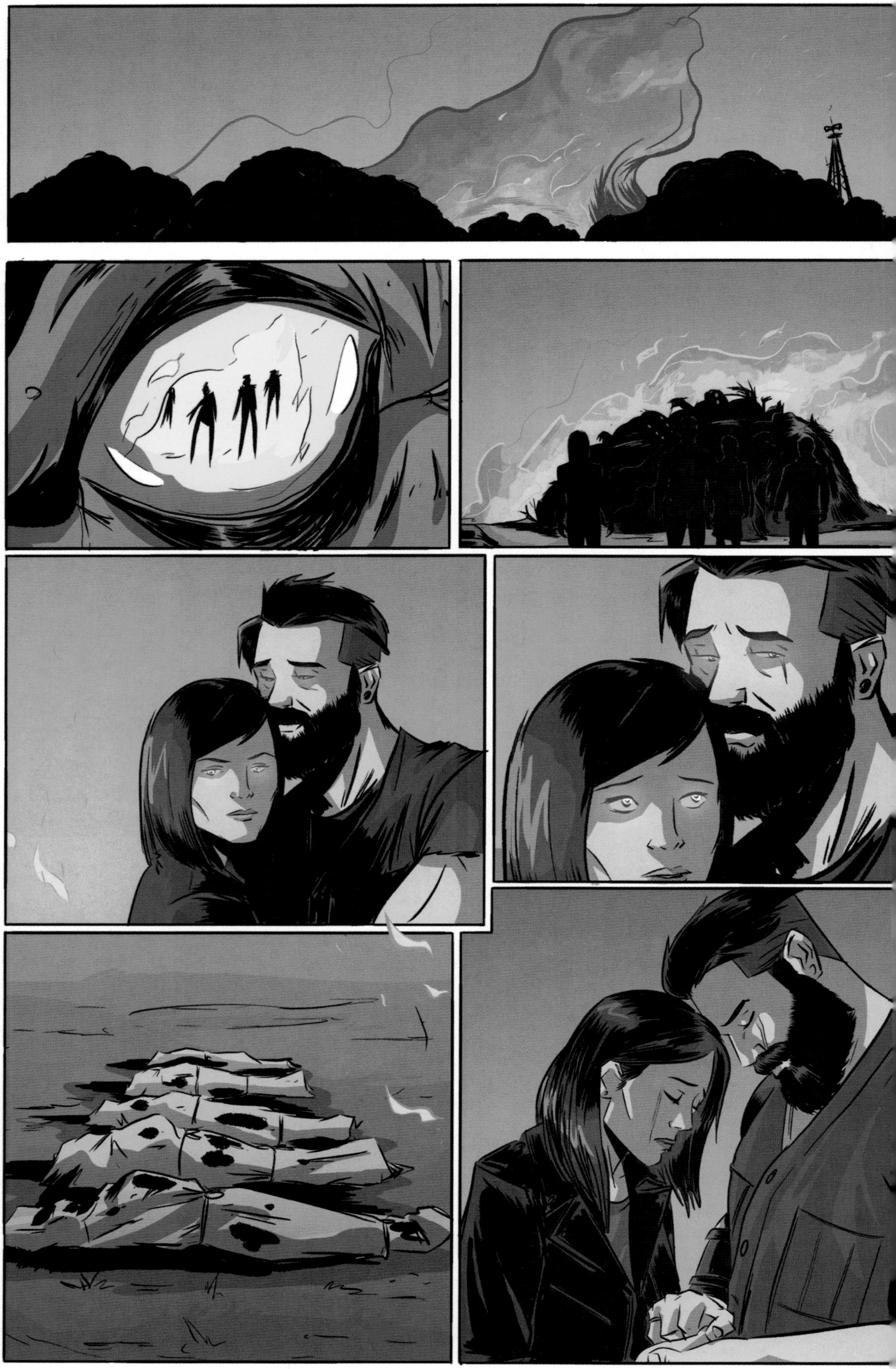

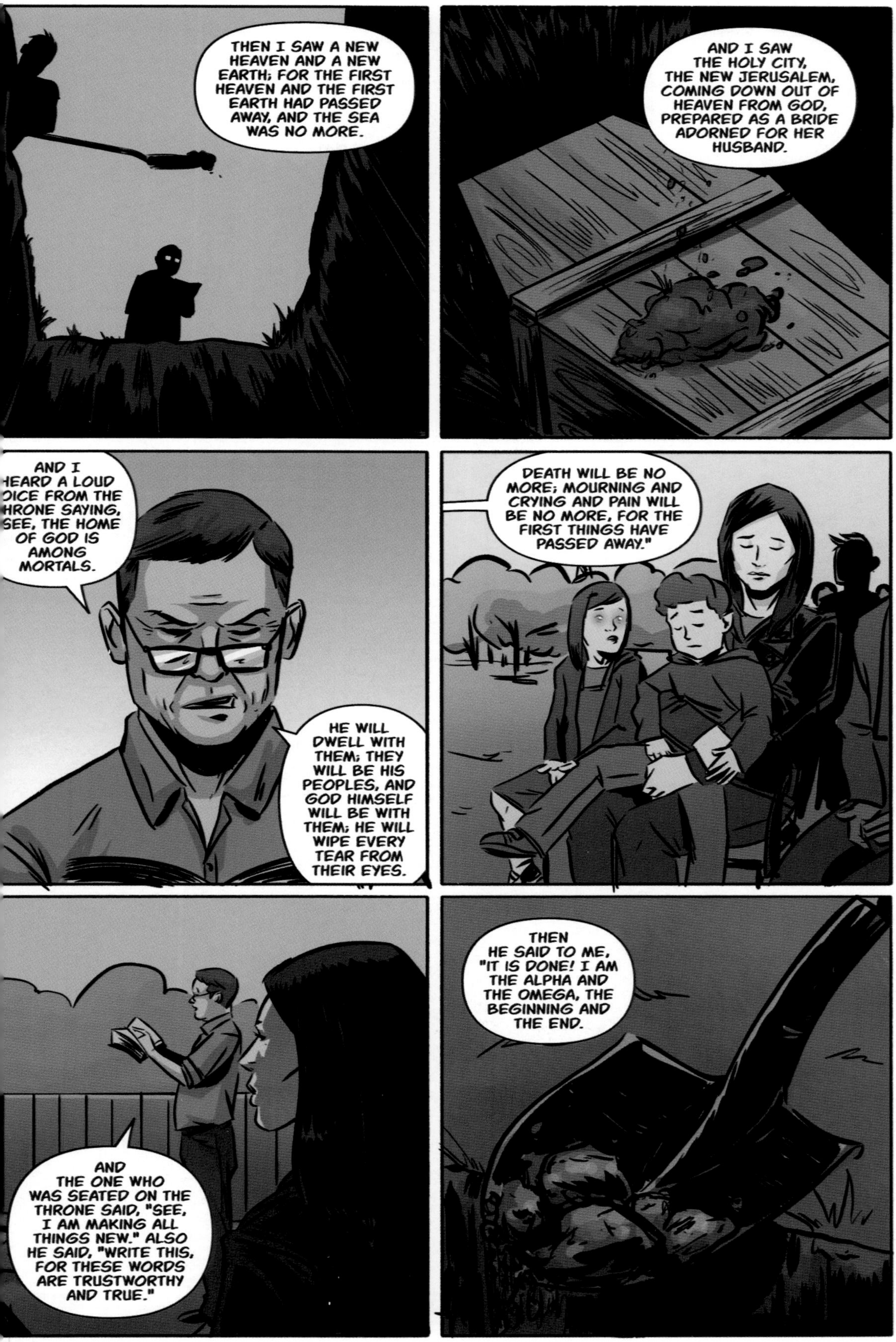
THEN I SAW A NEW HEAVEN AND A NEW EARTH; FOR THE FIRST HEAVEN AND THE FIRST EARTH HAD PASSED AWAY, AND THE SEA WAS NO MORE.
AND I SAW THE HOLY CITY, THE NEW JERUSALEM, COMING DOWN OUT OF HEAVEN FROM GOD, PREPARED AS A BRIDE ADORNED FOR HER HUSBAND.
AND I HEARD A LOUD VOICE FROM THE THRONE SAYING, SEE, THE HOME OF GOD IS AMONG MORTALS.
HE WILL DWELL WITH THEM; THEY WILL BE HIS PEOPLES, AND GOD HIMSELF WILL BE WITH THEM; HE WILL WIPE EVERY TEAR FROM THEIR EYES.
DEATH WILL BE NO MORE; MOURNING AND CRYING AND PAIN WILL BE NO MORE, FOR THE FIRST THINGS HAVE PASSED AWAY."
AND THE ONE WHO WAS SEATED ON THE THRONE SAID, "SEE, I AM MAKING ALL THINGS NEW." ALSO HE SAID, "WRITE THIS, FOR THESE WORDS ARE TRUSTWORTHY AND TRUE."
THEN HE SAID TO ME, "IT IS DONE! I AM THE ALPHA AND THE OMEGA, THE BEGINNING AND THE END.

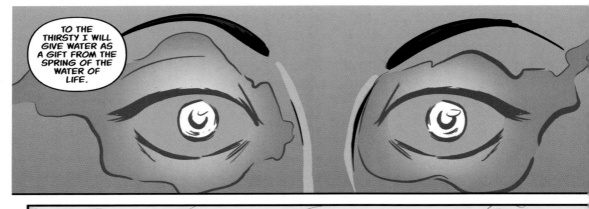

TO THE THIRSTY I WILL GIVE WATER AS A GIFT FROM THE SPRING OF THE WATER OF LIFE.

THOSE WHO CONQUER WILL INHERIT THESE THINGS, AND I WILL BE THEIR GOD AND THEY WILL BE MY CHILDREN.

THREE SOULS. THREE SOULS TAKEN FROM US; CUT DOWN SENSELESSLY BY BEASTS WITH NO UNDERSTANDING OF HONOR...

FAMILY...

COUNTRY.

BUT EVEN IN OUR GRIEF WE FIND COMFORT IN...

KOREY!

MOMMY, WHERE ARE WE GOING?!

≥SNFF≤ MOMMY JUST NEEDS SOME AIR, BABY.

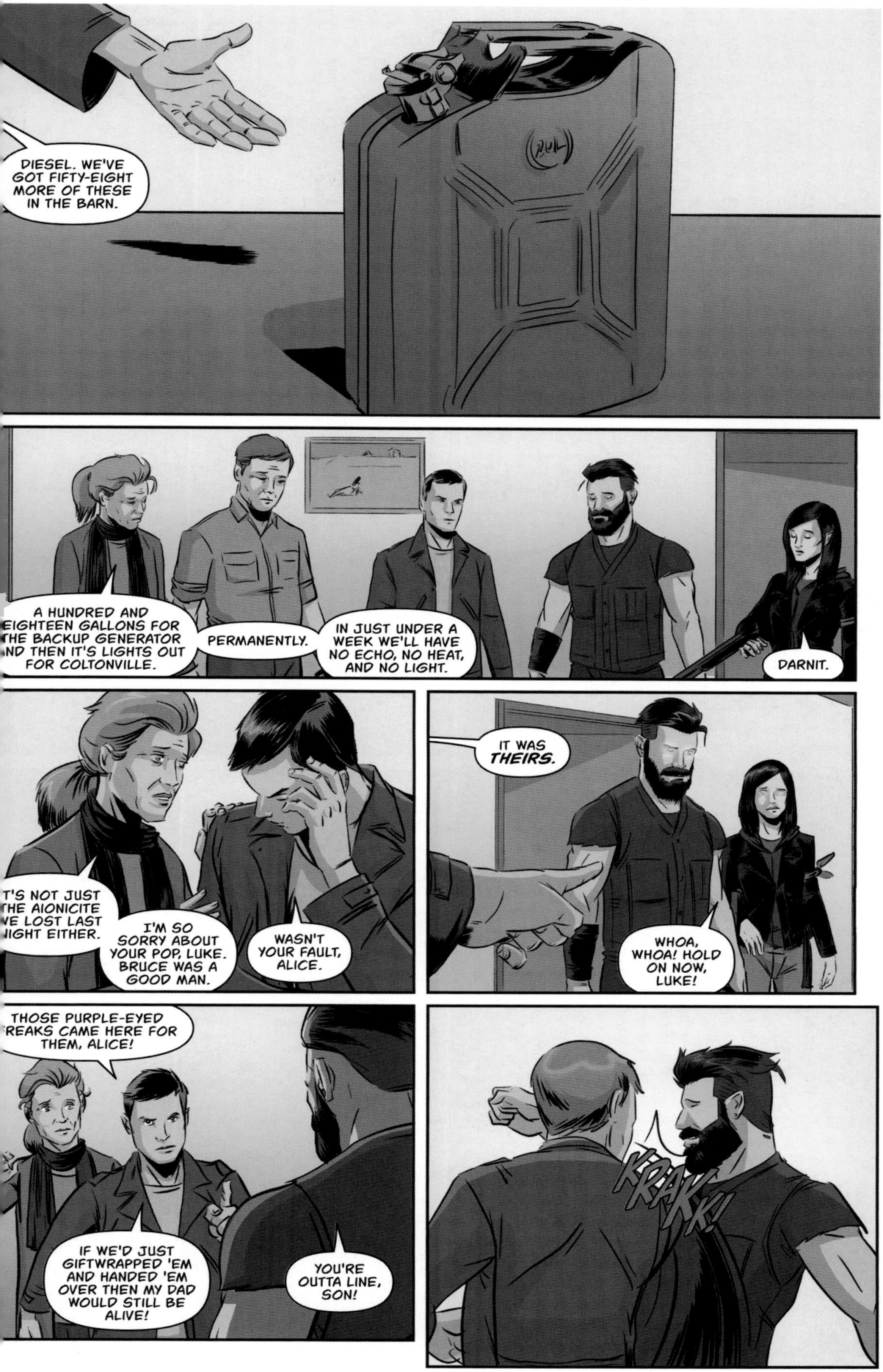
DIESEL. WE'VE GOT FIFTY-EIGHT MORE OF THESE IN THE BARN.
A HUNDRED AND EIGHTEEN GALLONS FOR THE BACKUP GENERATOR AND THEN IT'S LIGHTS OUT FOR COLTONVILLE.
PERMANENTLY.
IN JUST UNDER A WEEK WE'LL HAVE NO ECHO, NO HEAT, AND NO LIGHT.
DARNIT.
IT'S NOT JUST THE AIONICITE WE LOST LAST NIGHT EITHER.
I'M SO SORRY ABOUT YOUR POP, LUKE. BRUCE WAS A GOOD MAN.
WASN'T YOUR FAULT, ALICE.
IT WAS THEIRS.
WHOA, WHOA! HOLD ON NOW, LUKE!
THOSE PURPLE-EYED FREAKS CAME HERE FOR THEM, ALICE!
IF WE'D JUST GIFTWRAPPED 'EM AND HANDED 'EM OVER THEN MY DAD WOULD STILL BE ALIVE!
YOU'RE OUTTA LINE, SON!
KRAKK!

WHY DID YOU HAVE TO ⸝SNFF⸝ HAVE THOSE DUMB DREAMS, HUH?!

LUKE, I DON'T...

I KNOW HE DIDN'T ACT LIKE IT, BUT MY DAD *LOVED* YOU, MAN!

...

I'LL GO.

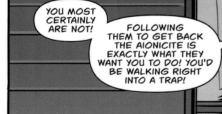

YOU MOST CERTAINLY ARE NOT!

FOLLOWING THEM TO GET BACK THE AIONICITE IS EXACTLY WHAT THEY WANT YOU TO DO! YOU'D BE WALKING RIGHT INTO A TRAP!

PERHAPS...

JOHN'S RIGHT, ALICE. THEY WERE HERE FOR US, AND THAT MEANS IT'S OUR RESPONSIBILITY WHETHER WE LIKE IT OR *NOT.*

WE'RE GOING.

HEY, WHO'S THIS "WE"? I'LL TAKE CARE OF IT.

OH PLEASE. YOU'RE A *HORRIBLE* SHOT.

YOU NEED ME.

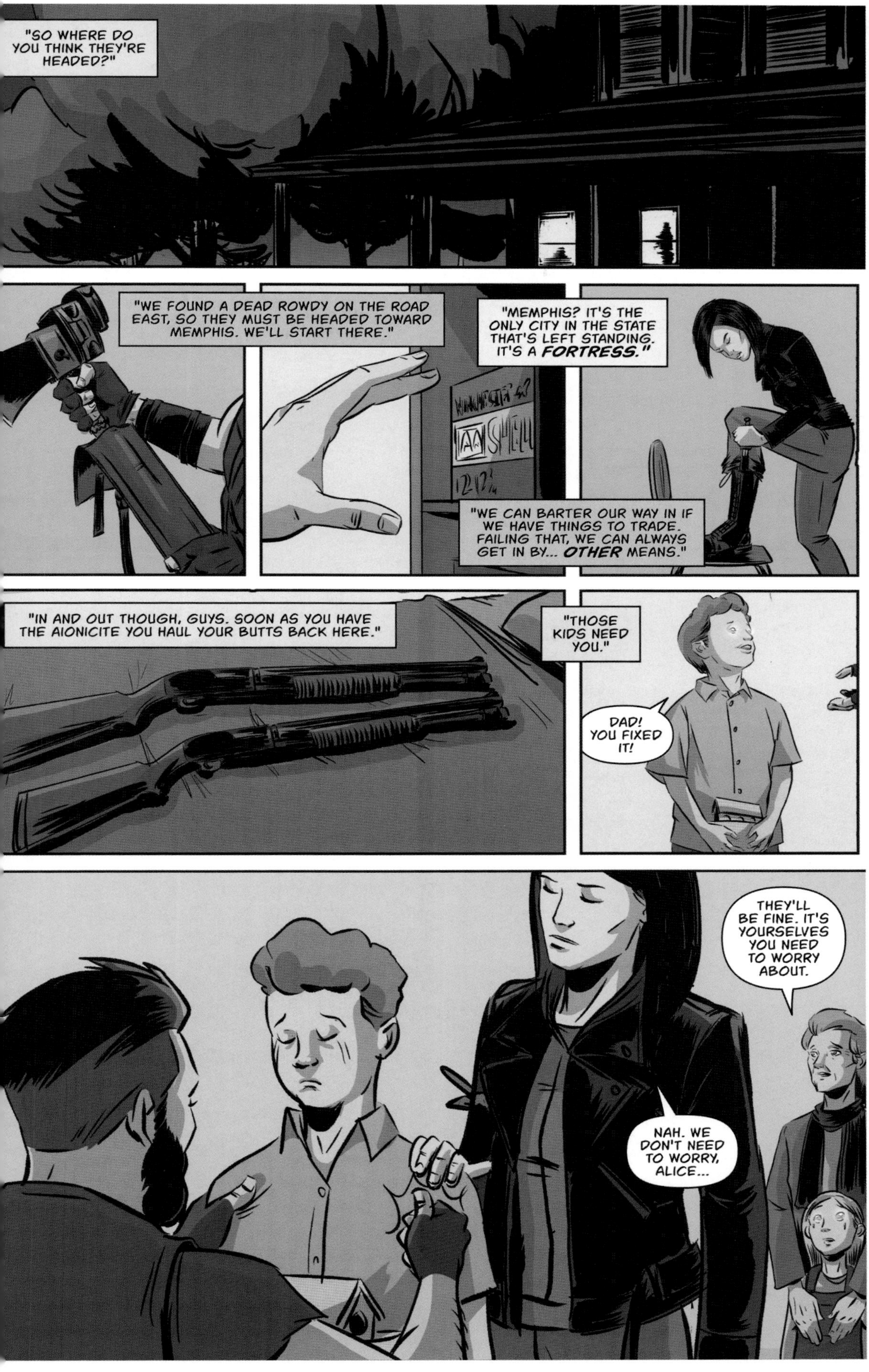
"SO WHERE DO YOU THINK THEY'RE HEADED?"
"WE FOUND A DEAD ROWDY ON THE ROAD EAST, SO THEY MUST BE HEADED TOWARD MEMPHIS. WE'LL START THERE."
"MEMPHIS? IT'S THE ONLY CITY IN THE STATE THAT'S LEFT STANDING. IT'S A FORTRESS."
"WE CAN BARTER OUR WAY IN IF WE HAVE THINGS TO TRADE. FAILING THAT, WE CAN ALWAYS GET IN BY... OTHER MEANS."
"IN AND OUT THOUGH, GUYS. SOON AS YOU HAVE THE AIONICITE YOU HAUL YOUR BUTTS BACK HERE."
"THOSE KIDS NEED YOU."
DAD! YOU FIXED IT!
THEY'LL BE FINE. IT'S YOURSELVES YOU NEED TO WORRY ABOUT.
NAH. WE DON'T NEED TO WORRY, ALICE...

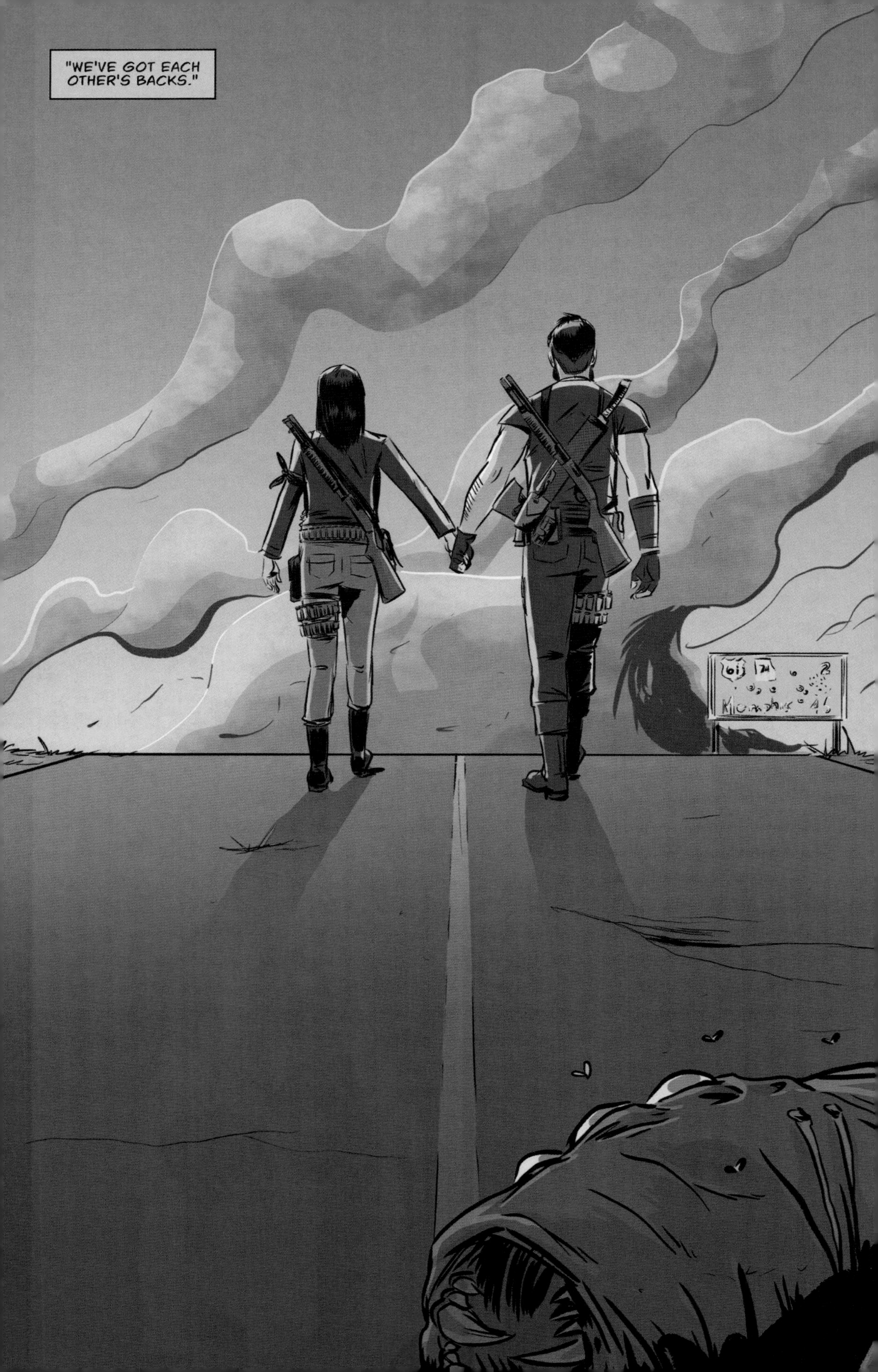
"WE'VE GOT EACH OTHER'S BACKS."

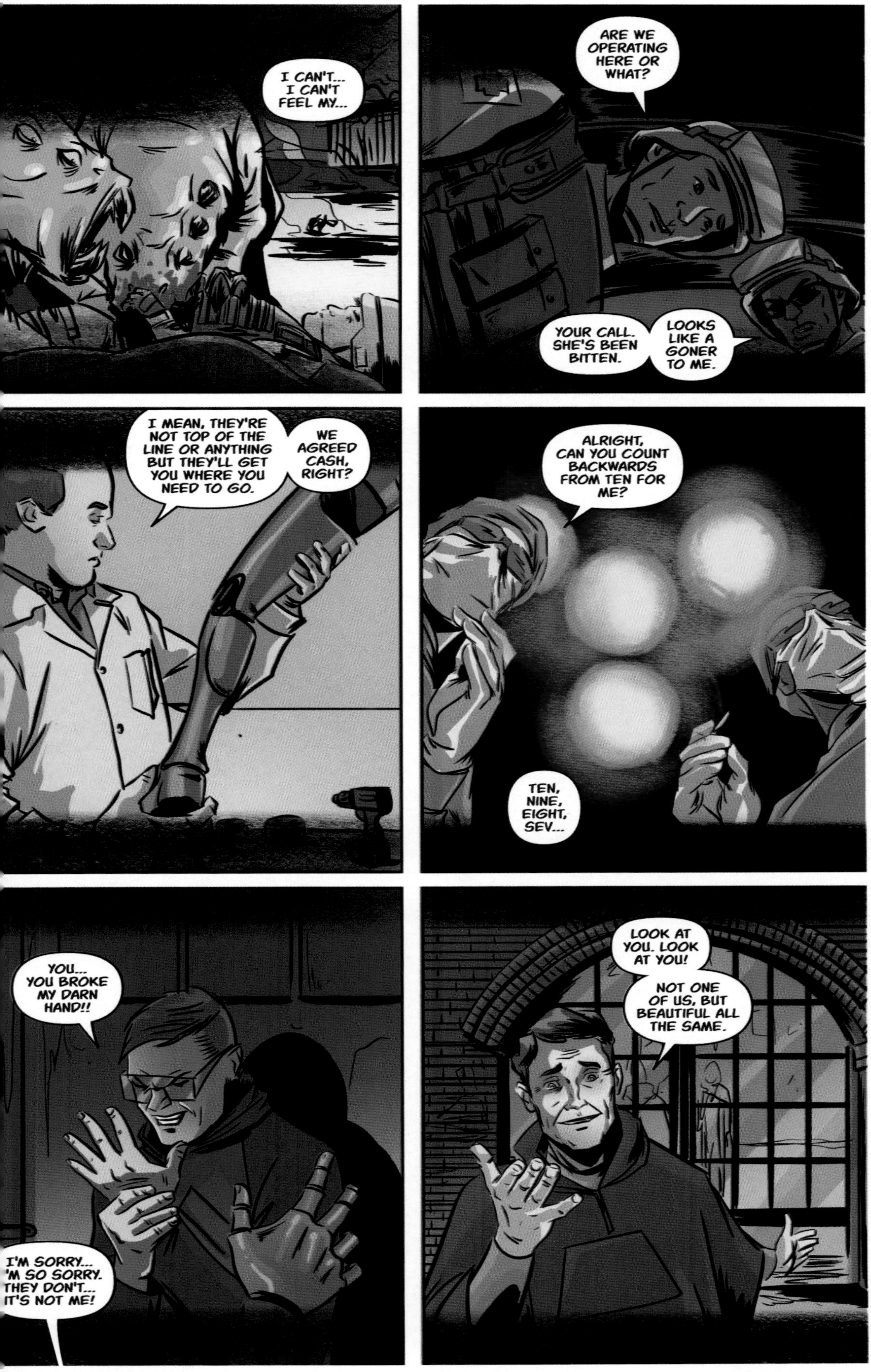
I CAN'T... I CAN'T FEEL MY...
ARE WE OPERATING HERE OR WHAT?
YOUR CALL. SHE'S BEEN BITTEN.
LOOKS LIKE A GONER TO ME.
I MEAN, THEY'RE NOT TOP OF THE LINE OR ANYTHING BUT THEY'LL GET YOU WHERE YOU NEED TO GO.
WE AGREED CASH, RIGHT?
ALRIGHT, CAN YOU COUNT BACKWARDS FROM TEN FOR ME?
TEN, NINE, EIGHT, SEV...
YOU... YOU BROKE MY DARN HAND!!
I'M SORRY... 'M SO SORRY. THEY DON'T... IT'S NOT ME!
LOOK AT YOU. LOOK AT YOU!
NOT ONE OF US, BUT BEAUTIFUL ALL THE SAME.

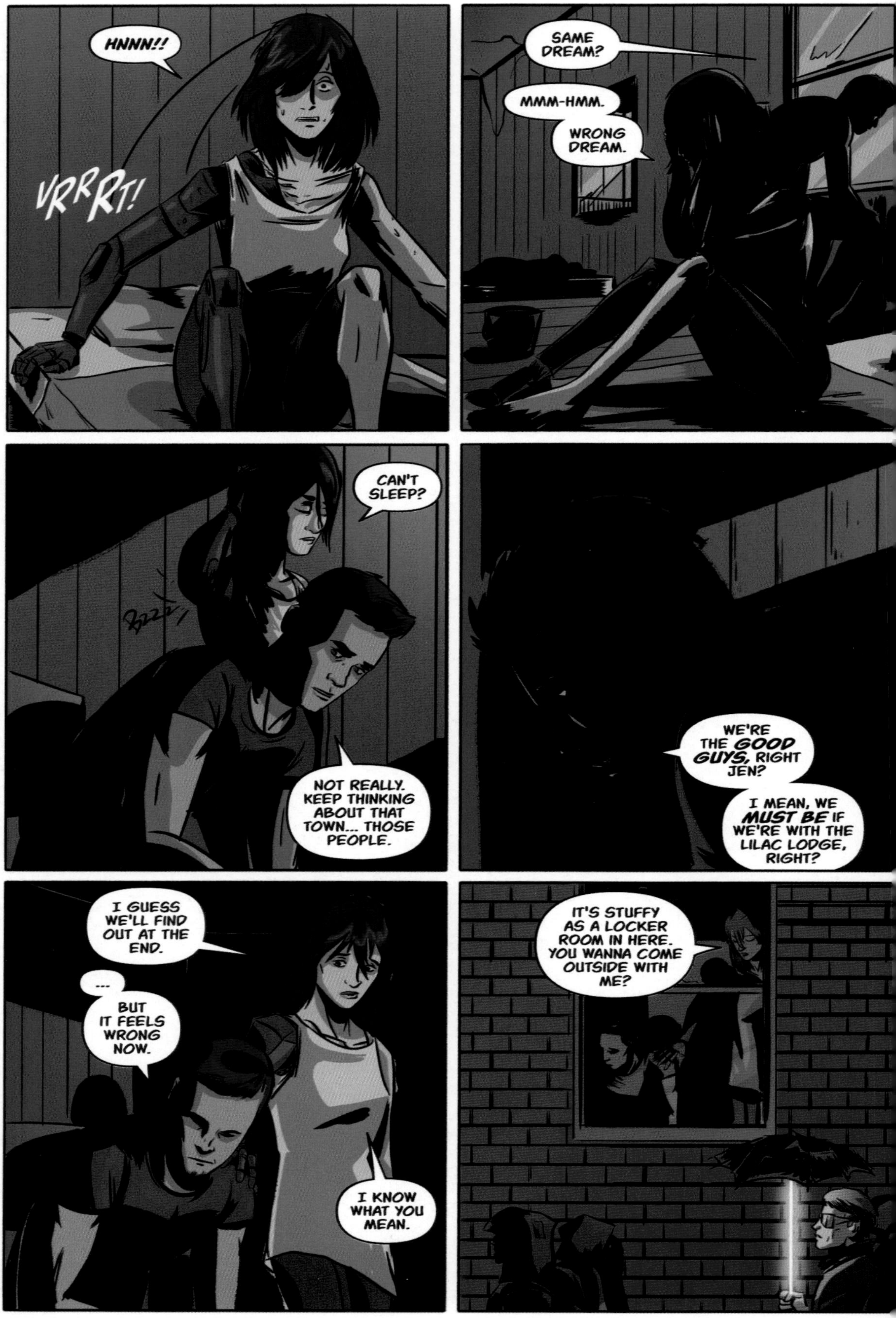
HNNN!!
VRRRT!
SAME DREAM?
MMM-HMM.
WRONG DREAM.
CAN'T SLEEP?
NOT REALLY. KEEP THINKING ABOUT THAT TOWN... THOSE PEOPLE.
WE'RE THE GOOD GUYS, RIGHT JEN?
I MEAN, WE MUST BE IF WE'RE WITH THE LILAC LODGE, RIGHT?
I GUESS WE'LL FIND OUT AT THE END.
...
BUT IT FEELS WRONG NOW.
I KNOW WHAT YOU MEAN.
IT'S STUFFY AS A LOCKER ROOM IN HERE. YOU WANNA COME OUTSIDE WITH ME?

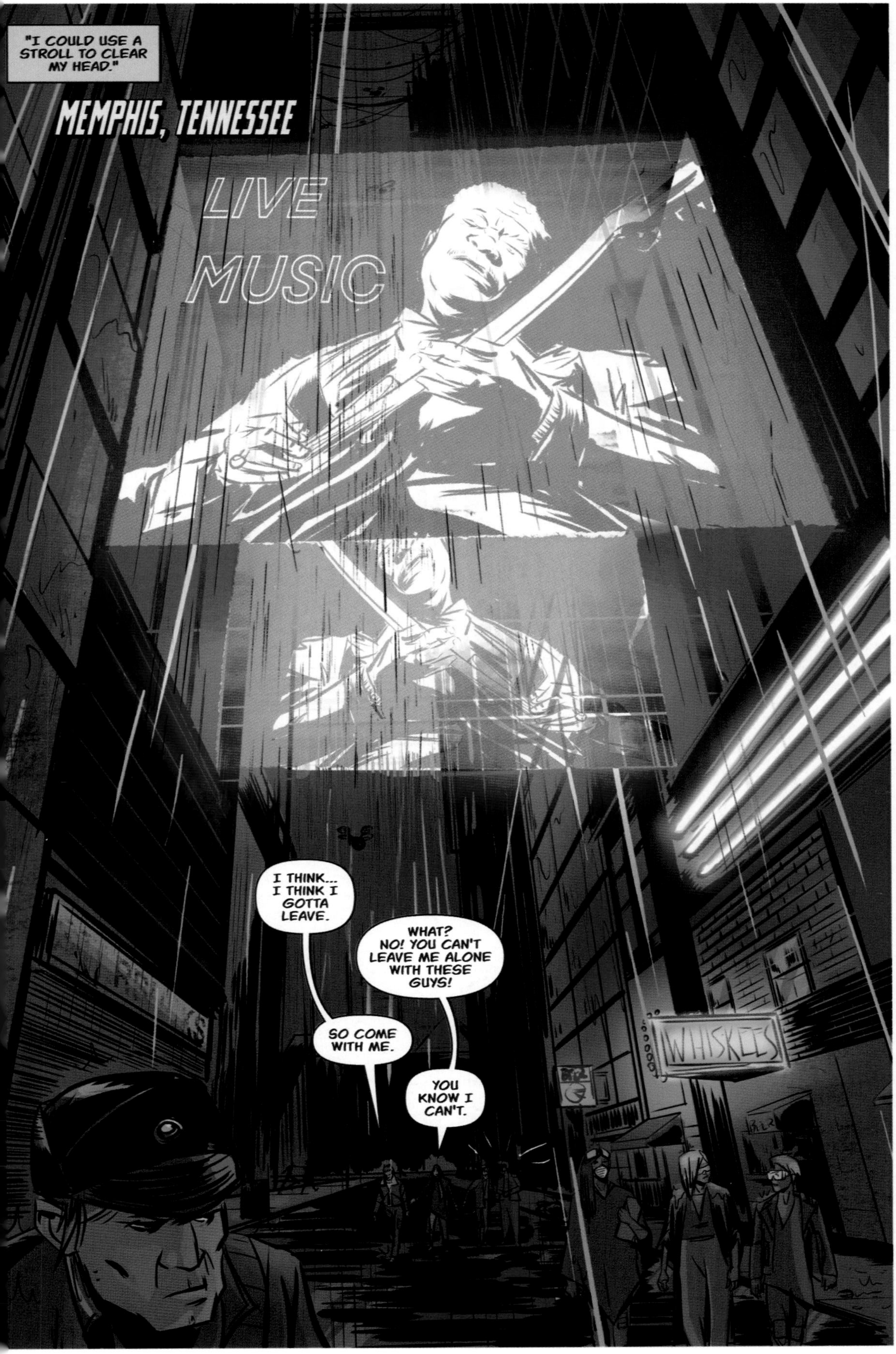
"I COULD USE A STROLL TO CLEAR MY HEAD."
MEMPHIS, TENNESSEE
LIVE MUSIC
I THINK... I THINK I GOTTA LEAVE.
WHAT? NO! YOU CAN'T LEAVE ME ALONE WITH THESE GUYS!
SO COME WITH ME.
YOU KNOW I CAN'T.
WHISKEES

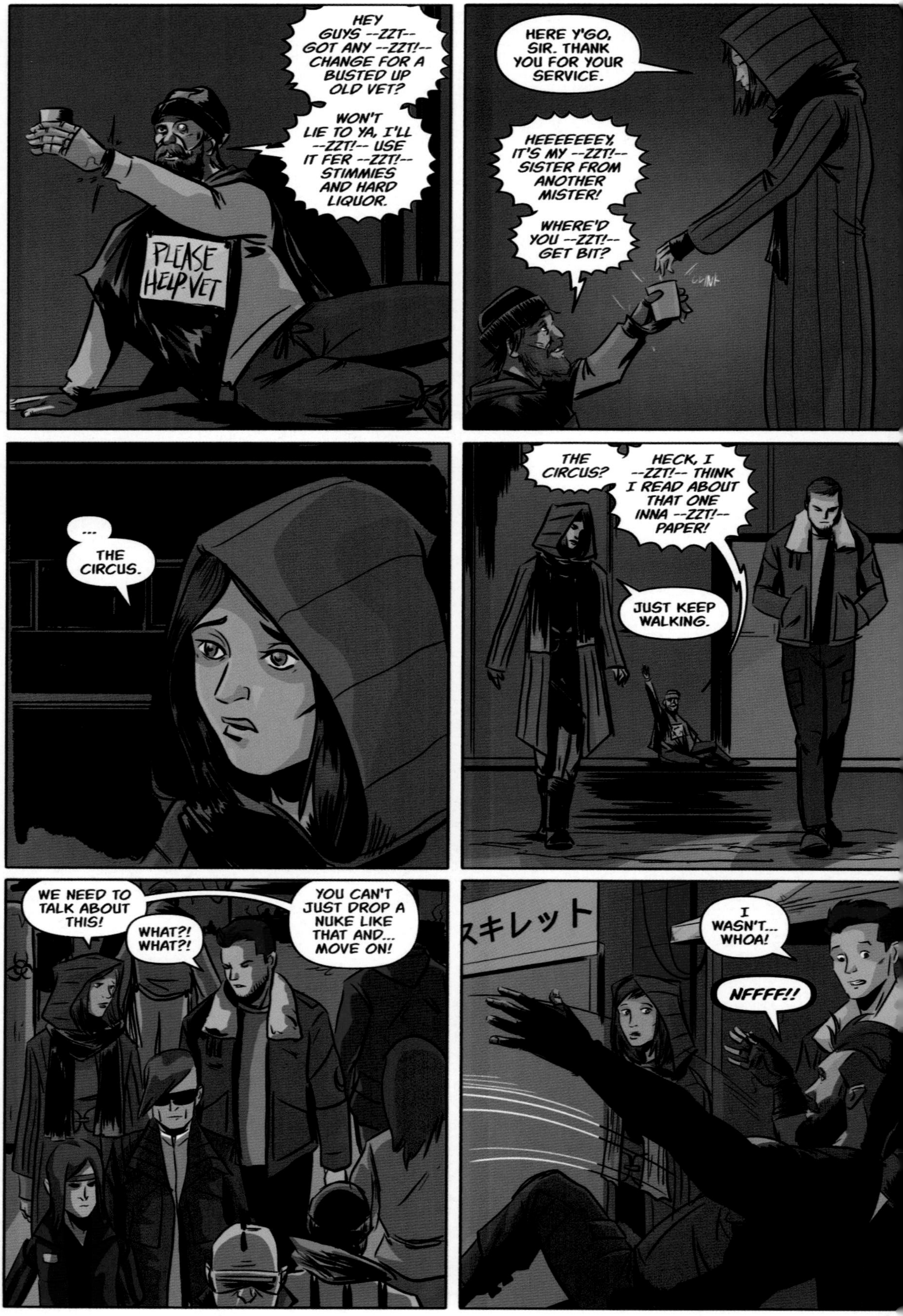
HEY GUYS --ZZT-- GOT ANY --ZZT!-- CHANGE FOR A BUSTED UP OLD VET?
WON'T LIE TO YA, I'LL --ZZT!-- USE IT FER --ZZT!-- STIMMIES AND HARD LIQUOR.
PLEASE HELP VET
HERE Y'GO, SIR. THANK YOU FOR YOUR SERVICE.
HEEEEEEEY, IT'S MY --ZZT!-- SISTER FROM ANOTHER MISTER!
WHERE'D YOU --ZZT!-- GET BIT?
... THE CIRCUS.
THE CIRCUS?
HECK, I --ZZT!-- THINK I READ ABOUT THAT ONE INNA --ZZT!-- PAPER!
JUST KEEP WALKING.
WE NEED TO TALK ABOUT THIS!
WHAT?! WHAT?!
YOU CAN'T JUST DROP A NUKE LIKE THAT AND... MOVE ON!
スキレット
I WASN'T... WHOA!
NFFFF!!

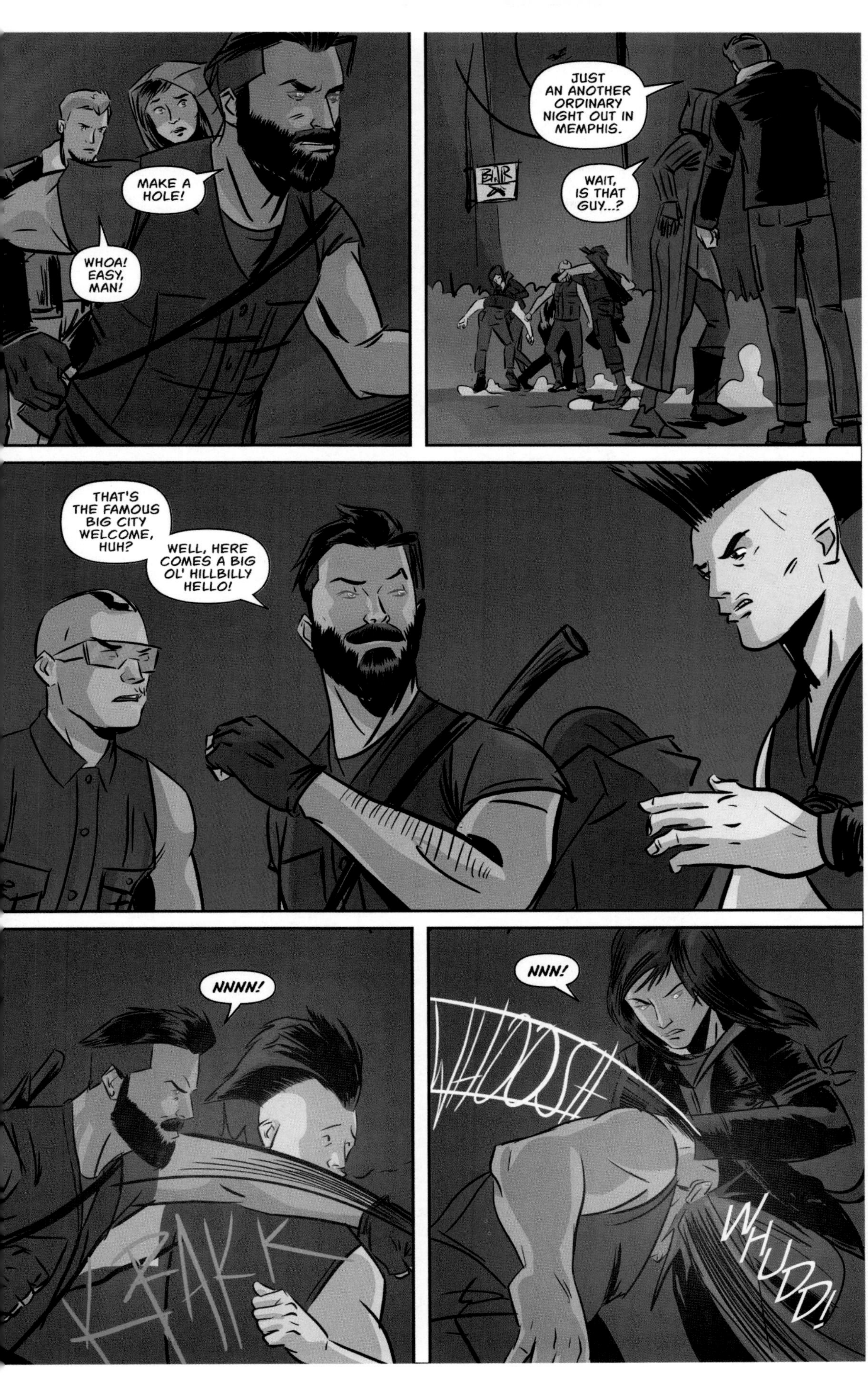
MAKE A HOLE!
WHOA! EASY, MAN!
JUST AN ANOTHER ORDINARY NIGHT OUT IN MEMPHIS.
WAIT, IS THAT GUY...?
BAR
THAT'S THE FAMOUS BIG CITY WELCOME, HUH?
WELL, HERE COMES A BIG OL' HILLBILLY HELLO!
NNNN!
KRAKK
NNN!
WHOOOSH
WHUDD!

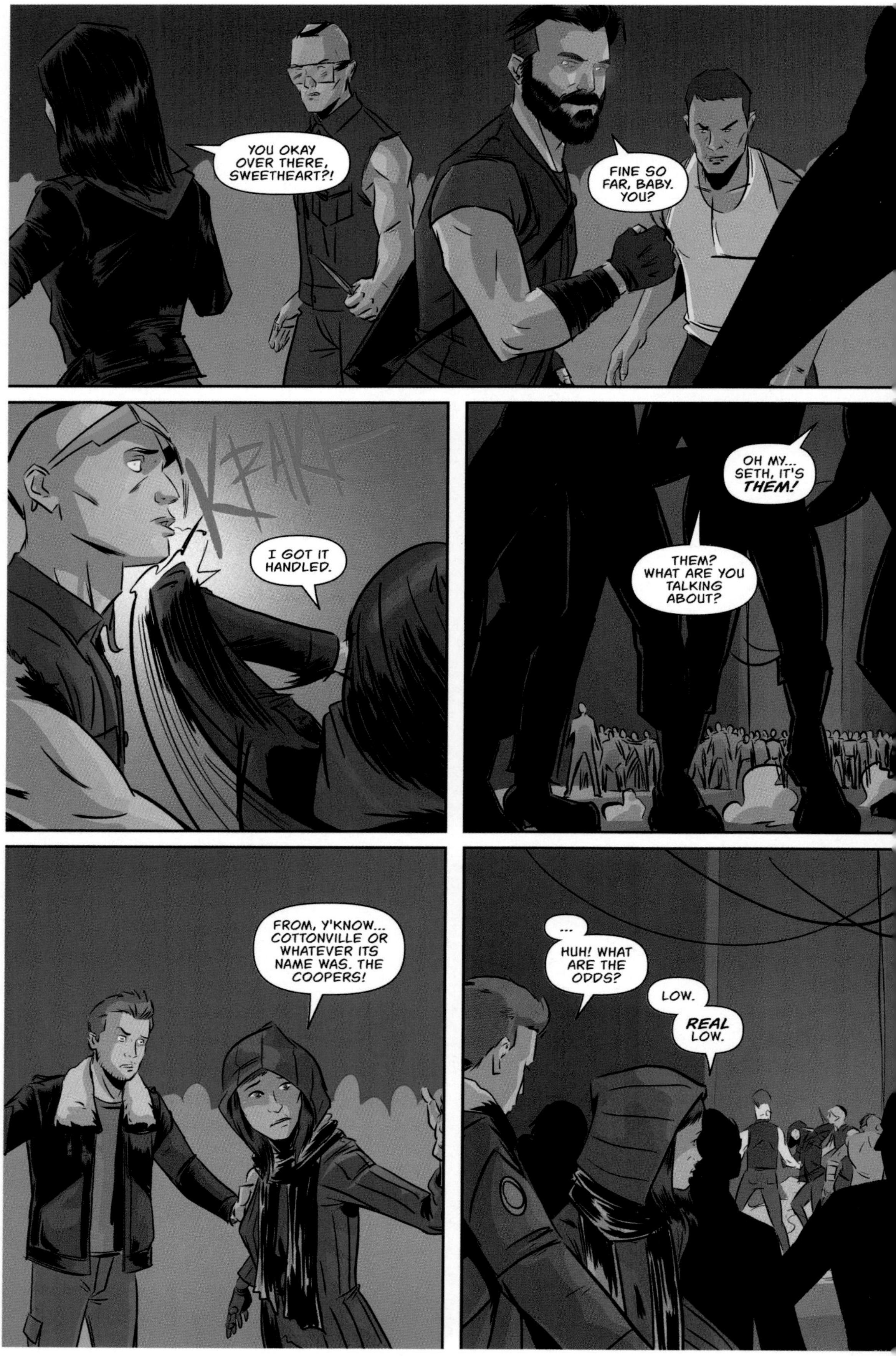
YOU OKAY OVER THERE, SWEETHEART?!
FINE SO FAR, BABY. YOU?
I GOT IT HANDLED.
OH MY... SETH, IT'S THEM!
THEM? WHAT ARE YOU TALKING ABOUT?
FROM, Y'KNOW... COTTONVILLE OR WHATEVER ITS NAME WAS. THE COOPERS!
...
HUH! WHAT ARE THE ODDS?
LOW.
REAL LOW.

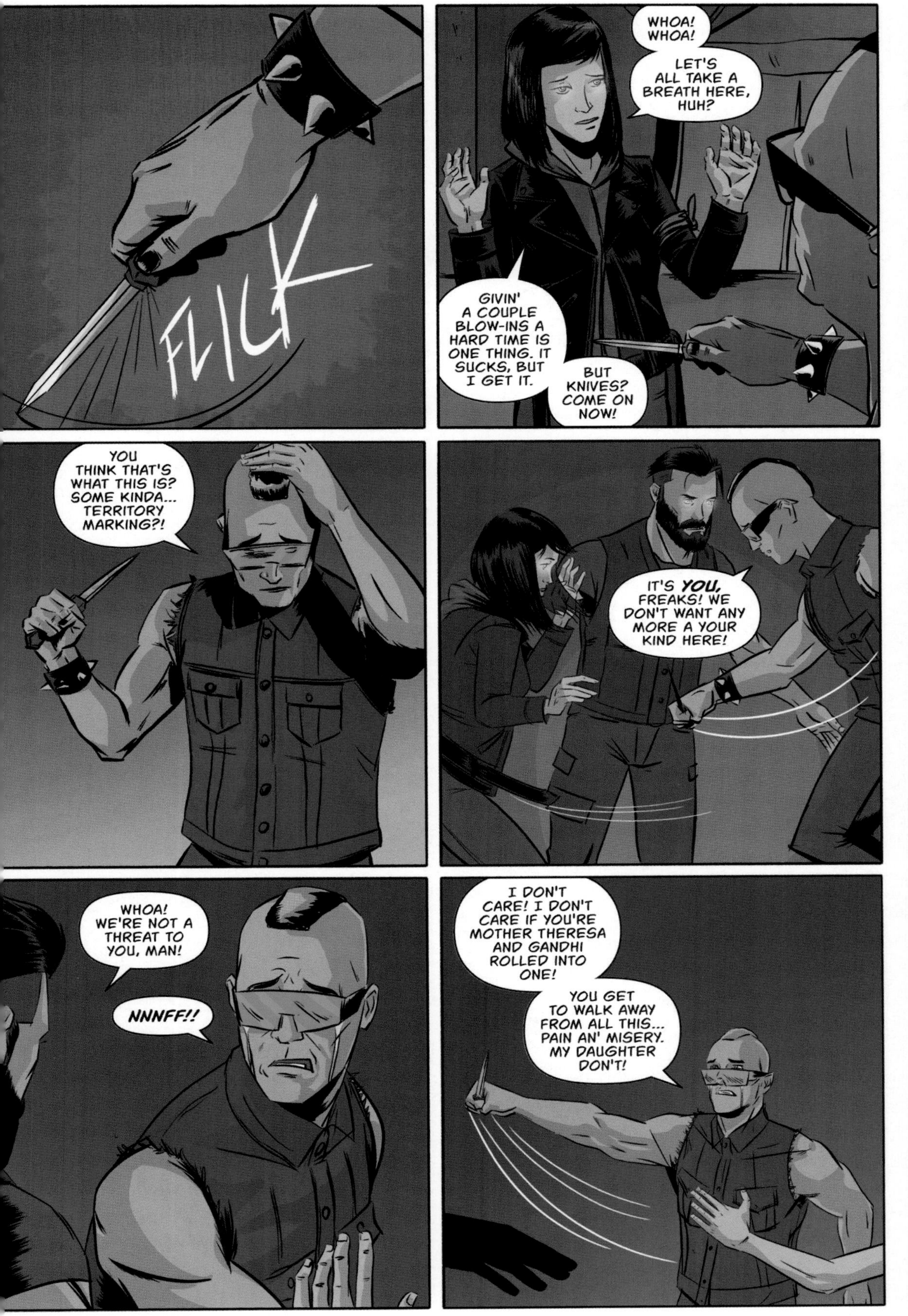
FLICK
WHOA! WHOA!
LET'S ALL TAKE A BREATH HERE, HUH?
GIVIN' A COUPLE BLOW-INS A HARD TIME IS ONE THING. IT SUCKS, BUT I GET IT.
BUT KNIVES? COME ON NOW!
YOU THINK THAT'S WHAT THIS IS? SOME KINDA... TERRITORY MARKING?!
IT'S YOU, FREAKS! WE DON'T WANT ANY MORE A YOUR KIND HERE!
WHOA! WE'RE NOT A THREAT TO YOU, MAN!
NNNFF!!
I DON'T CARE! I DON'T CARE IF YOU'RE MOTHER THERESA AND GANDHI ROLLED INTO ONE!
YOU GET TO WALK AWAY FROM ALL THIS... PAIN AN' MISERY. MY DAUGHTER DON'T!

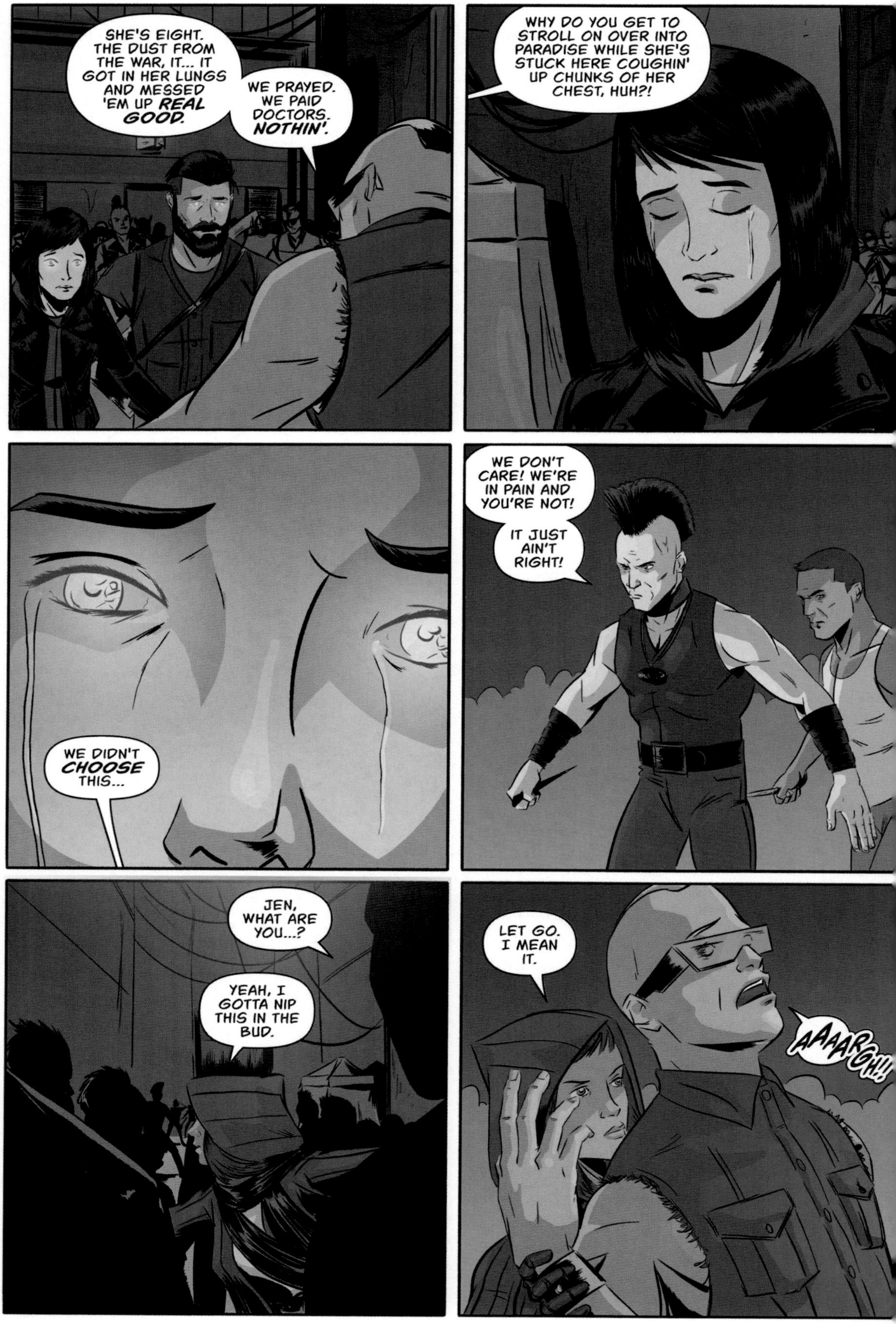
SHE'S EIGHT. THE DUST FROM THE WAR, IT... IT GOT IN HER LUNGS AND MESSED 'EM UP REAL GOOD.
WE PRAYED. WE PAID DOCTORS. NOTHIN'.
WHY DO YOU GET TO STROLL ON OVER INTO PARADISE WHILE SHE'S STUCK HERE COUGHIN' UP CHUNKS OF HER CHEST, HUH?!
WE DIDN'T CHOOSE THIS...
WE DON'T CARE! WE'RE IN PAIN AND YOU'RE NOT!
IT JUST AIN'T RIGHT!
JEN, WHAT ARE YOU...?
YEAH, I GOTTA NIP THIS IN THE BUD.
LET GO. I MEAN IT.
AAAARGH!!

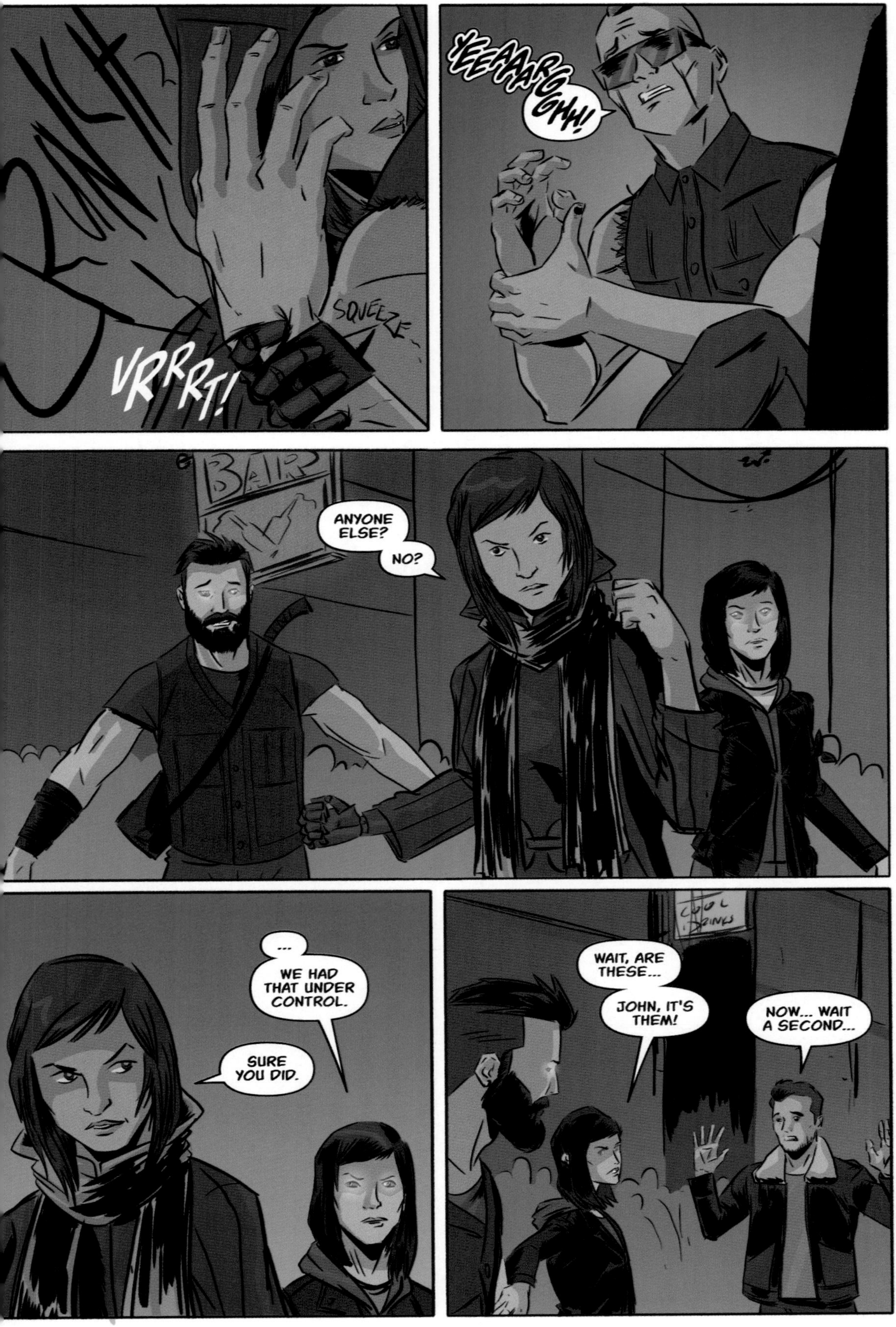
SQUEEZE
VRRRT!
YEEAAARGHH!
BAR
ANYONE ELSE?
NO?
...
WE HAD THAT UNDER CONTROL.
SURE YOU DID.
COOL DRINKS
WAIT, ARE THESE...
JOHN, IT'S THEM!
NOW... WAIT A SECOND...

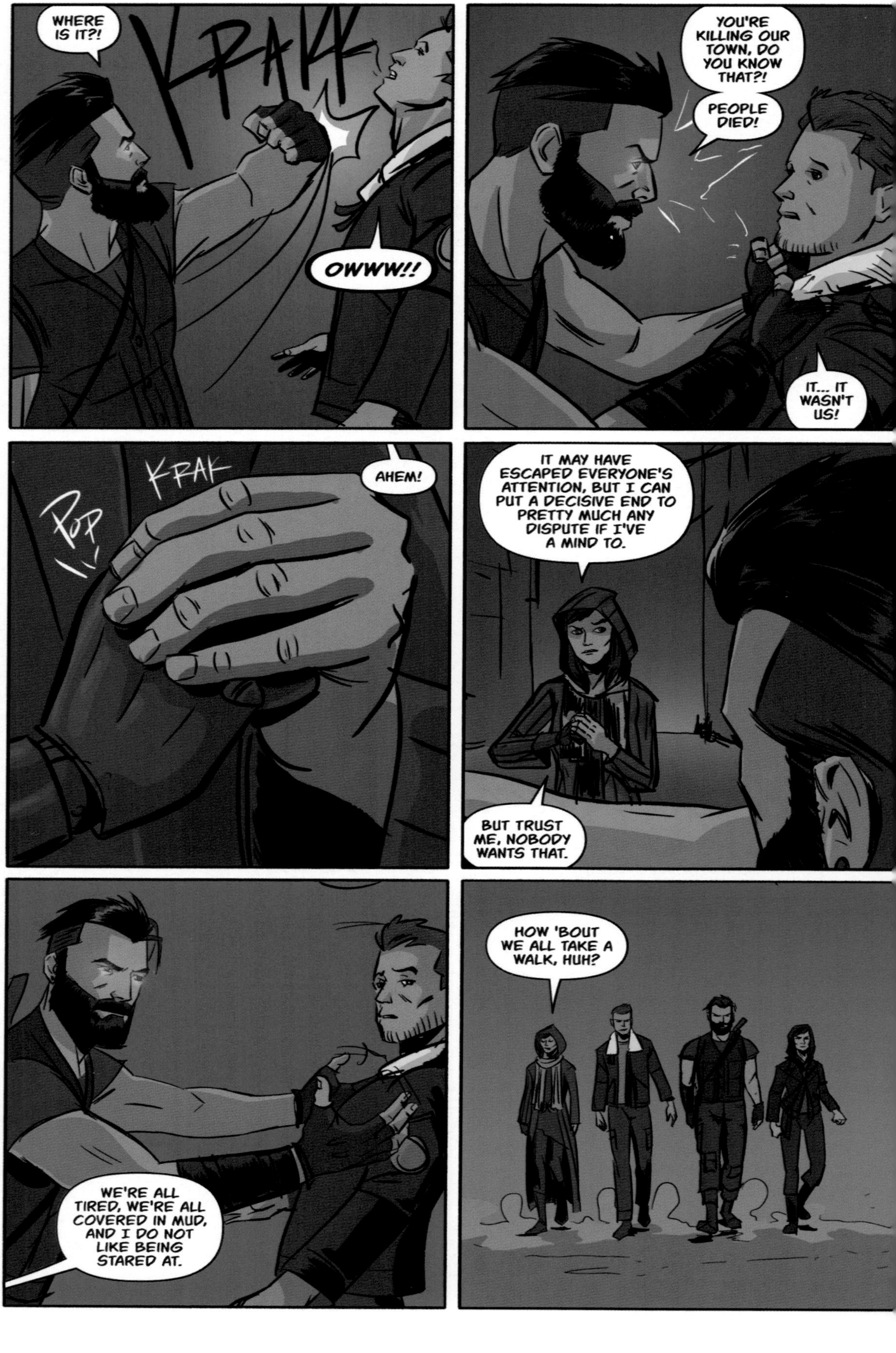
WHERE IS IT?!
KRAKK
OWWW!!
YOU'RE KILLING OUR TOWN, DO YOU KNOW THAT?!
PEOPLE DIED!
IT... IT WASN'T US!
KRAK
POP
AHEM!
IT MAY HAVE ESCAPED EVERYONE'S ATTENTION, BUT I CAN PUT A DECISIVE END TO PRETTY MUCH ANY DISPUTE IF I'VE A MIND TO.
BUT TRUST ME, NOBODY WANTS THAT.
WE'RE ALL TIRED, WE'RE ALL COVERED IN MUD, AND I DO NOT LIKE BEING STARED AT.
HOW 'BOUT WE ALL TAKE A WALK, HUH?

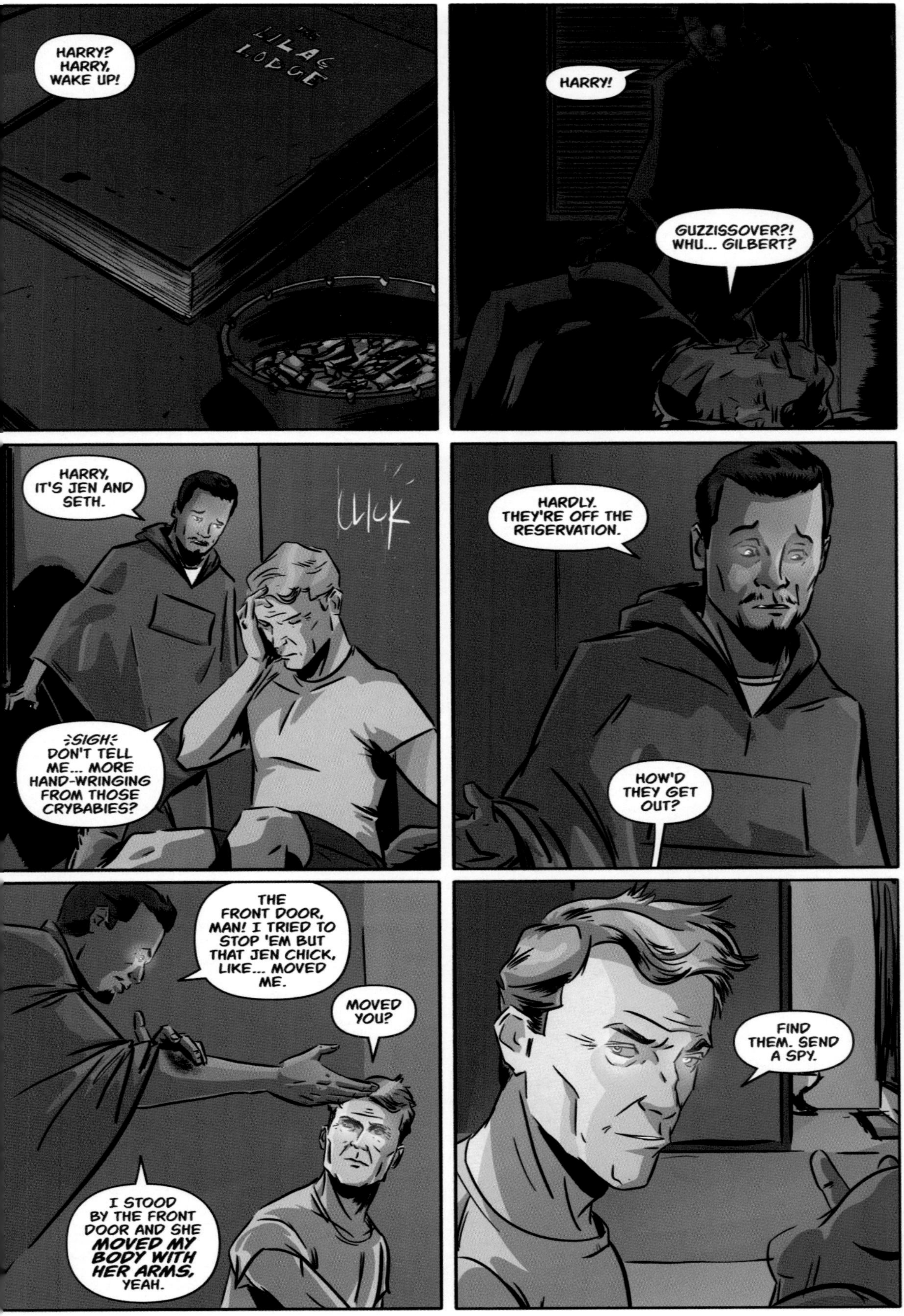
HARRY? HARRY, WAKE UP!
LILAC LODGE
HARRY!
GUZZISSOVER?! WHU... GILBERT?
HARRY, IT'S JEN AND SETH.
CLICK
:SIGH: DON'T TELL ME... MORE HAND-WRINGING FROM THOSE CRYBABIES?
HARDLY. THEY'RE OFF THE RESERVATION.
HOW'D THEY GET OUT?
THE FRONT DOOR, MAN! I TRIED TO STOP 'EM BUT THAT JEN CHICK, LIKE... MOVED ME.
MOVED YOU?
I STOOD BY THE FRONT DOOR AND SHE *MOVED MY BODY WITH HER ARMS,* YEAH.
FIND THEM. SEND A SPY.

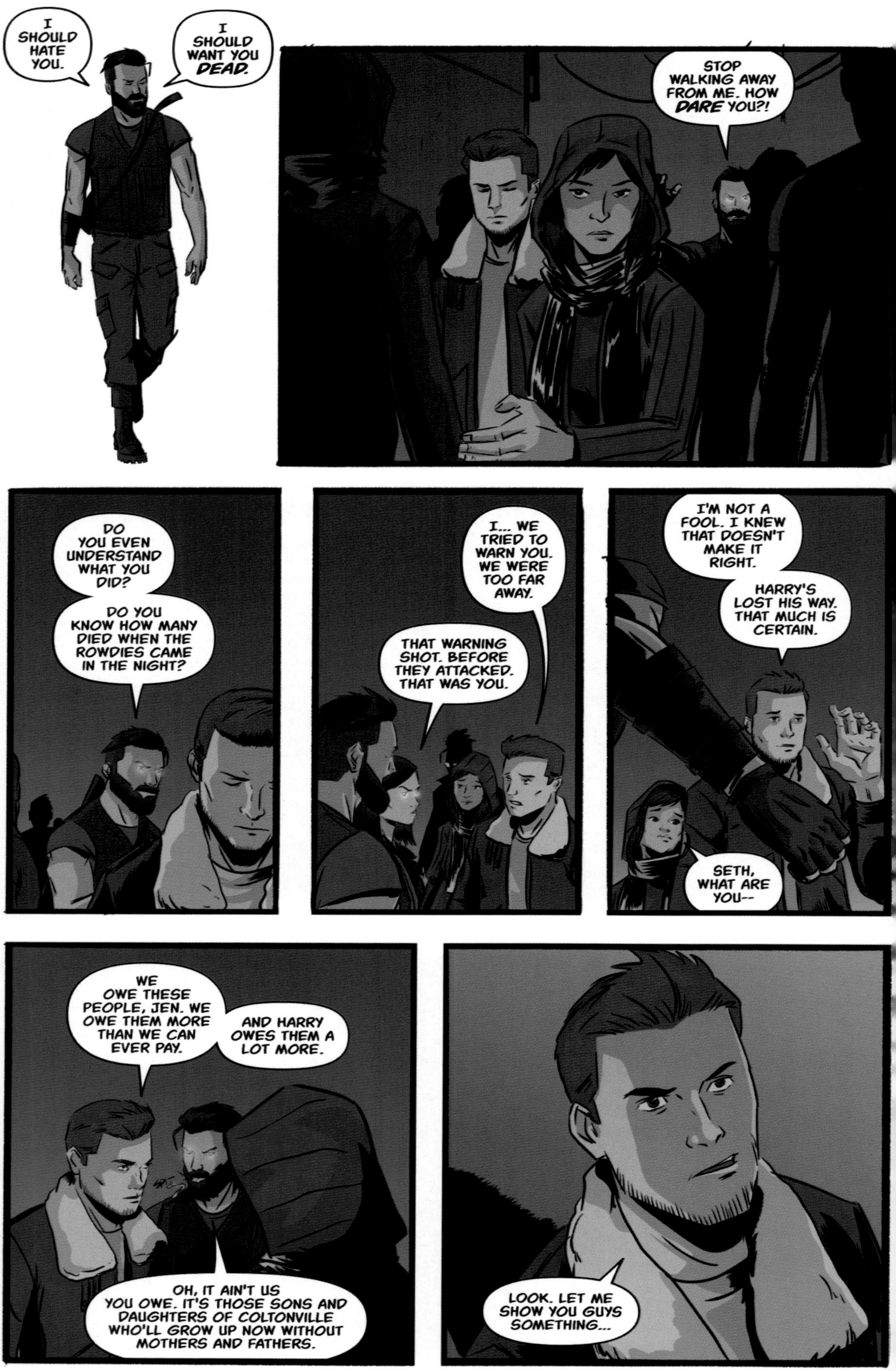
I SHOULD HATE YOU.
I SHOULD WANT YOU DEAD.
STOP WALKING AWAY FROM ME. HOW DARE YOU?!
DO YOU EVEN UNDERSTAND WHAT YOU DID?
DO YOU KNOW HOW MANY DIED WHEN THE ROWDIES CAME IN THE NIGHT?
I... WE TRIED TO WARN YOU. WE WERE TOO FAR AWAY.
THAT WARNING SHOT. BEFORE THEY ATTACKED. THAT WAS YOU.
I'M NOT A FOOL. I KNEW THAT DOESN'T MAKE IT RIGHT.
HARRY'S LOST HIS WAY. THAT MUCH IS CERTAIN.
SETH, WHAT ARE YOU--
WE OWE THESE PEOPLE, JEN. WE OWE THEM MORE THAN WE CAN EVER PAY.
AND HARRY OWES THEM A LOT MORE.
OH, IT AIN'T US YOU OWE. IT'S THOSE SONS AND DAUGHTERS OF COLTONVILLE WHO'LL GROW UP NOW WITHOUT MOTHERS AND FATHERS.
LOOK. LET ME SHOW YOU GUYS SOMETHING...

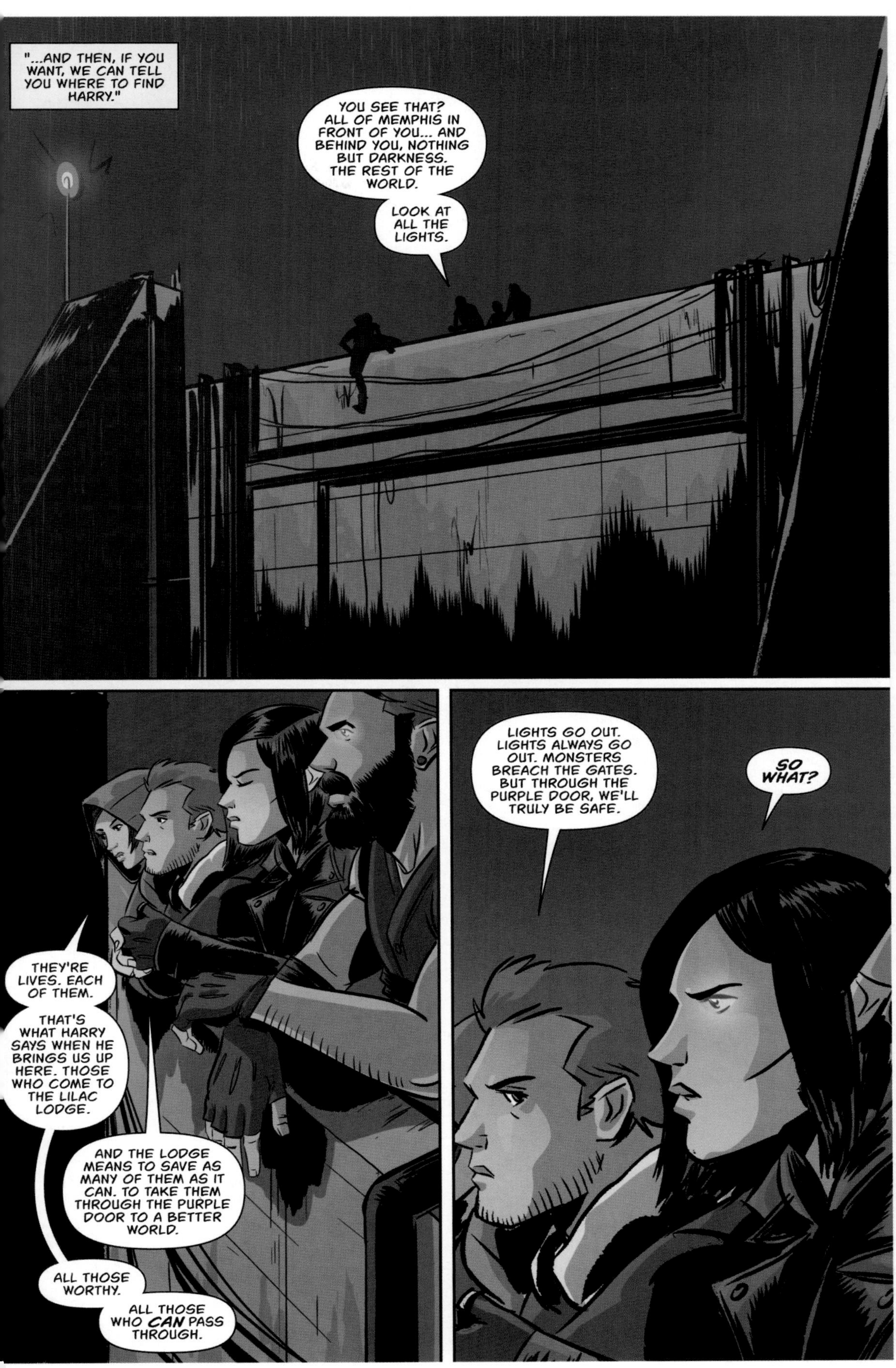
"...AND THEN, IF YOU WANT, WE CAN TELL YOU WHERE TO FIND HARRY."
YOU SEE THAT? ALL OF MEMPHIS IN FRONT OF YOU... AND BEHIND YOU, NOTHING BUT DARKNESS. THE REST OF THE WORLD.
LOOK AT ALL THE LIGHTS.
THEY'RE LIVES. EACH OF THEM.
THAT'S WHAT HARRY SAYS WHEN HE BRINGS US UP HERE. THOSE WHO COME TO THE LILAC LODGE.
AND THE LODGE MEANS TO SAVE AS MANY OF THEM AS IT CAN. TO TAKE THEM THROUGH THE PURPLE DOOR TO A BETTER WORLD.
ALL THOSE WORTHY.
ALL THOSE WHO CAN PASS THROUGH.
LIGHTS GO OUT. LIGHTS ALWAYS GO OUT. MONSTERS BREACH THE GATES. BUT THROUGH THE PURPLE DOOR, WE'LL TRULY BE SAFE.
SO WHAT?

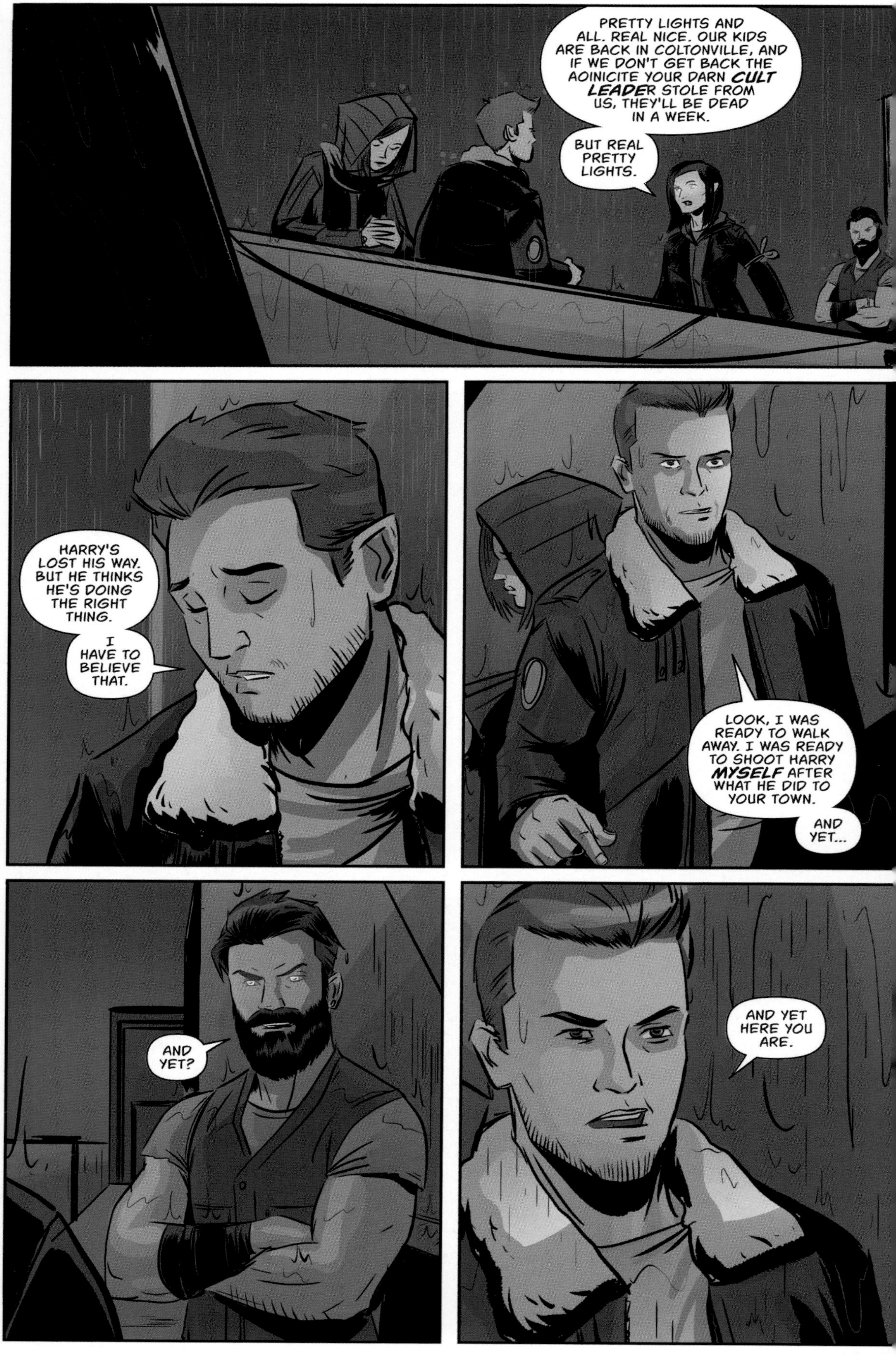
PRETTY LIGHTS AND ALL. REAL NICE. OUR KIDS ARE BACK IN COLTONVILLE, AND IF WE DON'T GET BACK THE AOINICITE YOUR DARN *CULT LEADER* STOLE FROM US, THEY'LL BE DEAD IN A WEEK.
BUT REAL PRETTY LIGHTS.
HARRY'S LOST HIS WAY. BUT HE THINKS HE'S DOING THE RIGHT THING.
I HAVE TO BELIEVE THAT.
LOOK, I WAS READY TO WALK AWAY. I WAS READY TO SHOOT HARRY *MYSELF* AFTER WHAT HE DID TO YOUR TOWN.
AND YET...
AND YET?
AND YET HERE YOU ARE.

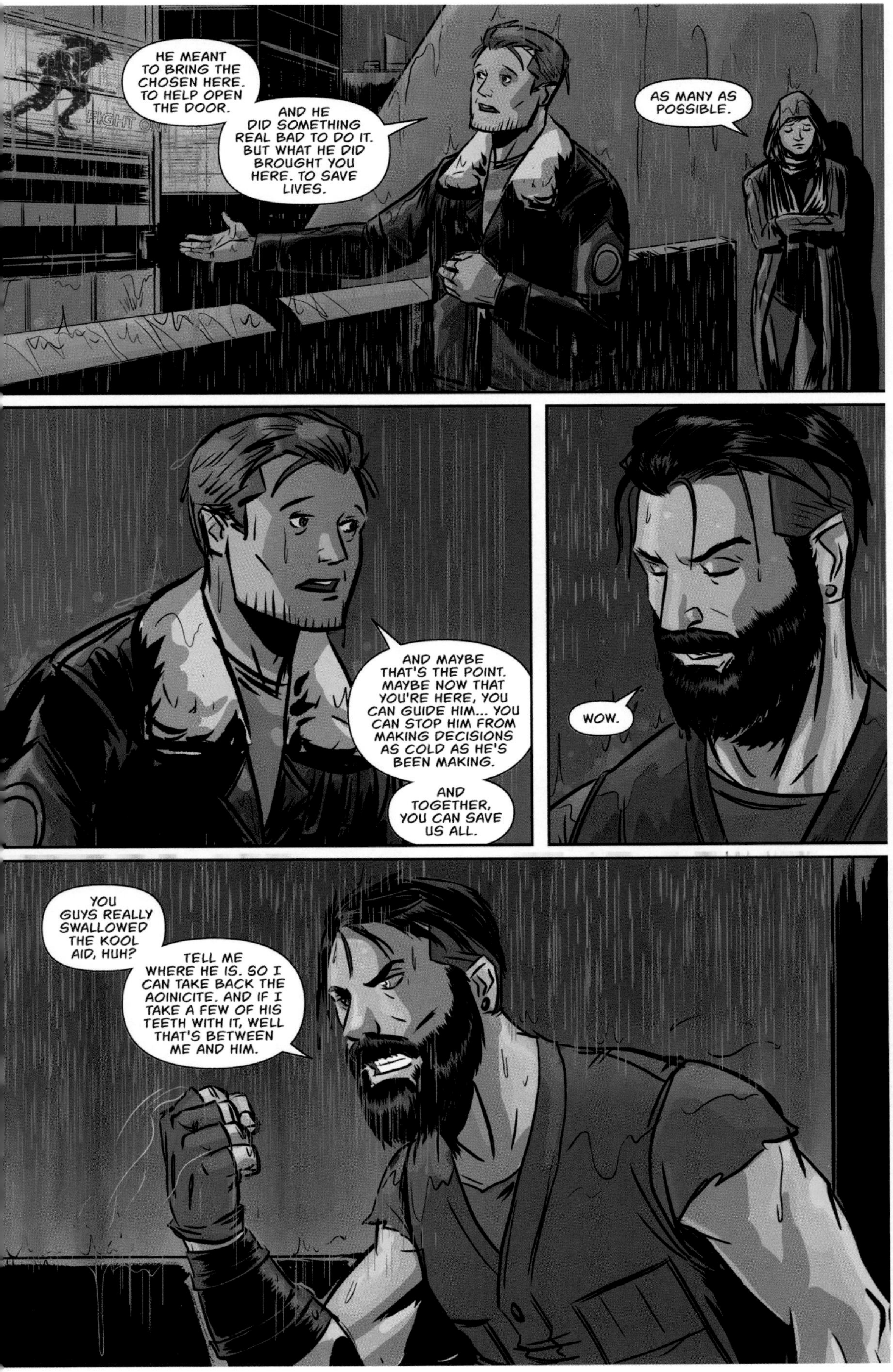
HE MEANT TO BRING THE CHOSEN HERE. TO HELP OPEN THE DOOR.
AND HE DID SOMETHING REAL BAD TO DO IT. BUT WHAT HE DID BROUGHT YOU HERE. TO SAVE LIVES.
AS MANY AS POSSIBLE.
AND MAYBE THAT'S THE POINT. MAYBE NOW THAT YOU'RE HERE, YOU CAN GUIDE HIM... YOU CAN STOP HIM FROM MAKING DECISIONS AS COLD AS HE'S BEEN MAKING.
AND TOGETHER, YOU CAN SAVE US ALL.
WOW.
YOU GUYS REALLY SWALLOWED THE KOOL AID, HUH?
TELL ME WHERE HE IS. SO I CAN TAKE BACK THE AOINICITE. AND IF I TAKE A FEW OF HIS TEETH WITH IT, WELL THAT'S BETWEEN ME AND HIM.

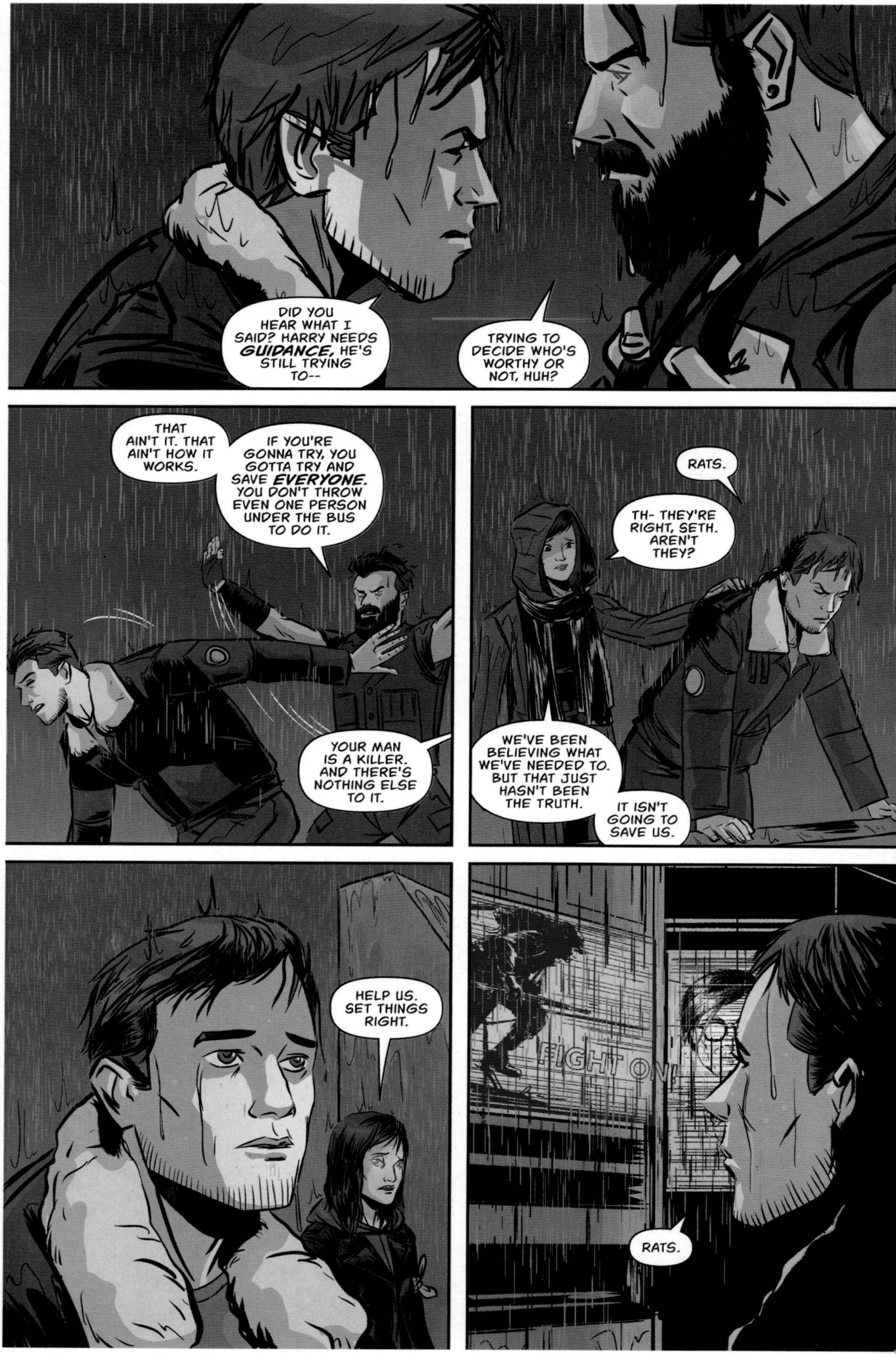
DID YOU HEAR WHAT I SAID? HARRY NEEDS **GUIDANCE,** HE'S STILL TRYING TO--
TRYING TO DECIDE WHO'S WORTHY OR NOT, HUH?
THAT AIN'T IT. THAT AIN'T HOW IT WORKS.
IF YOU'RE GONNA TRY, YOU GOTTA TRY AND SAVE **EVERYONE.** YOU DON'T THROW EVEN ONE PERSON UNDER THE BUS TO DO IT.
YOUR MAN IS A KILLER. AND THERE'S NOTHING ELSE TO IT.
RATS.
TH- THEY'RE RIGHT, SETH. AREN'T THEY?
WE'VE BEEN BELIEVING WHAT WE'VE NEEDED TO. BUT THAT JUST HASN'T BEEN THE TRUTH.
IT ISN'T GOING TO SAVE US.
HELP US. SET THINGS RIGHT.
FIGHT ON!
RATS.

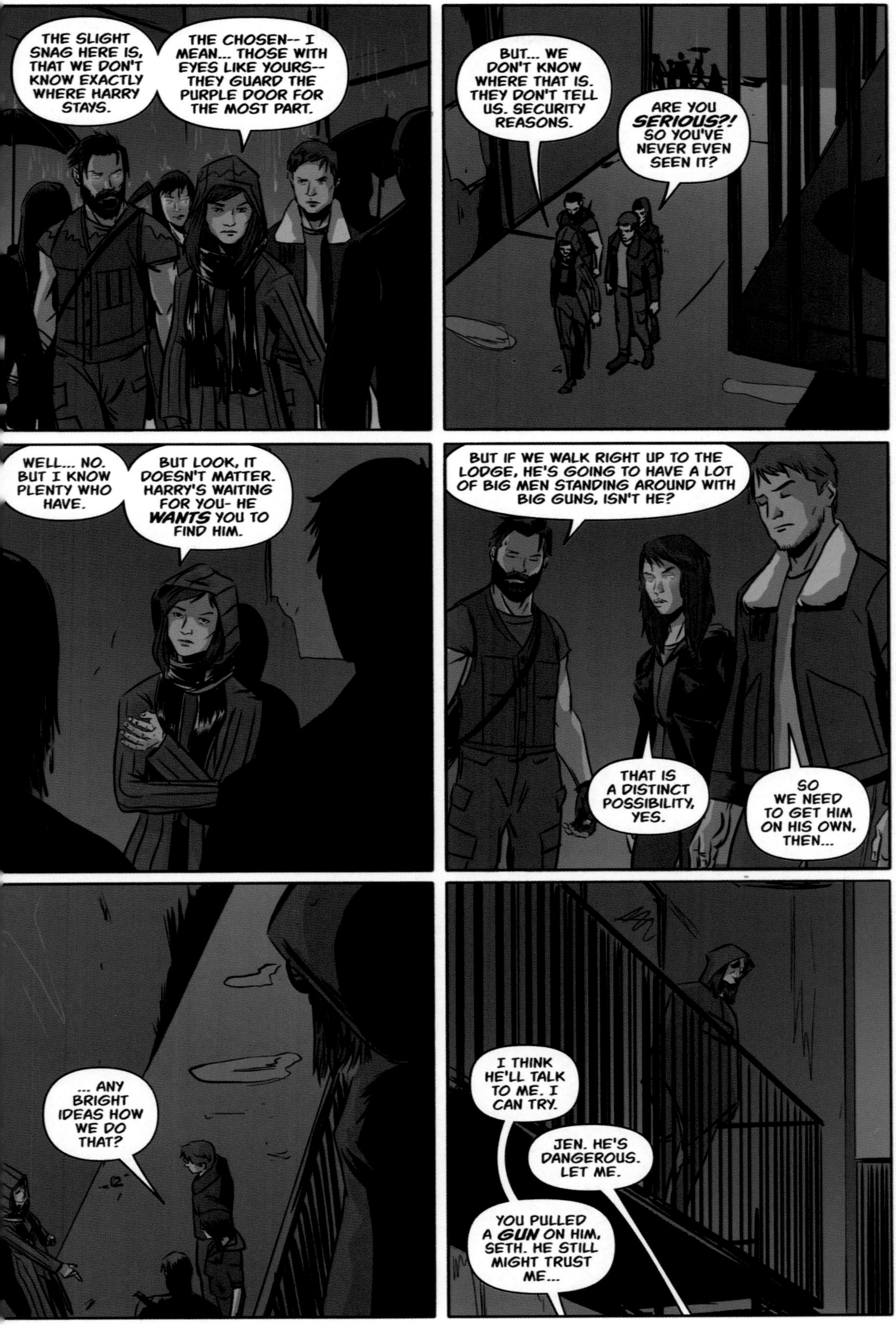
THE SLIGHT SNAG HERE IS, THAT WE DON'T KNOW EXACTLY WHERE HARRY STAYS.
THE CHOSEN-- I MEAN... THOSE WITH EYES LIKE YOURS-- THEY GUARD THE PURPLE DOOR FOR THE MOST PART.
BUT... WE DON'T KNOW WHERE THAT IS. THEY DON'T TELL US. SECURITY REASONS.
ARE YOU SERIOUS?! SO YOU'VE NEVER EVEN SEEN IT?
WELL... NO. BUT I KNOW PLENTY WHO HAVE.
BUT LOOK, IT DOESN'T MATTER. HARRY'S WAITING FOR YOU- HE WANTS YOU TO FIND HIM.
BUT IF WE WALK RIGHT UP TO THE LODGE, HE'S GOING TO HAVE A LOT OF BIG MEN STANDING AROUND WITH BIG GUNS, ISN'T HE?
THAT IS A DISTINCT POSSIBILITY, YES.
SO WE NEED TO GET HIM ON HIS OWN, THEN...
... ANY BRIGHT IDEAS HOW WE DO THAT?
I THINK HE'LL TALK TO ME. I CAN TRY.
JEN. HE'S DANGEROUS. LET ME.
YOU PULLED A GUN ON HIM, SETH. HE STILL MIGHT TRUST ME...

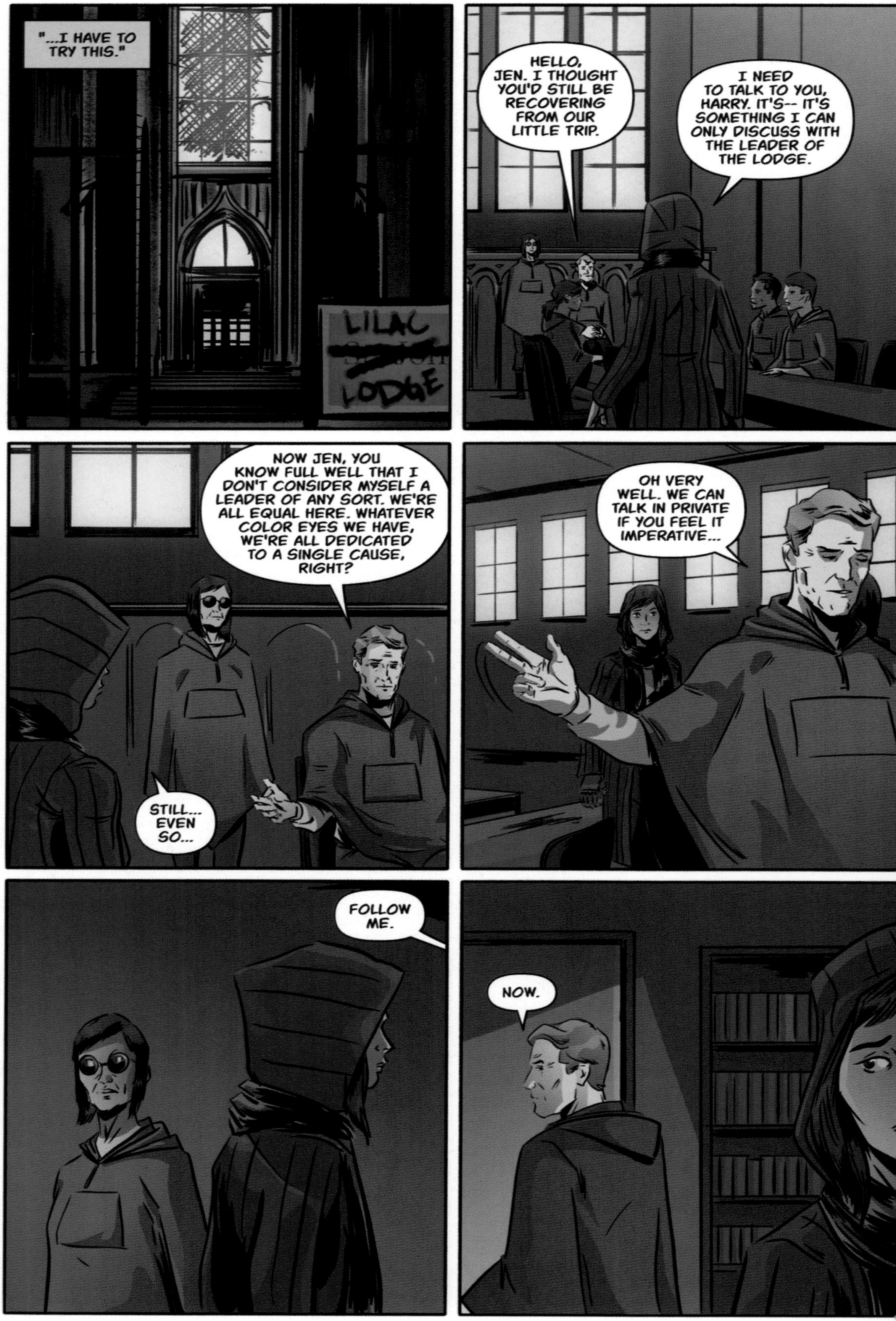
"...I HAVE TO TRY THIS."
LILAC LODGE
HELLO, JEN. I THOUGHT YOU'D STILL BE RECOVERING FROM OUR LITTLE TRIP.
I NEED TO TALK TO YOU, HARRY. IT'S-- IT'S SOMETHING I CAN ONLY DISCUSS WITH THE LEADER OF THE LODGE.
NOW JEN, YOU KNOW FULL WELL THAT I DON'T CONSIDER MYSELF A LEADER OF ANY SORT. WE'RE ALL EQUAL HERE. WHATEVER COLOR EYES WE HAVE, WE'RE ALL DEDICATED TO A SINGLE CAUSE, RIGHT?
STILL... EVEN SO...
OH VERY WELL. WE CAN TALK IN PRIVATE IF YOU FEEL IT IMPERATIVE...
FOLLOW ME.
NOW.

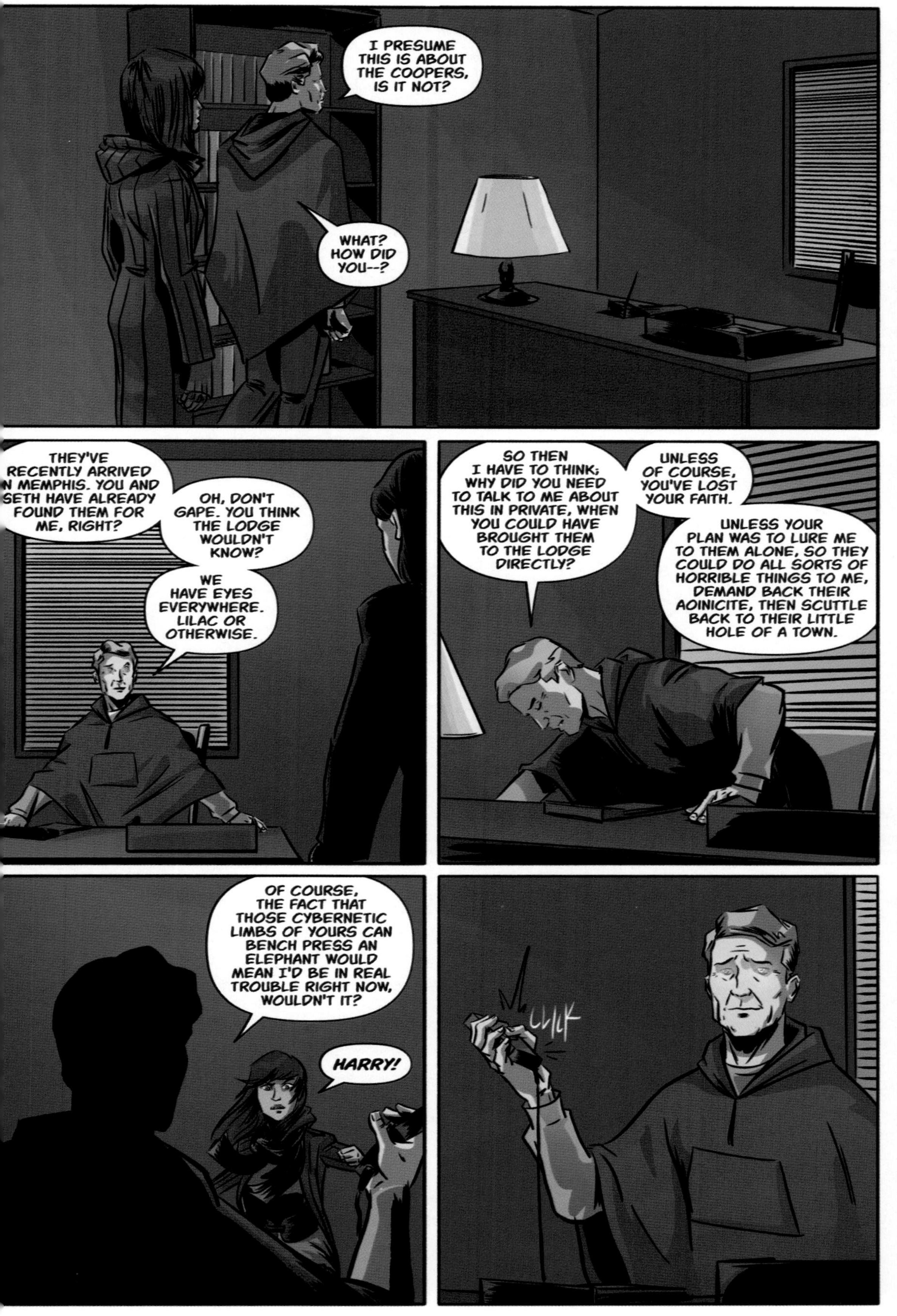
I PRESUME THIS IS ABOUT THE COOPERS, IS IT NOT?
WHAT? HOW DID YOU--?
THEY'VE RECENTLY ARRIVED N MEMPHIS. YOU AND SETH HAVE ALREADY FOUND THEM FOR ME, RIGHT?
OH, DON'T GAPE. YOU THINK THE LODGE WOULDN'T KNOW?
WE HAVE EYES EVERYWHERE. LILAC OR OTHERWISE.
SO THEN I HAVE TO THINK; WHY DID YOU NEED TO TALK TO ME ABOUT THIS IN PRIVATE, WHEN YOU COULD HAVE BROUGHT THEM TO THE LODGE DIRECTLY?
UNLESS OF COURSE, YOU'VE LOST YOUR FAITH.
UNLESS YOUR PLAN WAS TO LURE ME TO THEM ALONE, SO THEY COULD DO ALL SORTS OF HORRIBLE THINGS TO ME, DEMAND BACK THEIR AOINICITE, THEN SCUTTLE BACK TO THEIR LITTLE HOLE OF A TOWN.
OF COURSE, THE FACT THAT THOSE CYBERNETIC LIMBS OF YOURS CAN BENCH PRESS AN ELEPHANT WOULD MEAN I'D BE IN REAL TROUBLE RIGHT NOW, WOULDN'T IT?
HARRY!
CLICK

AAARGH!

VOOOOOOOOOOOOOOM

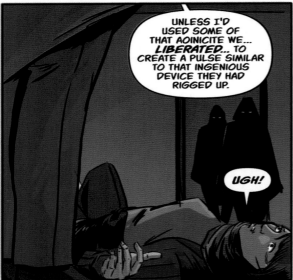

UNLESS I'D USED SOME OF THAT AOINICITE WE... *LIBERATED*... TO CREATE A PULSE SIMILAR TO THAT INGENIOUS DEVICE THEY HAD RIGGED UP.

UGH!

TOO SMALL TO REPULSE A ROWDY, I'D IMAGINE, BUT EASILY ENOUGH TO INTERRUPT THE NEURAL LINK BETWEEN A BRAIN AND A COUPLE OF CYBERNETIC LIMBS.

THIS IS SUCH A DISAPPOINTMENT, JEN.

I THOUGHT YOU HAD A STRONGER STOMACH. I THOUGHT YOU UNDERSTOOD WHAT HAS TO BE DONE.

I THOUGHT YOU UNDERSTOOD MY *SACRIFICE*.

UU-UCK...

I'M NOT THE BAD GUY, JEN.

YOU'RE HAVING A CRISIS OF FAITH, BUT WE'RE STILL GOING TO TRY AND HELP YOU.

COME WITH US. COME AND SEE THE PURPLE DOOR WITH YOUR UNWORTHY EYES.

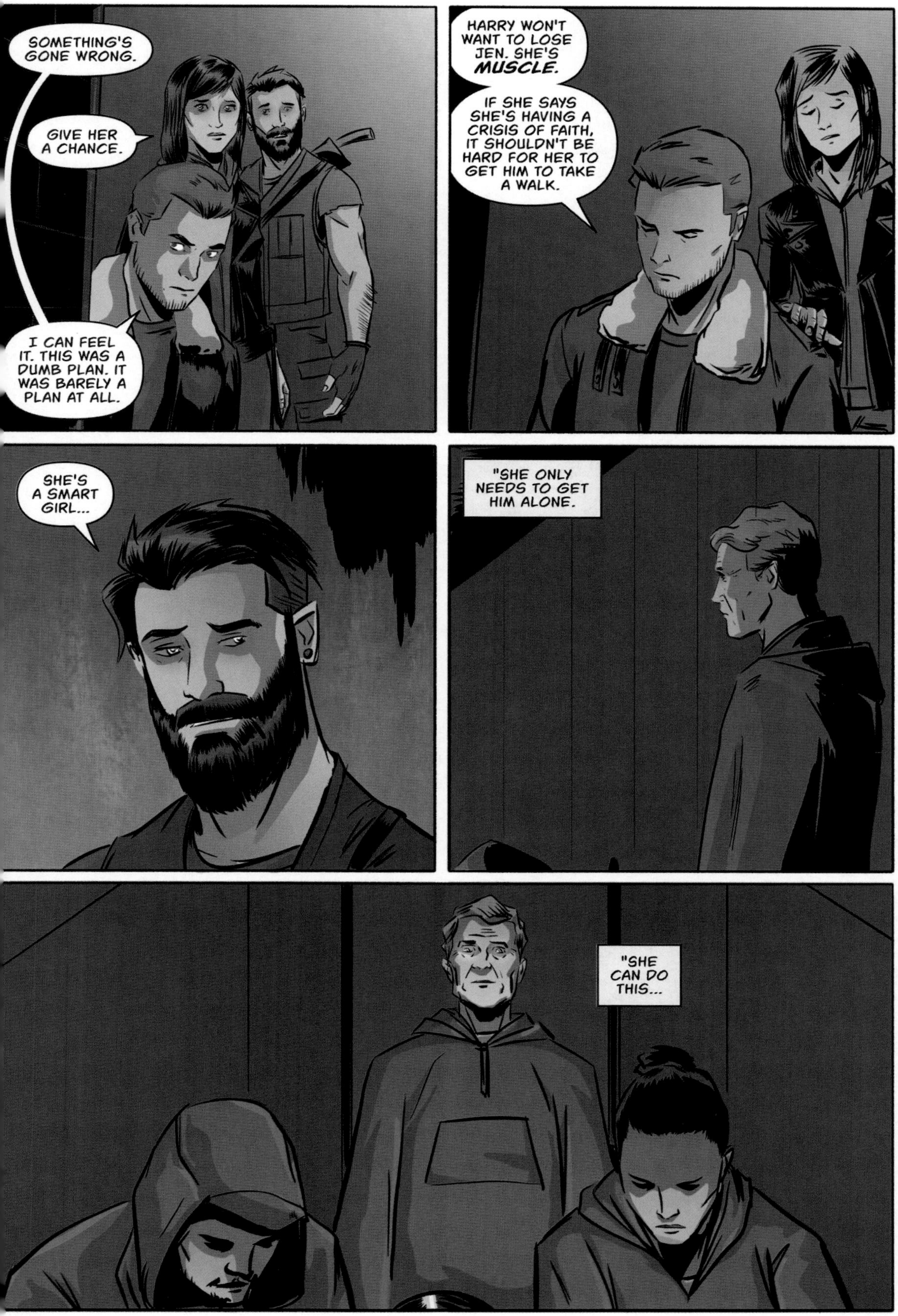
SOMETHING'S GONE WRONG.
GIVE HER A CHANCE.
I CAN FEEL IT. THIS WAS A DUMB PLAN. IT WAS BARELY A PLAN AT ALL.
HARRY WON'T WANT TO LOSE JEN. SHE'S MUSCLE.
IF SHE SAYS SHE'S HAVING A CRISIS OF FAITH, IT SHOULDN'T BE HARD FOR HER TO GET HIM TO TAKE A WALK.
SHE'S A SMART GIRL...
"SHE ONLY NEEDS TO GET HIM ALONE.
"SHE CAN DO THIS...

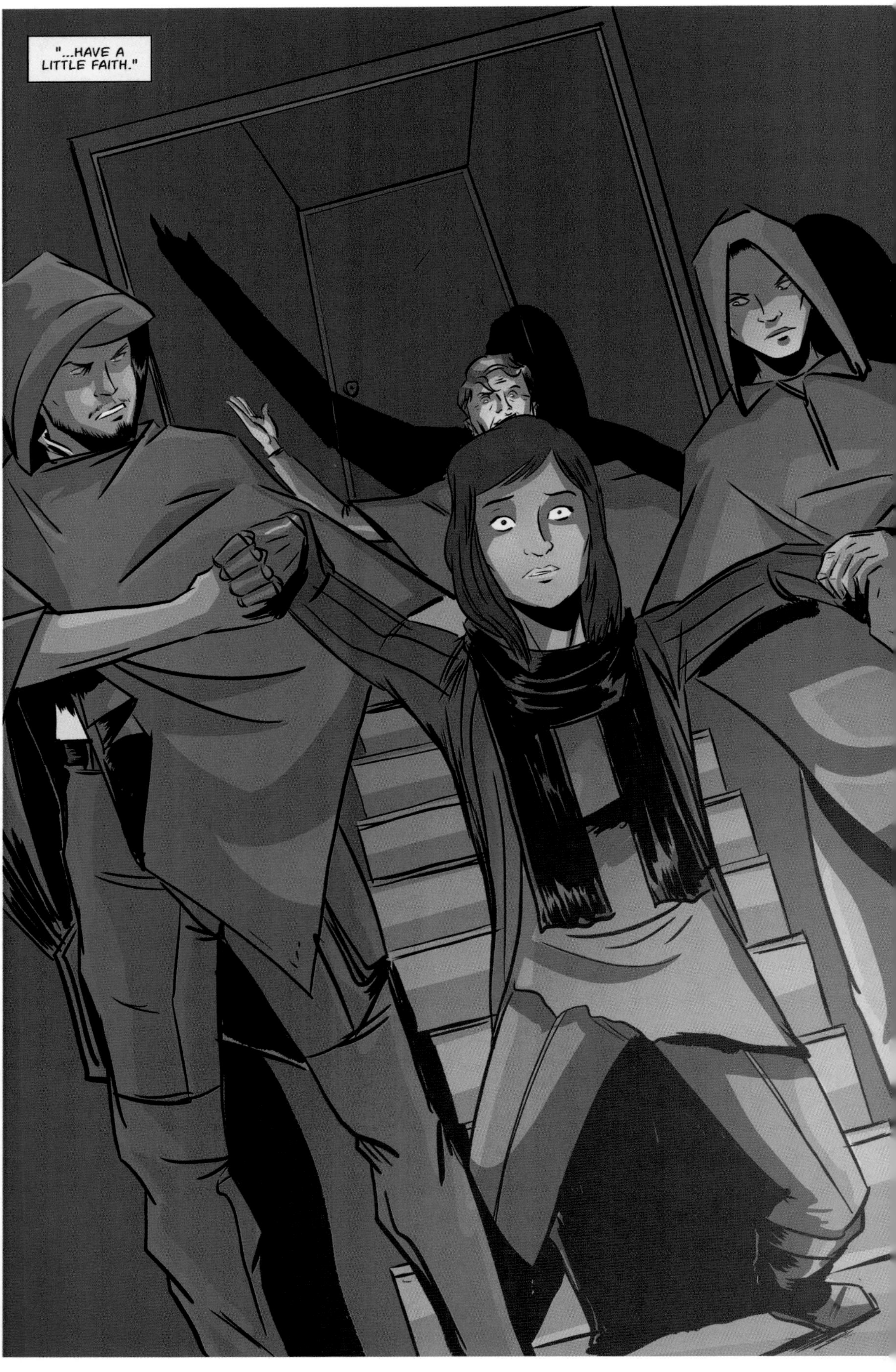
"...HAVE A LITTLE FAITH."

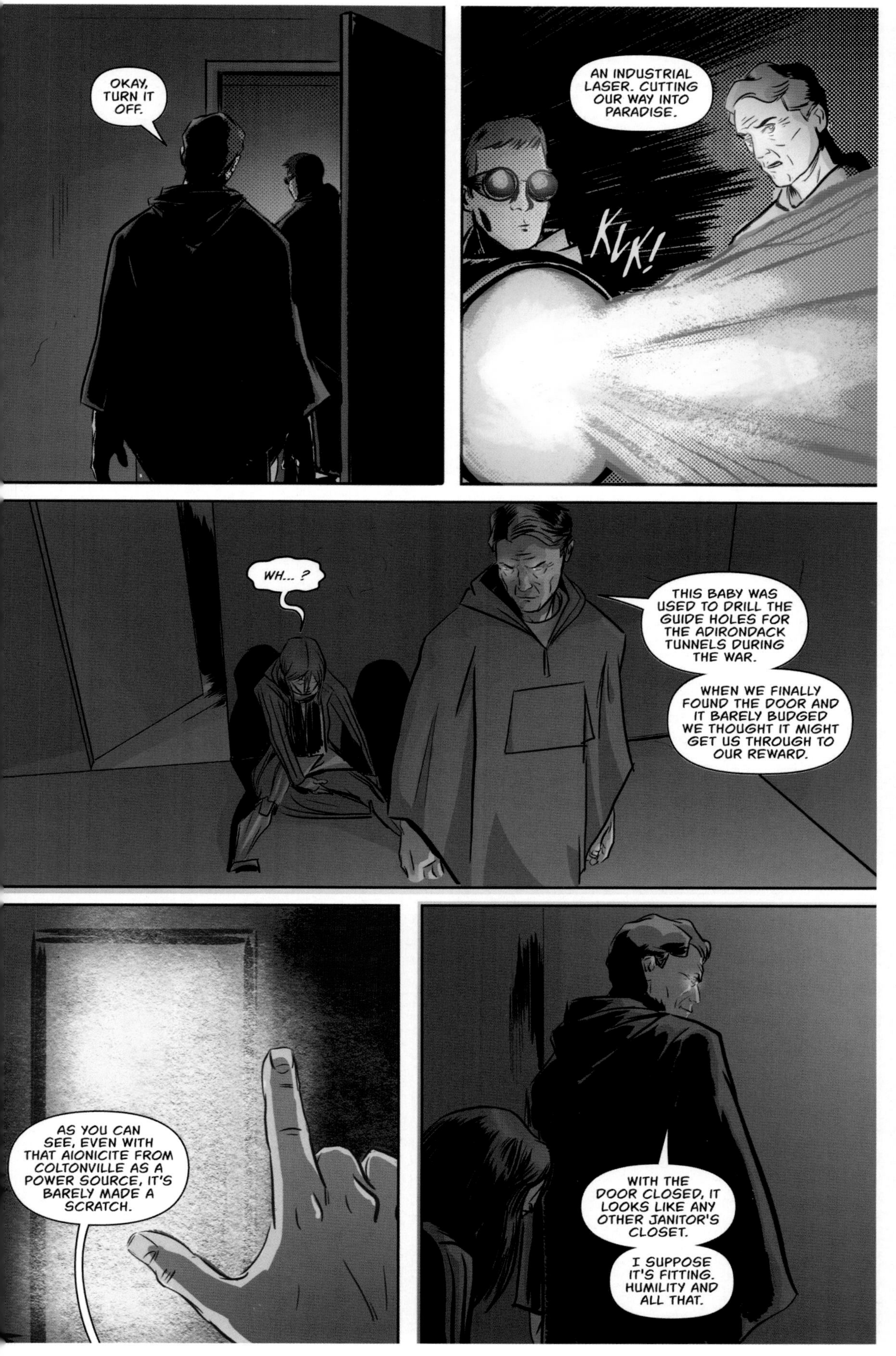
OKAY, TURN IT OFF.
AN INDUSTRIAL LASER. CUTTING OUR WAY INTO PARADISE.
KLIK!
WH... ?
THIS BABY WAS USED TO DRILL THE GUIDE HOLES FOR THE ADIRONDACK TUNNELS DURING THE WAR.
WHEN WE FINALLY FOUND THE DOOR AND IT BARELY BUDGED WE THOUGHT IT MIGHT GET US THROUGH TO OUR REWARD.
AS YOU CAN SEE, EVEN WITH THAT AIONICITE FROM COLTONVILLE AS A POWER SOURCE, IT'S BARELY MADE A SCRATCH.
WITH THE DOOR CLOSED, IT LOOKS LIKE ANY OTHER JANITOR'S CLOSET.
I SUPPOSE IT'S FITTING. HUMILITY AND ALL THAT.

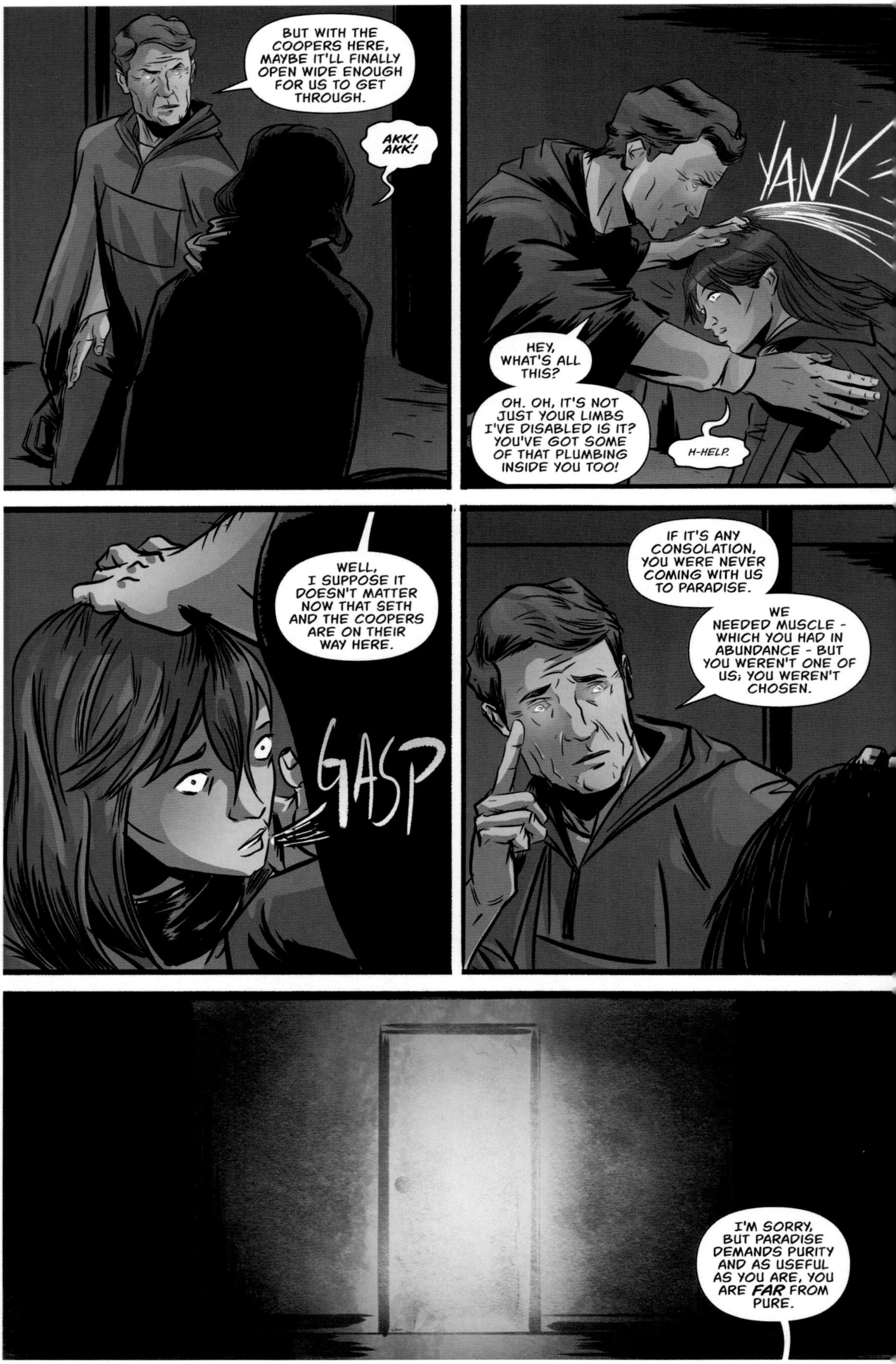
BUT WITH THE COOPERS HERE, MAYBE IT'LL FINALLY OPEN WIDE ENOUGH FOR US TO GET THROUGH.
AKK! AKK!
YANK
HEY, WHAT'S ALL THIS?
OH. OH, IT'S NOT JUST YOUR LIMBS I'VE DISABLED IS IT? YOU'VE GOT SOME OF THAT PLUMBING INSIDE YOU TOO!
H-HELP.
WELL, I SUPPOSE IT DOESN'T MATTER NOW THAT SETH AND THE COOPERS ARE ON THEIR WAY HERE.
GASP
IF IT'S ANY CONSOLATION, YOU WERE NEVER COMING WITH US TO PARADISE.
WE NEEDED MUSCLE - WHICH YOU HAD IN ABUNDANCE - BUT YOU WEREN'T ONE OF US; YOU WEREN'T CHOSEN.
I'M SORRY, BUT PARADISE DEMANDS PURITY AND AS USEFUL AS YOU ARE, YOU ARE *FAR* FROM PURE.

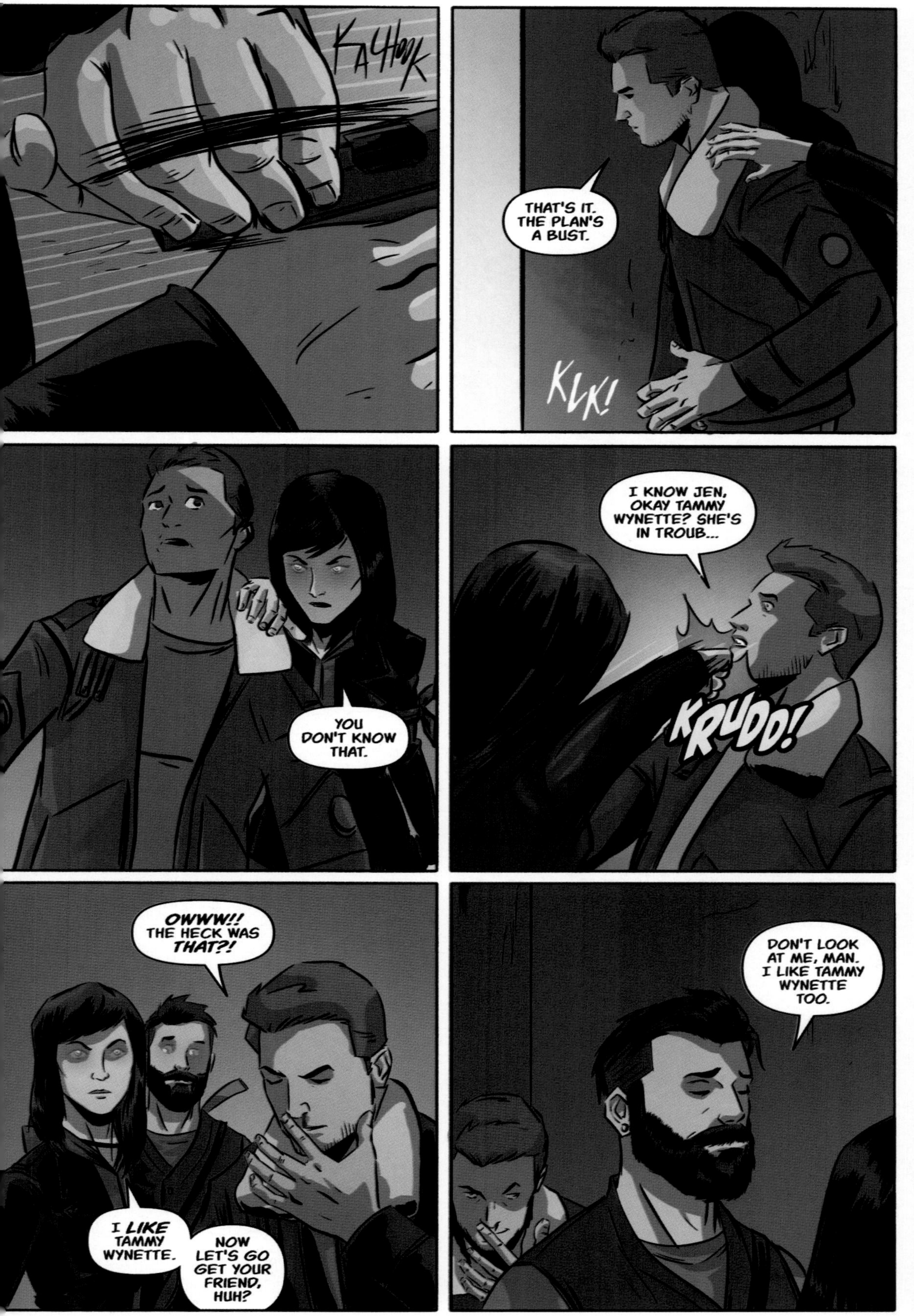
KACHOOK
THAT'S IT. THE PLAN'S A BUST.
KLIK!
YOU DON'T KNOW THAT.
I KNOW JEN, OKAY TAMMY WYNETTE? SHE'S IN TROUB...
KRUDD!
OWWW!! THE HECK WAS THAT?!
I LIKE TAMMY WYNETTE.
NOW LET'S GO GET YOUR FRIEND, HUH?
DON'T LOOK AT ME, MAN. I LIKE TAMMY WYNETTE TOO.

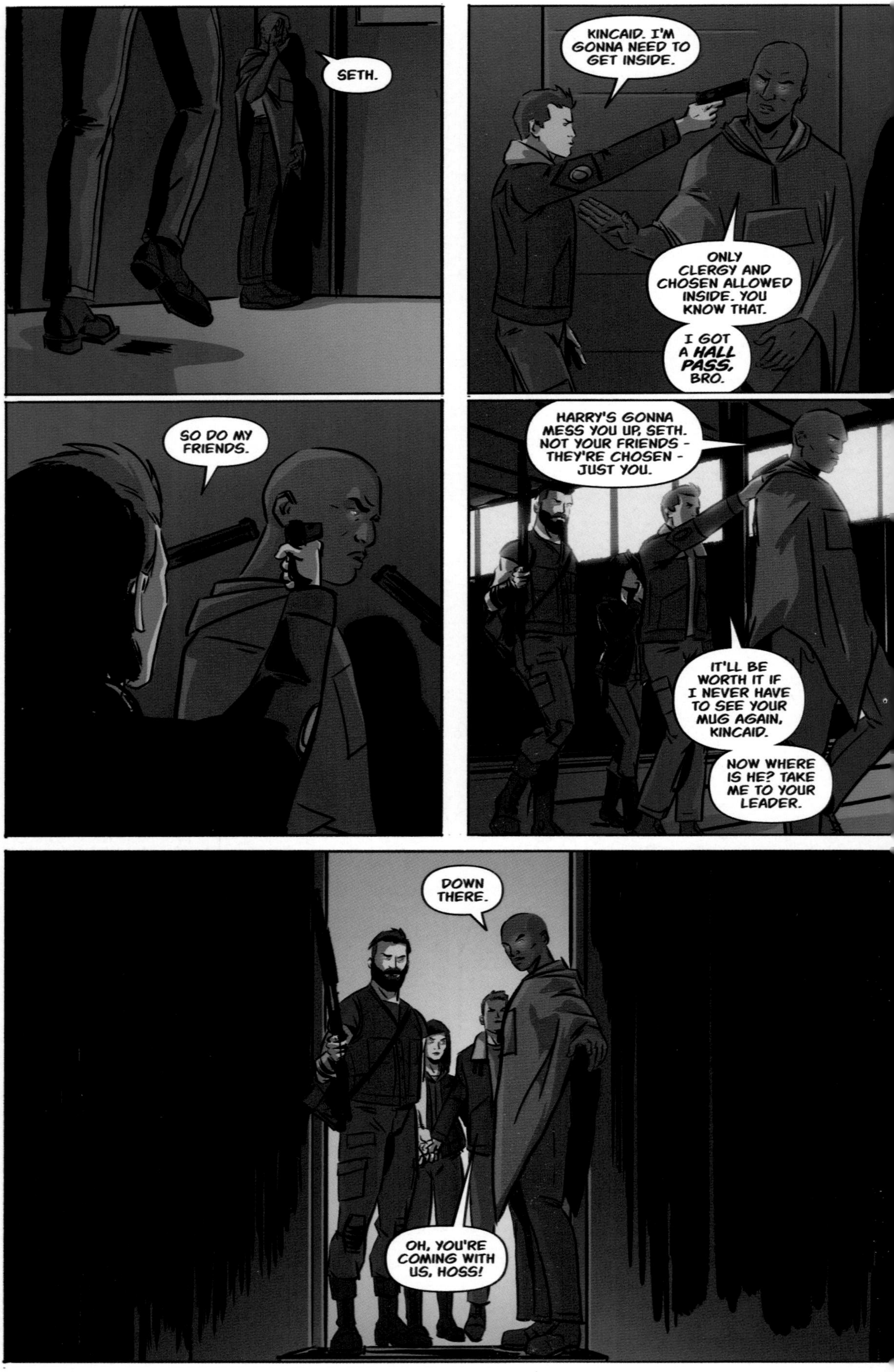
SETH.
KINCAID. I'M GONNA NEED TO GET INSIDE.
ONLY CLERGY AND CHOSEN ALLOWED INSIDE. YOU KNOW THAT.
I GOT A HALL PASS, BRO.
SO DO MY FRIENDS.
HARRY'S GONNA MESS YOU UP, SETH. NOT YOUR FRIENDS - THEY'RE CHOSEN - JUST YOU.
IT'LL BE WORTH IT IF I NEVER HAVE TO SEE YOUR MUG AGAIN, KINCAID.
NOW WHERE IS HE? TAKE ME TO YOUR LEADER.
DOWN THERE.
OH, YOU'RE COMING WITH US, HOSS!

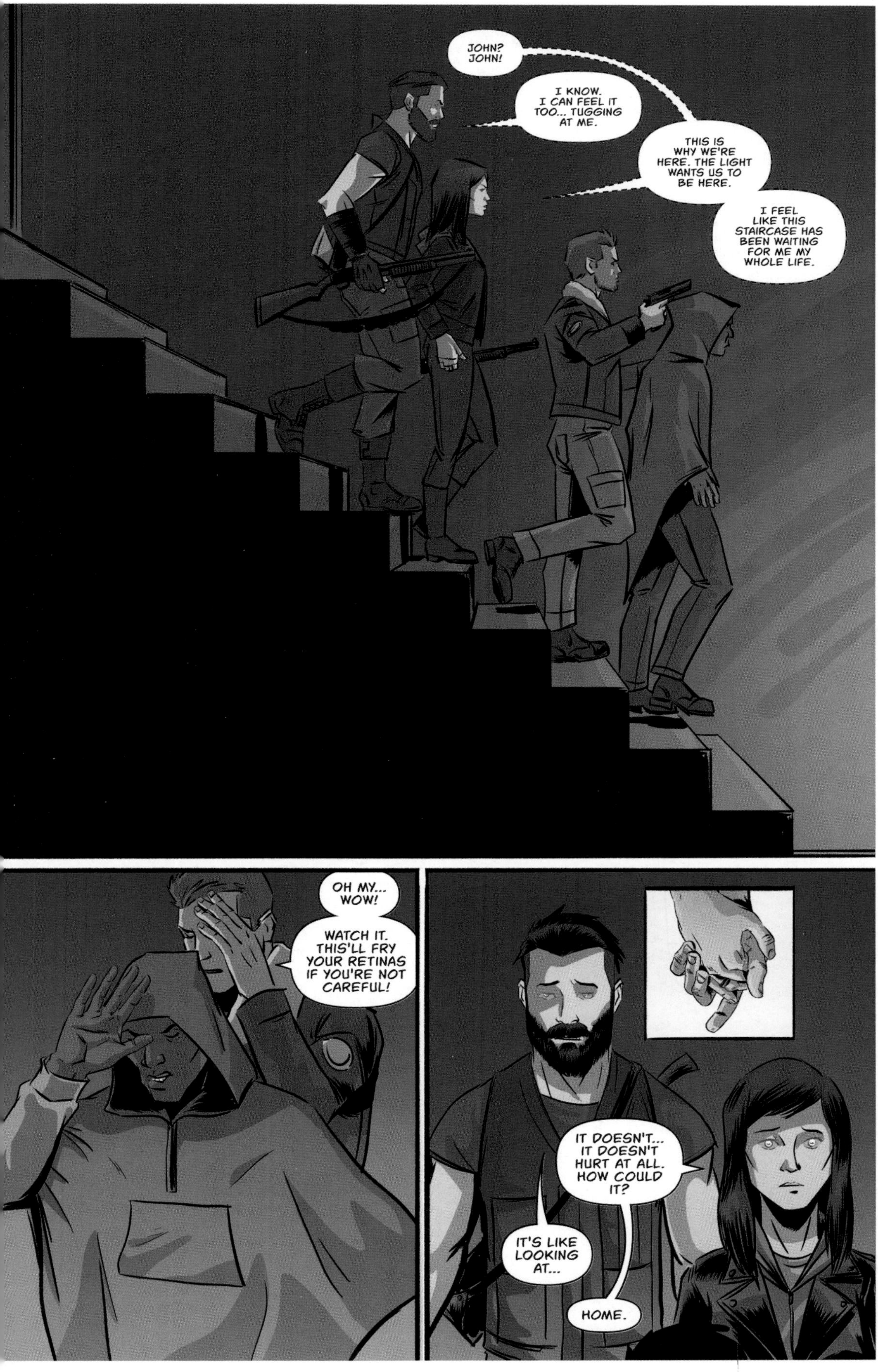
JOHN? JOHN!
I KNOW. I CAN FEEL IT TOO... TUGGING AT ME.
THIS IS WHY WE'RE HERE. THE LIGHT WANTS US TO BE HERE.
I FEEL LIKE THIS STAIRCASE HAS BEEN WAITING FOR ME MY WHOLE LIFE.
OH MY... WOW!
WATCH IT. THIS'LL FRY YOUR RETINAS IF YOU'RE NOT CAREFUL!
IT DOESN'T... IT DOESN'T HURT AT ALL. HOW COULD IT?
IT'S LIKE LOOKING AT...
HOME.

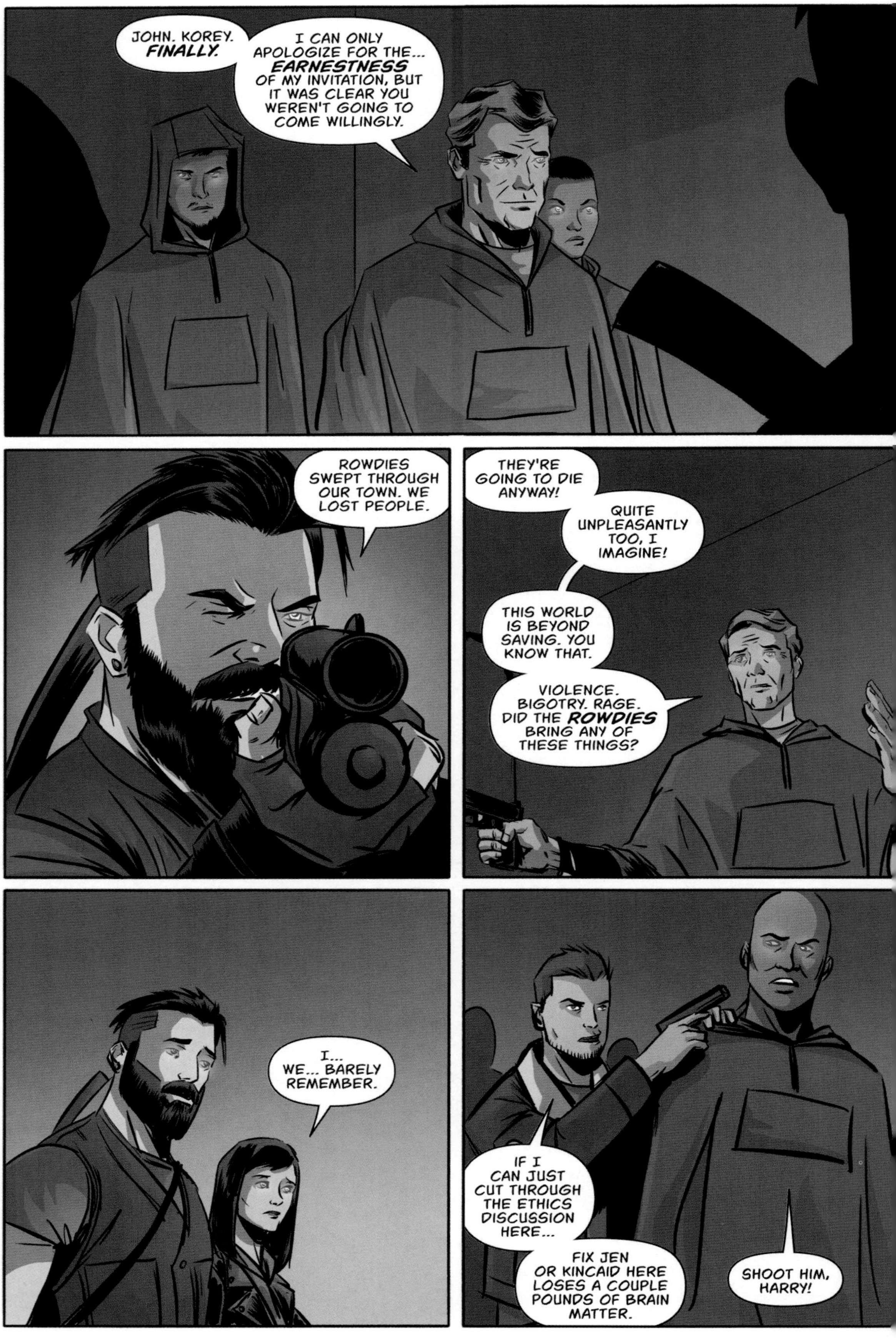
JOHN. KOREY. FINALLY.
I CAN ONLY APOLOGIZE FOR THE... EARNESTNESS OF MY INVITATION, BUT IT WAS CLEAR YOU WEREN'T GOING TO COME WILLINGLY.
ROWDIES SWEPT THROUGH OUR TOWN. WE LOST PEOPLE.
THEY'RE GOING TO DIE ANYWAY!
QUITE UNPLEASANTLY TOO, I IMAGINE!
THIS WORLD IS BEYOND SAVING. YOU KNOW THAT.
VIOLENCE. BIGOTRY. RAGE. DID THE ROWDIES BRING ANY OF THESE THINGS?
I... WE... BARELY REMEMBER.
IF I CAN JUST CUT THROUGH THE ETHICS DISCUSSION HERE...
FIX JEN OR KINCAID HERE LOSES A COUPLE POUNDS OF BRAIN MATTER.
SHOOT HIM, HARRY!

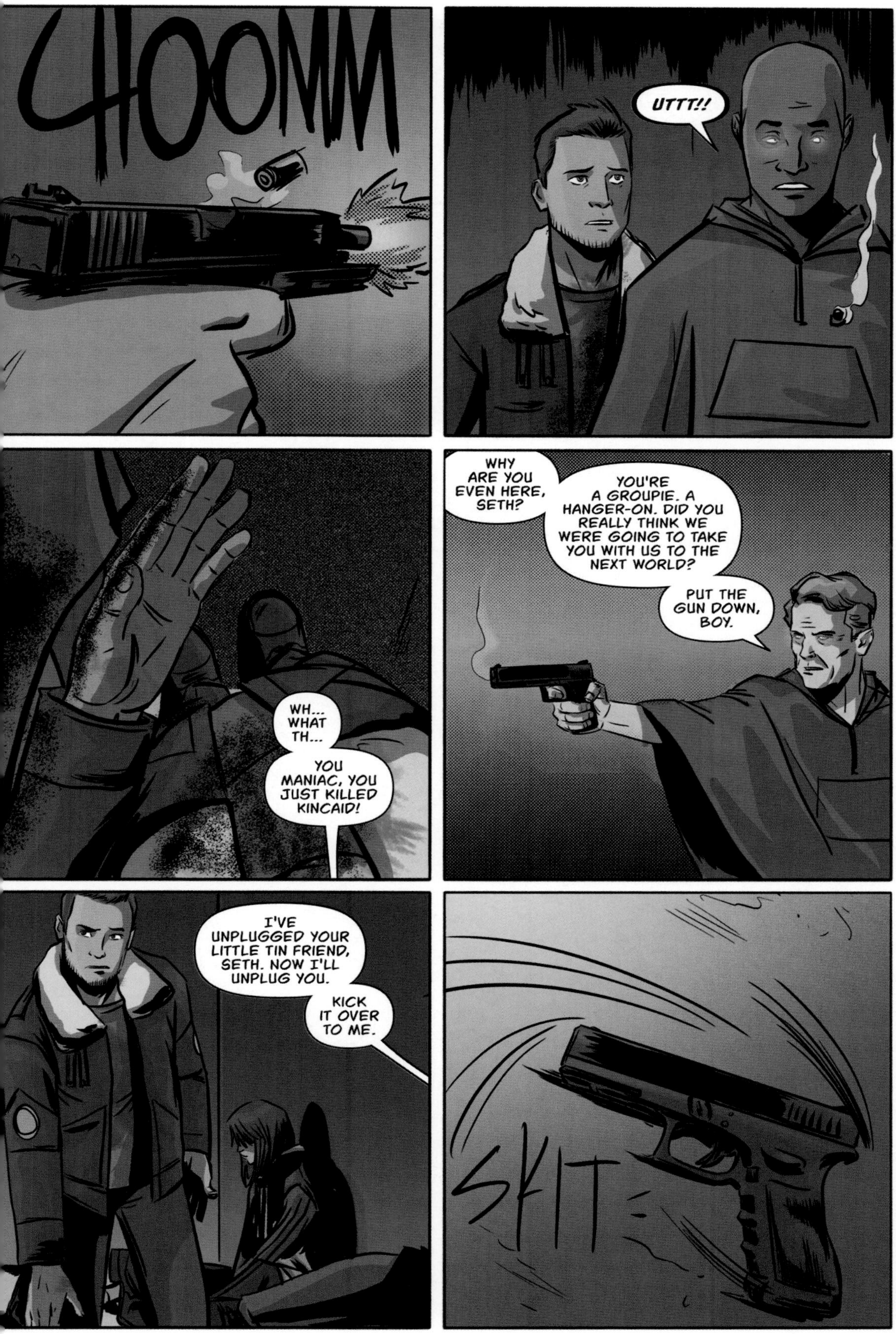
CHOOMM
UTTT!!
WH... WHAT TH...
YOU MANIAC, YOU JUST KILLED KINCAID!
WHY ARE YOU EVEN HERE, SETH?
YOU'RE A GROUPIE. A HANGER-ON. DID YOU REALLY THINK WE WERE GOING TO TAKE YOU WITH US TO THE NEXT WORLD?
PUT THE GUN DOWN, BOY.
I'VE UNPLUGGED YOUR LITTLE TIN FRIEND, SETH. NOW I'LL UNPLUG YOU.
KICK IT OVER TO ME.
SKIT

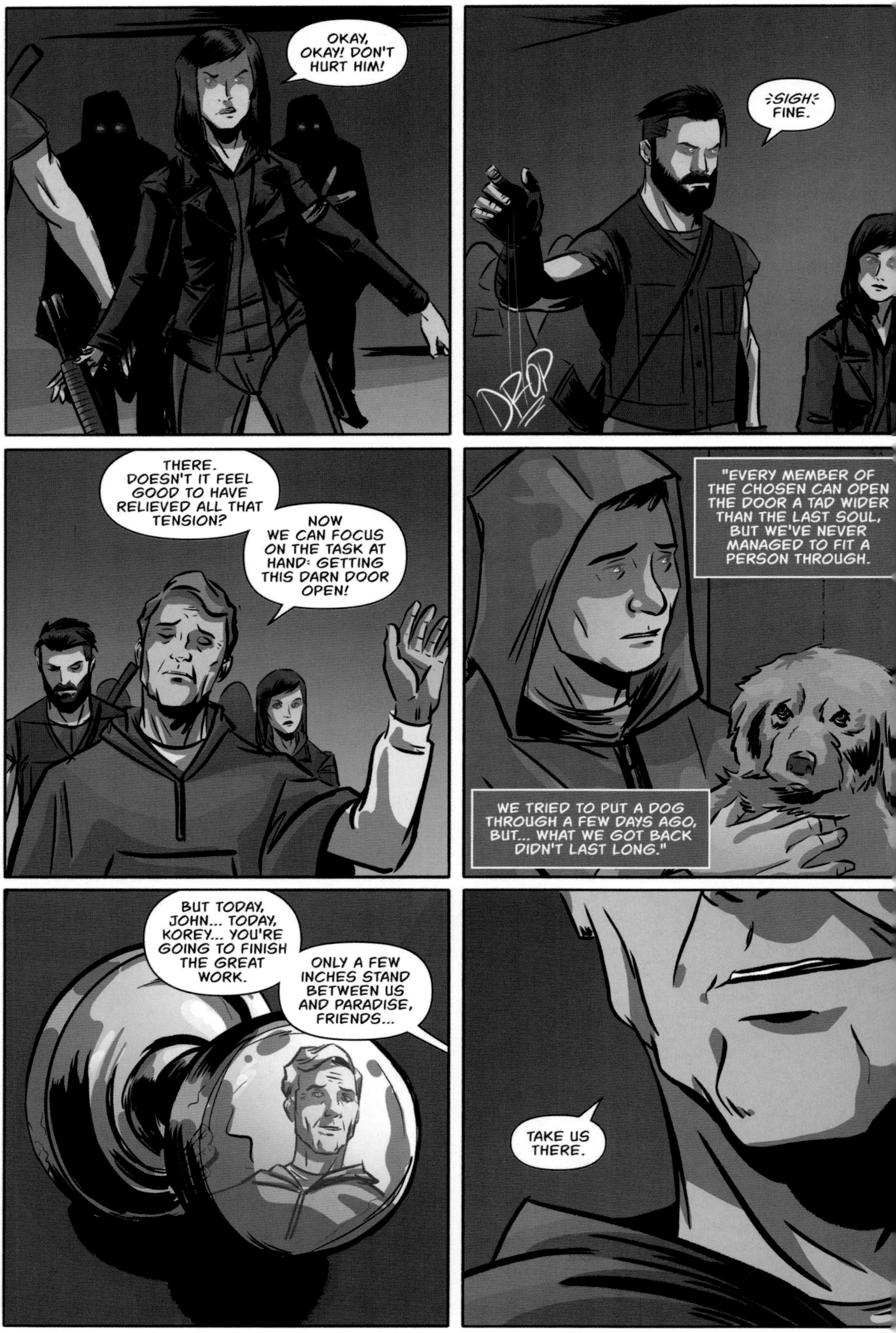
OKAY, OKAY! DON'T HURT HIM!
SIGH FINE.
DROP
THERE. DOESN'T IT FEEL GOOD TO HAVE RELIEVED ALL THAT TENSION?
NOW WE CAN FOCUS ON THE TASK AT HAND: GETTING THIS DARN DOOR OPEN!
"EVERY MEMBER OF THE CHOSEN CAN OPEN THE DOOR A TAD WIDER THAN THE LAST SOUL, BUT WE'VE NEVER MANAGED TO FIT A PERSON THROUGH.
WE TRIED TO PUT A DOG THROUGH A FEW DAYS AGO, BUT... WHAT WE GOT BACK DIDN'T LAST LONG."
BUT TODAY, JOHN... TODAY, KOREY... YOU'RE GOING TO FINISH THE GREAT WORK.
ONLY A FEW INCHES STAND BETWEEN US AND PARADISE, FRIENDS...
TAKE US THERE.

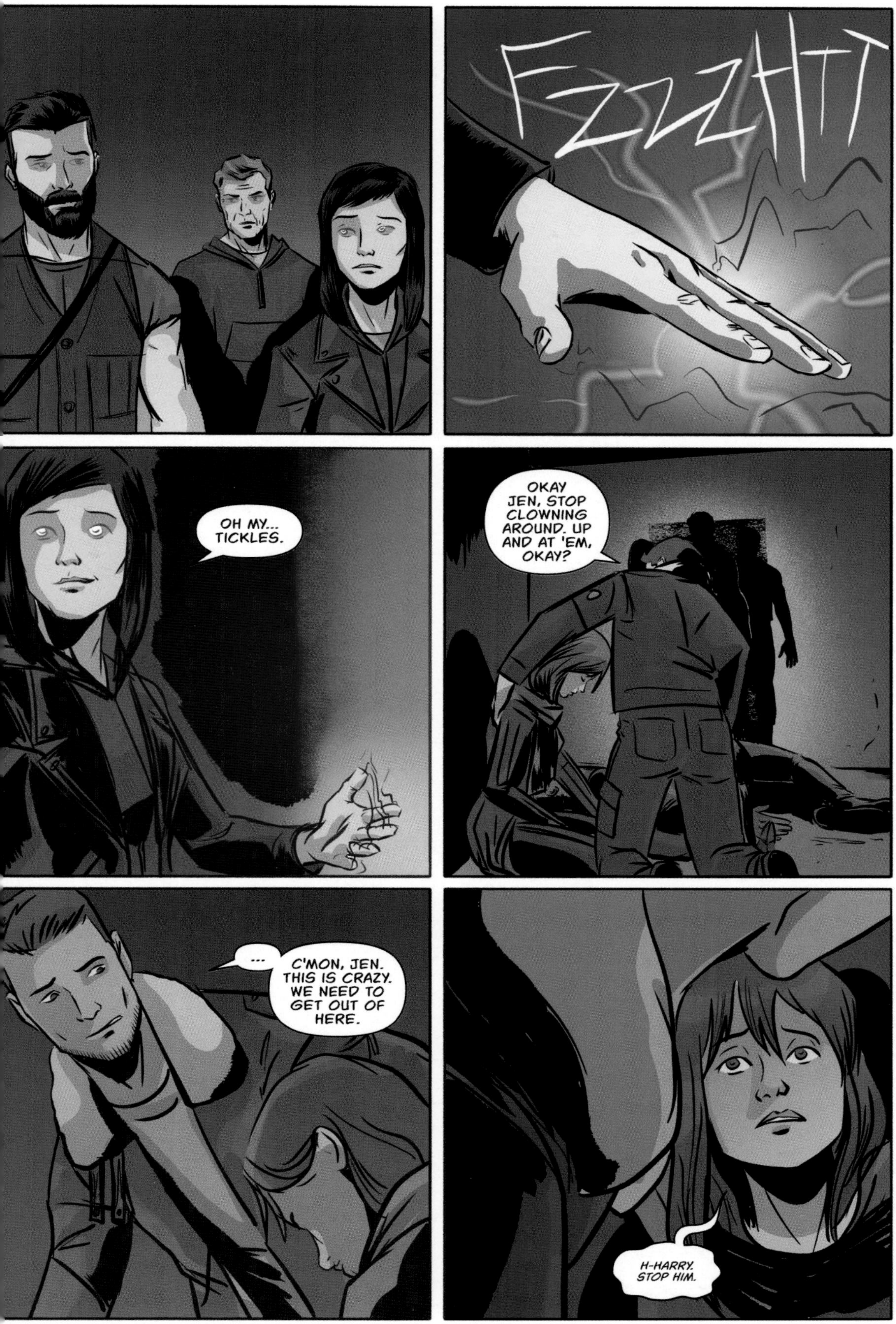
FZZZHTT
OH MY... TICKLES.
OKAY JEN, STOP CLOWNING AROUND. UP AND AT 'EM, OKAY?
...
C'MON, JEN. THIS IS CRAZY. WE NEED TO GET OUT OF HERE.
H-HARRY. STOP HIM.

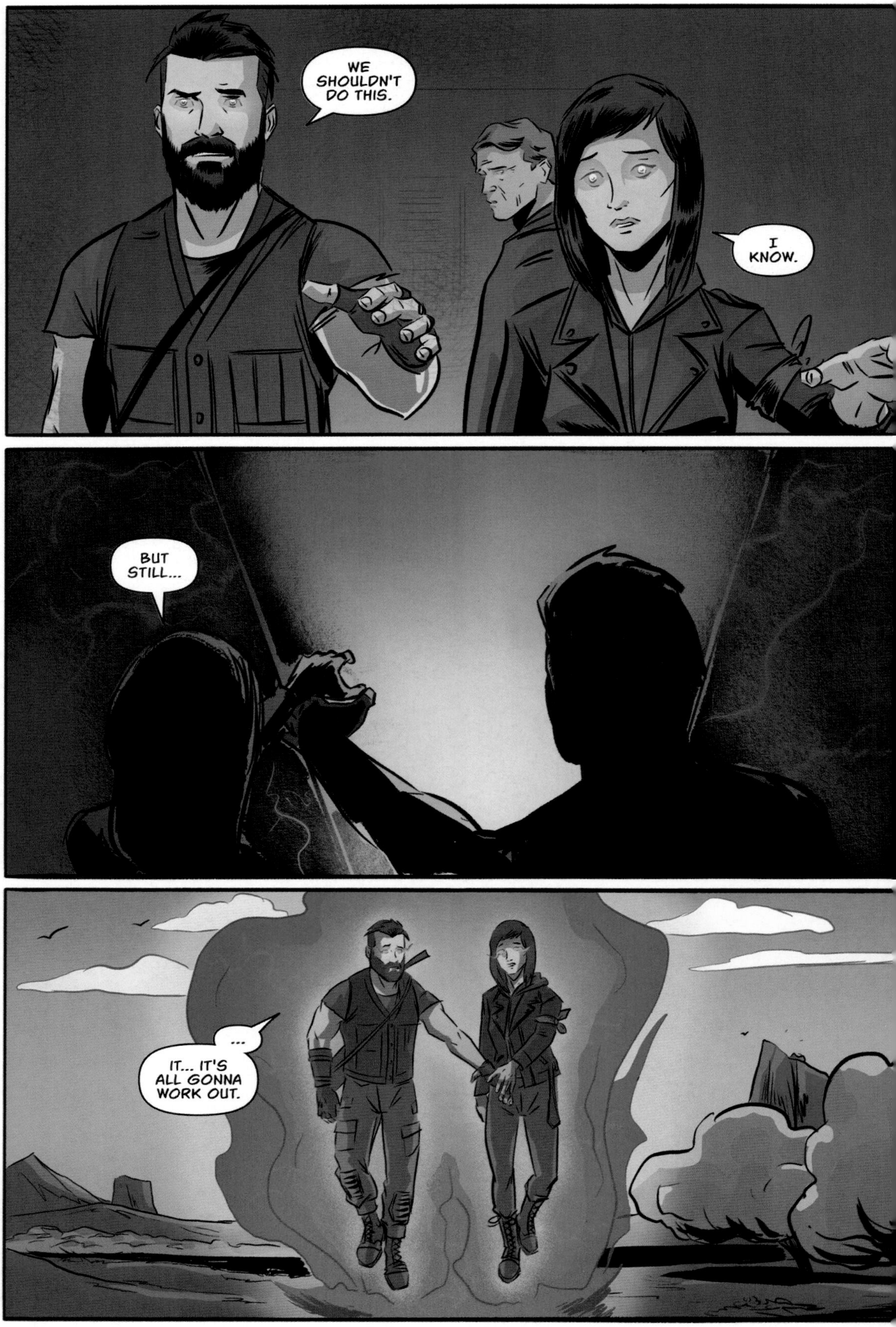
WE SHOULDN'T DO THIS.
I KNOW.
BUT STILL...
...
IT... IT'S ALL GONNA WORK OUT.

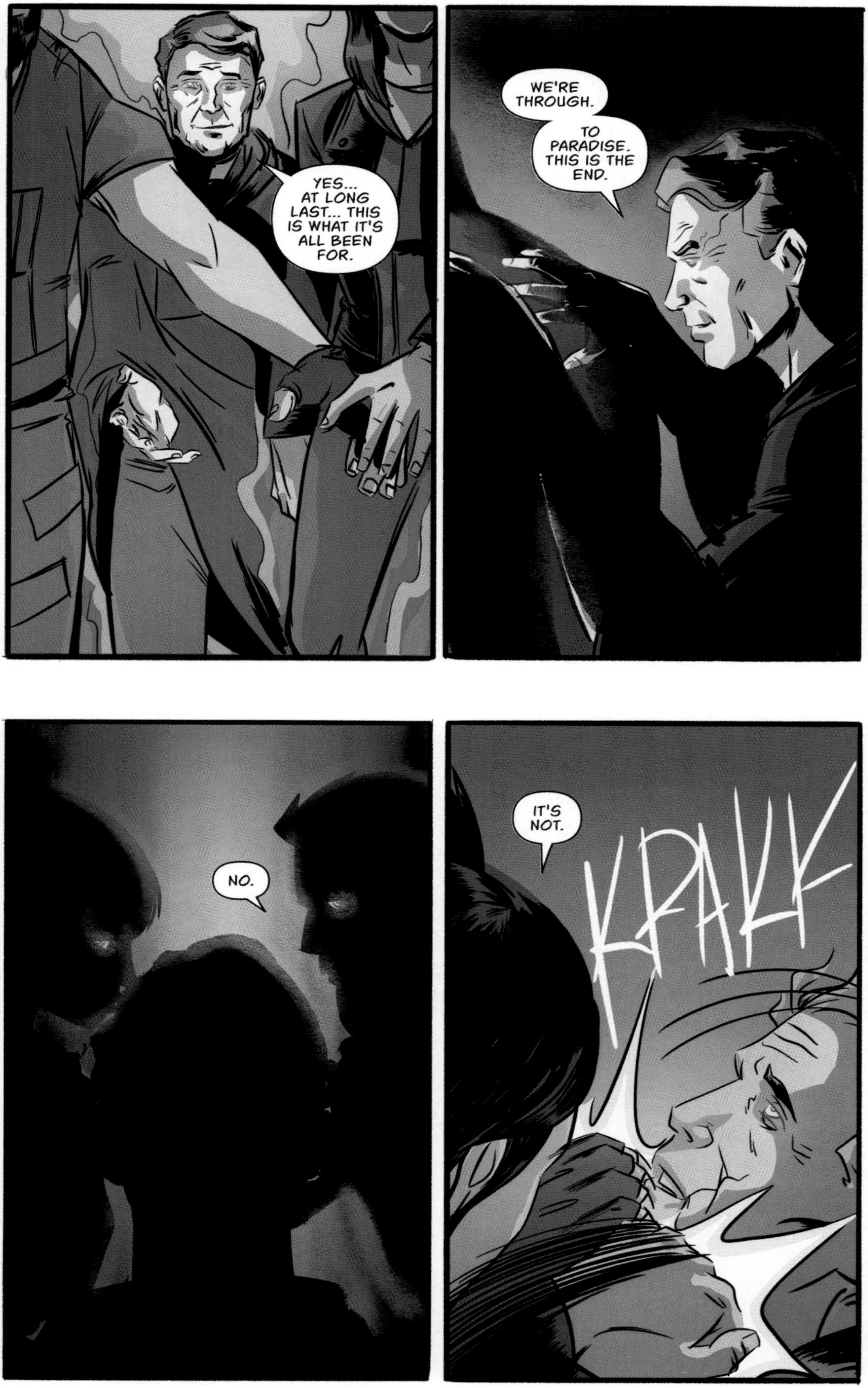
YES... AT LONG LAST... THIS IS WHAT IT'S ALL BEEN FOR.
WE'RE THROUGH.
TO PARADISE. THIS IS THE END.
NO.
IT'S NOT.
KRAKK

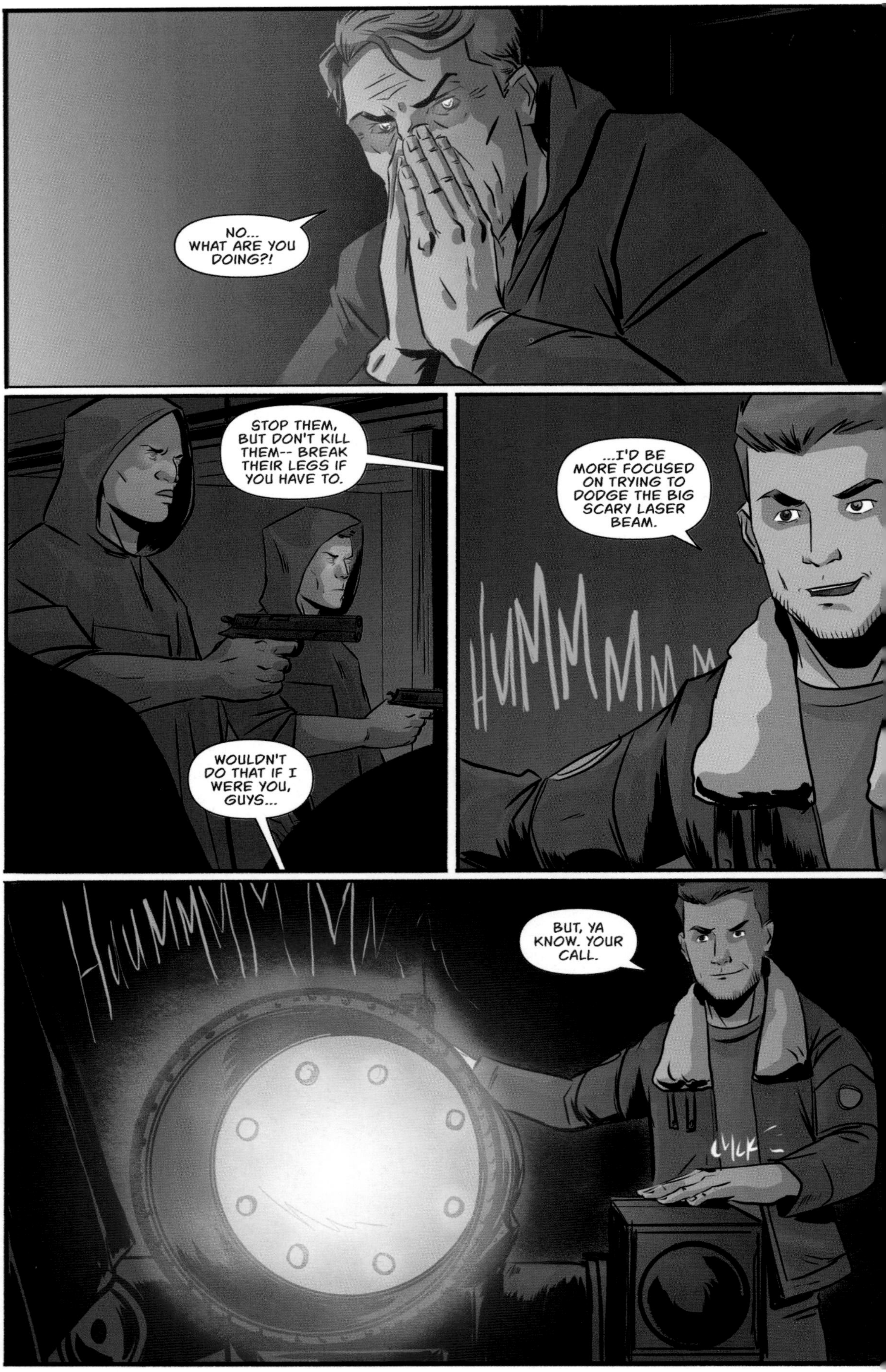
NO... WHAT ARE YOU DOING?!
STOP THEM, BUT DON'T KILL THEM-- BREAK THEIR LEGS IF YOU HAVE TO.
WOULDN'T DO THAT IF I WERE YOU, GUYS...
...I'D BE MORE FOCUSED ON TRYING TO DODGE THE BIG SCARY LASER BEAM.
HUMMMMMM
BUT, YA KNOW. YOUR CALL.
CLICK

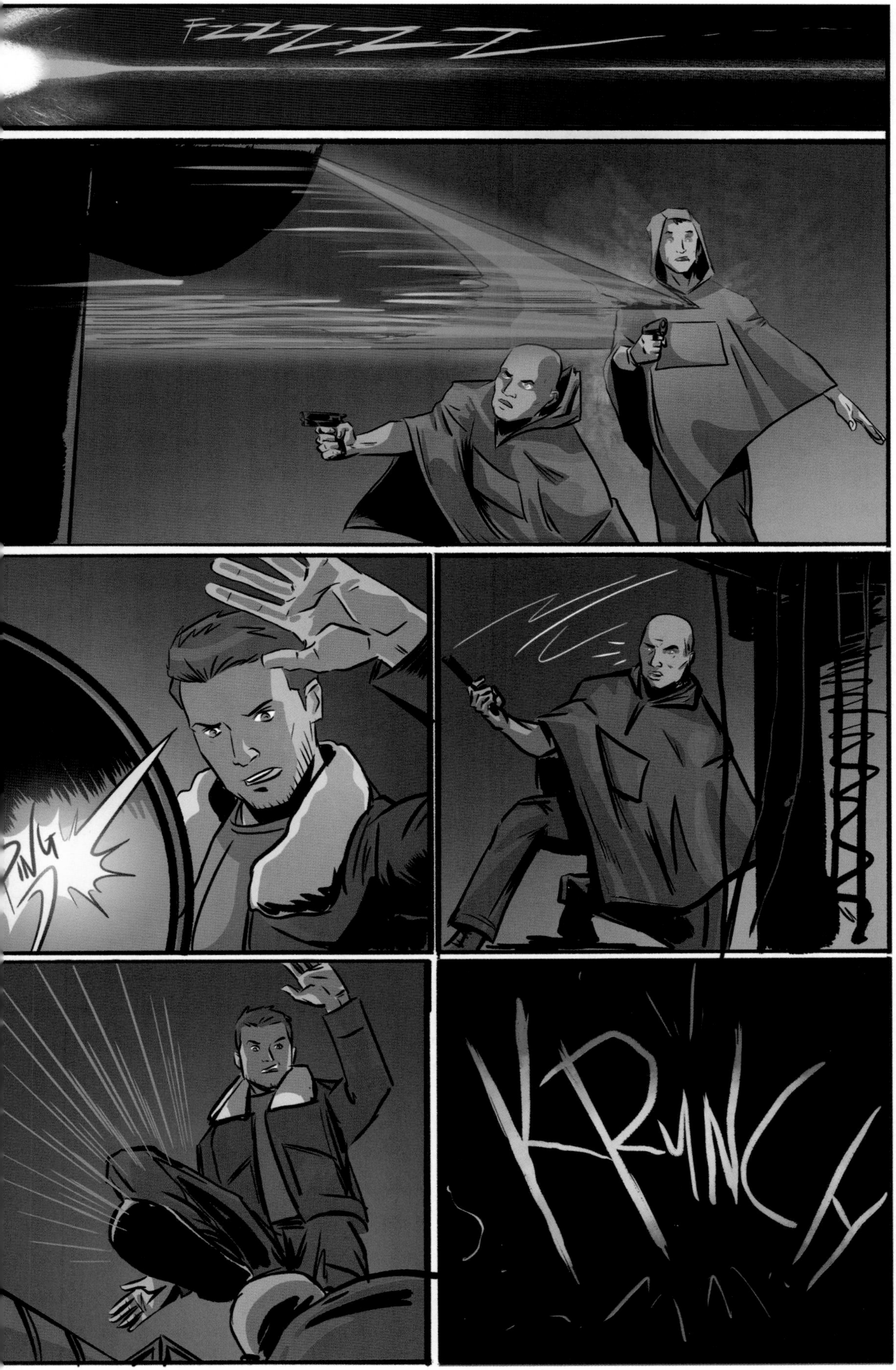
FZZZZZ
PING
KRUNCH

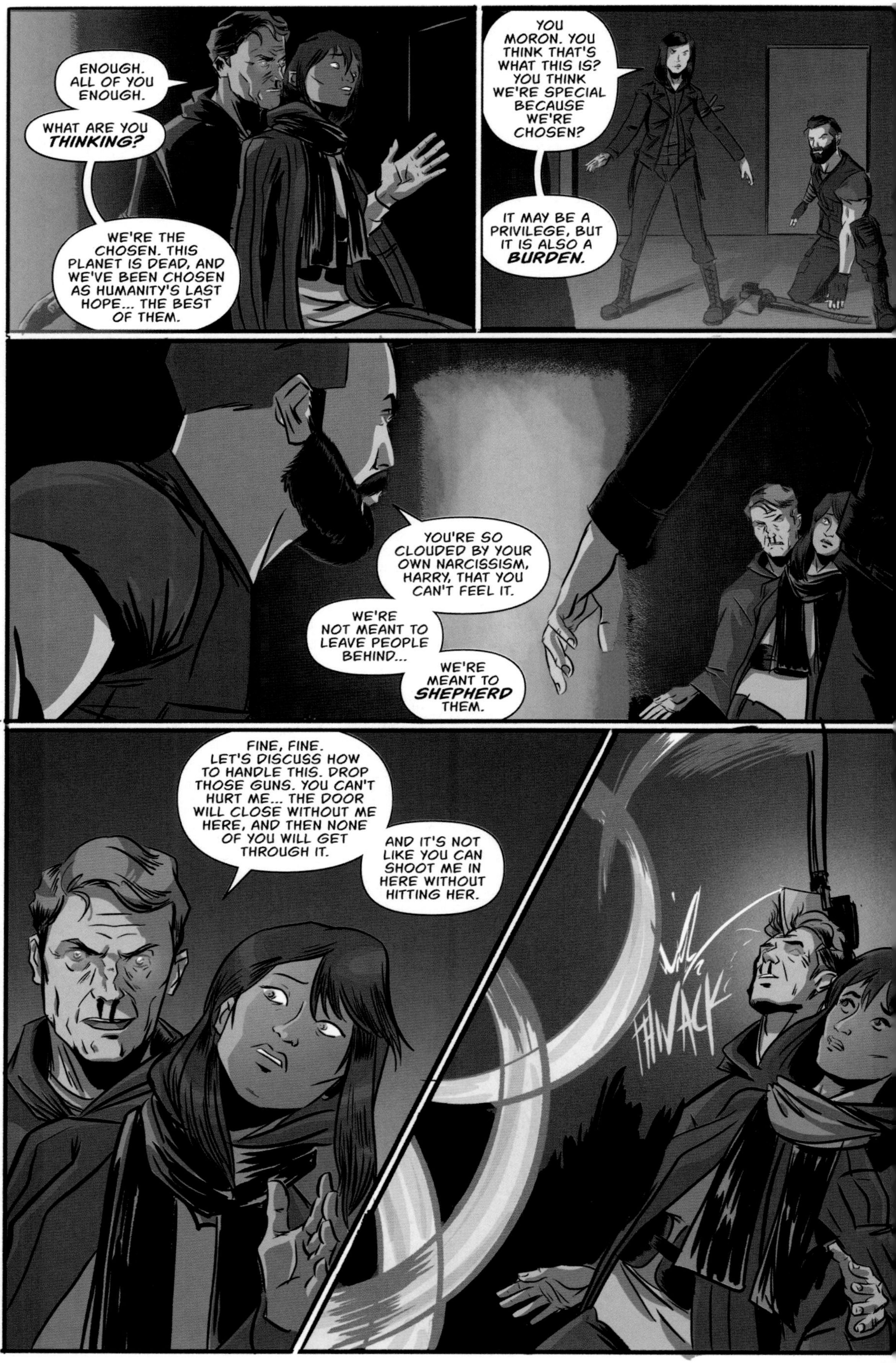
ENOUGH. ALL OF YOU ENOUGH.
WHAT ARE YOU *THINKING?*
WE'RE THE CHOSEN. THIS PLANET IS DEAD, AND WE'VE BEEN CHOSEN AS HUMANITY'S LAST HOPE... THE BEST OF THEM.
YOU MORON. YOU THINK THAT'S WHAT THIS IS? YOU THINK WE'RE SPECIAL BECAUSE WE'RE CHOSEN?
IT MAY BE A PRIVILEGE, BUT IT IS ALSO A *BURDEN.*
YOU'RE SO CLOUDED BY YOUR OWN NARCISSISM, HARRY, THAT YOU CAN'T FEEL IT.
WE'RE NOT MEANT TO LEAVE PEOPLE BEHIND...
WE'RE MEANT TO *SHEPHERD* THEM.
FINE, FINE. LET'S DISCUSS HOW TO HANDLE THIS. DROP THOSE GUNS. YOU CAN'T HURT ME... THE DOOR WILL CLOSE WITHOUT ME HERE, AND THEN NONE OF YOU WILL GET THROUGH IT.
AND IT'S NOT LIKE YOU CAN SHOOT ME IN HERE WITHOUT HITTING HER.
THWACK

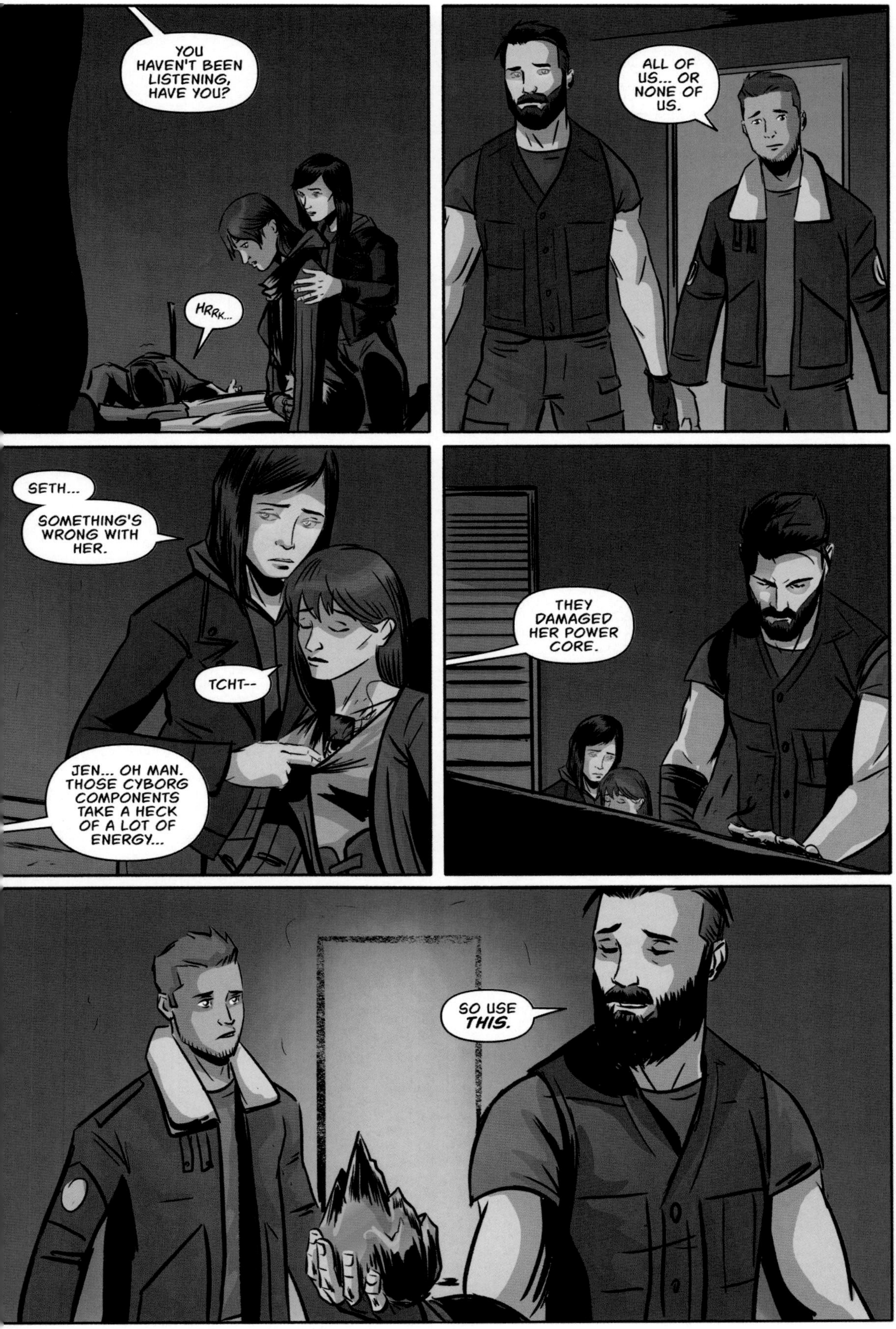

YOU HAVEN'T BEEN LISTENING, HAVE YOU?
HRRK...
ALL OF US... OR NONE OF US.
SETH...
SOMETHING'S WRONG WITH HER.
TCHT--
JEN... OH MAN. THOSE CYBORG COMPONENTS TAKE A HECK OF A LOT OF ENERGY...
THEY DAMAGED HER POWER CORE.
SO USE *THIS.*

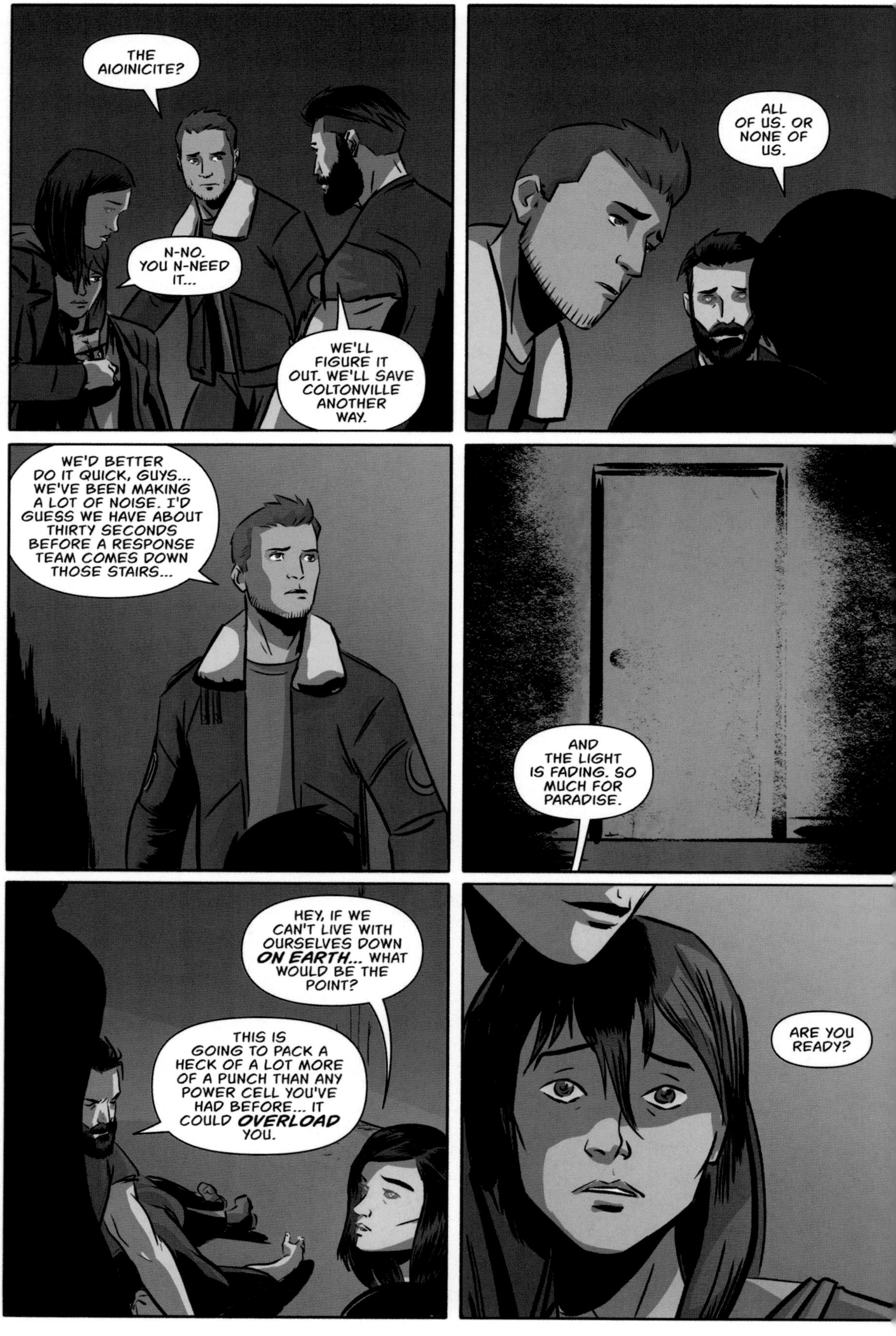
THE AIOINICITE?
N-NO. YOU N-NEED IT...
WE'LL FIGURE IT OUT. WE'LL SAVE COLTONVILLE ANOTHER WAY.
ALL OF US. OR NONE OF US.
WE'D BETTER DO IT QUICK, GUYS... WE'VE BEEN MAKING A LOT OF NOISE. I'D GUESS WE HAVE ABOUT THIRTY SECONDS BEFORE A RESPONSE TEAM COMES DOWN THOSE STAIRS...
AND THE LIGHT IS FADING. SO MUCH FOR PARADISE.
HEY, IF WE CAN'T LIVE WITH OURSELVES DOWN ON EARTH... WHAT WOULD BE THE POINT?
THIS IS GOING TO PACK A HECK OF A LOT MORE OF A PUNCH THAN ANY POWER CELL YOU'VE HAD BEFORE... IT COULD OVERLOAD YOU.
ARE YOU READY?

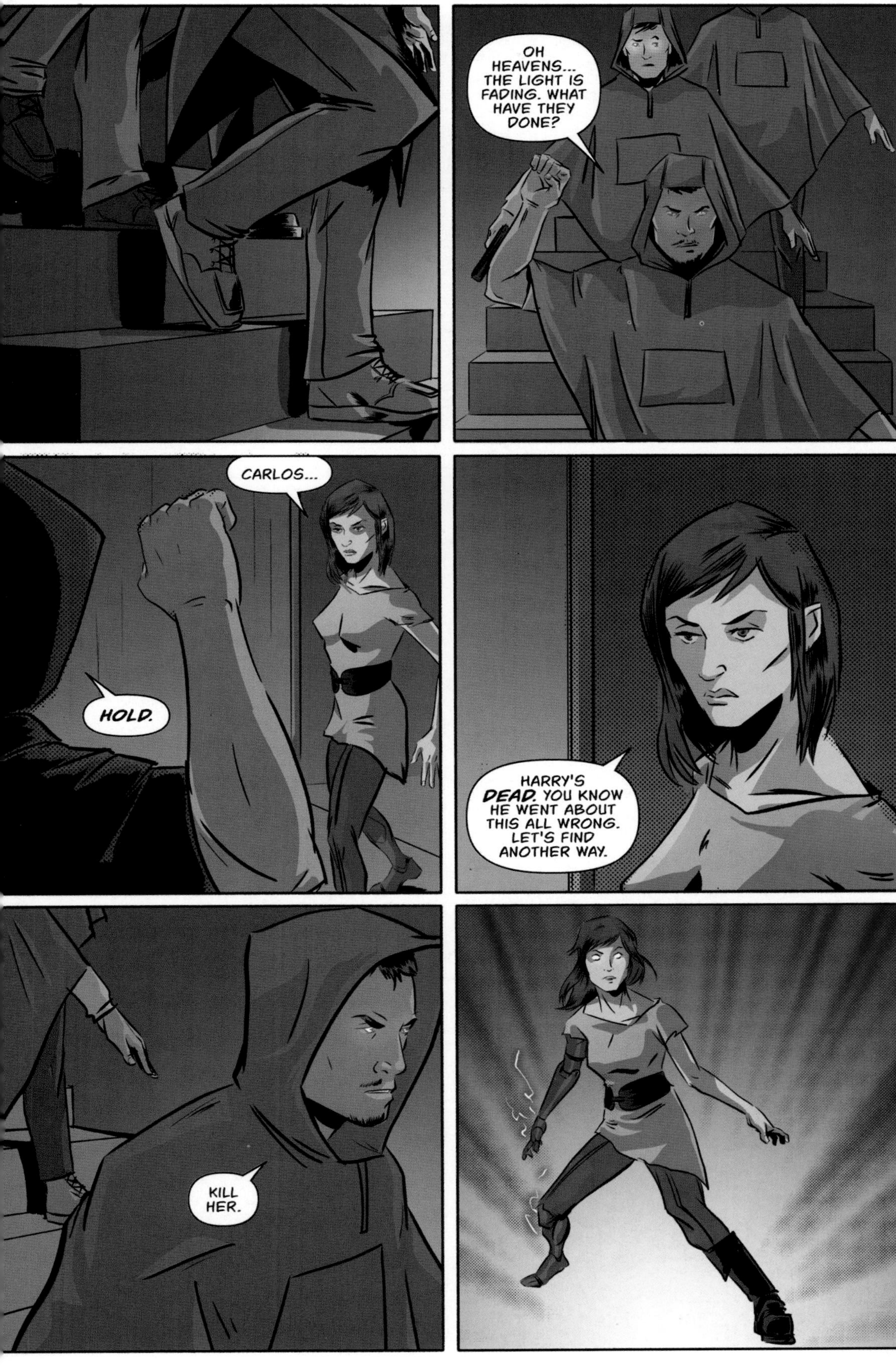
OH HEAVENS... THE LIGHT IS FADING. WHAT HAVE THEY DONE?
CARLOS...
HOLD.
HARRY'S DEAD. YOU KNOW HE WENT ABOUT THIS ALL WRONG. LET'S FIND ANOTHER WAY.
KILL HER.

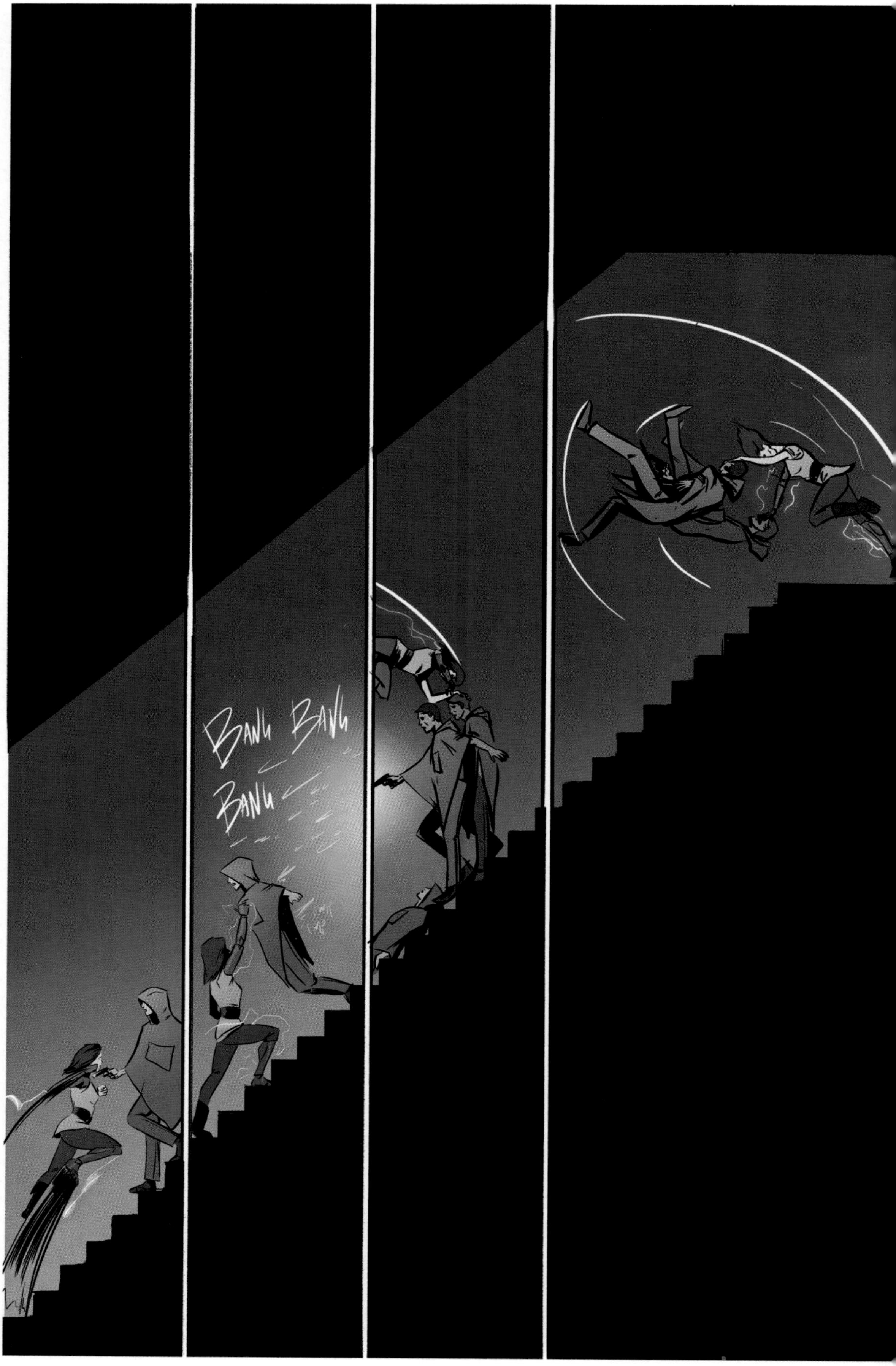
BANG BANG
BANG

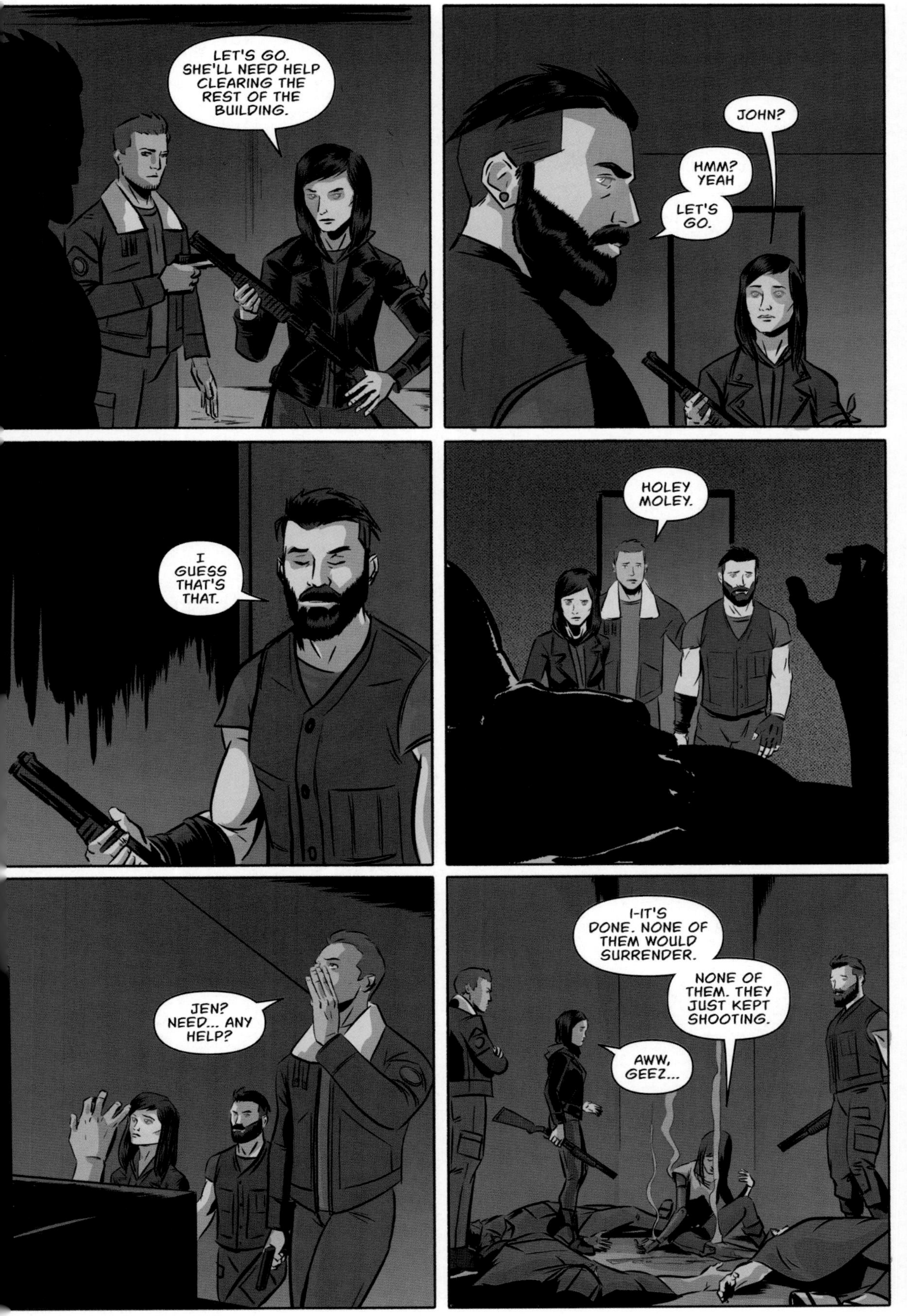
LET'S GO. SHE'LL NEED HELP CLEARING THE REST OF THE BUILDING.
JOHN?
HMM? YEAH
LET'S GO.
I GUESS THAT'S THAT.
HOLEY MOLEY.
JEN? NEED... ANY HELP?
I-IT'S DONE. NONE OF THEM WOULD SURRENDER.
NONE OF THEM. THEY JUST KEPT SHOOTING.
AWW, GEEZ...

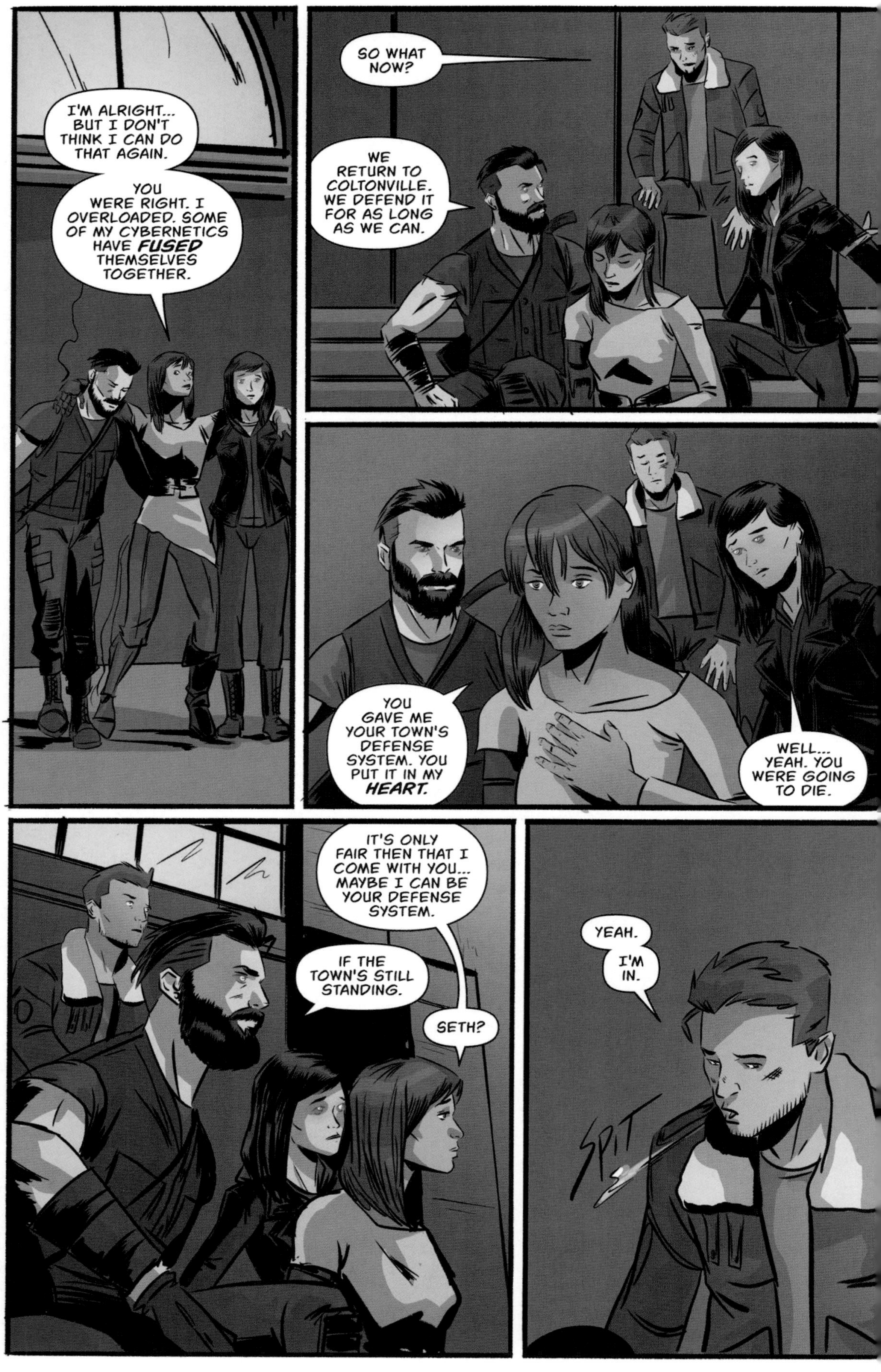
I'M ALRIGHT... BUT I DON'T THINK I CAN DO THAT AGAIN.
YOU WERE RIGHT. I OVERLOADED. SOME OF MY CYBERNETICS HAVE FUSED THEMSELVES TOGETHER.
SO WHAT NOW?
WE RETURN TO COLTONVILLE. WE DEFEND IT FOR AS LONG AS WE CAN.
YOU GAVE ME YOUR TOWN'S DEFENSE SYSTEM. YOU PUT IT IN MY HEART.
WELL... YEAH. YOU WERE GOING TO DIE.
IT'S ONLY FAIR THEN THAT I COME WITH YOU... MAYBE I CAN BE YOUR DEFENSE SYSTEM.
IF THE TOWN'S STILL STANDING.
SETH?
YEAH.
I'M IN.
SPIT

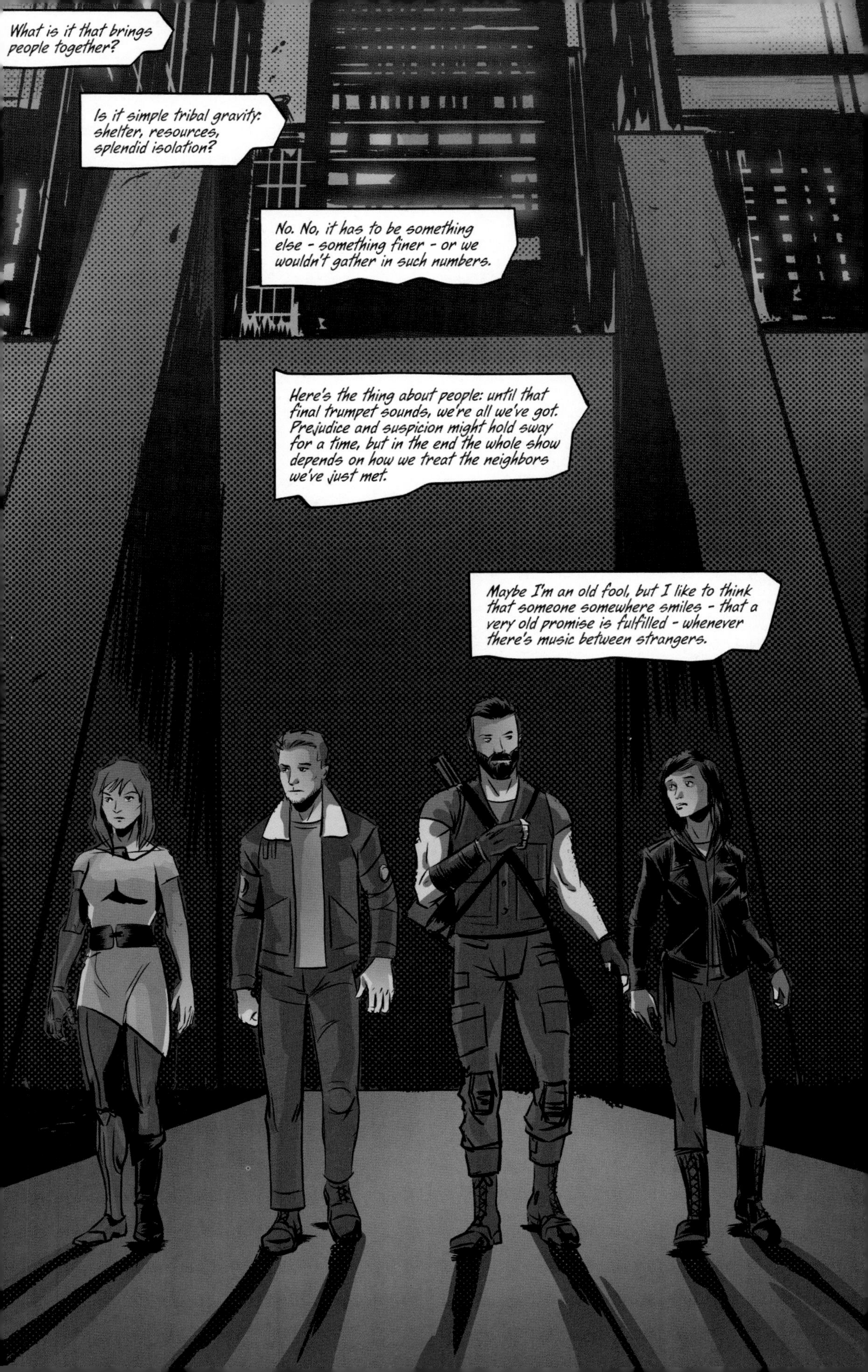
What is it that brings people together?
Is it simple tribal gravity: shelter, resources, splendid isolation?
No. No, it has to be something else - something finer - or we wouldn't gather in such numbers.
Here's the thing about people: until that final trumpet sounds, we're all we've got. Prejudice and suspicion might hold sway for a time, but in the end the whole show depends on how we treat the neighbors we've just met.
Maybe I'm an old fool, but I like to think that someone somewhere smiles - that a very old promise is fulfilled - whenever there's music between strangers.

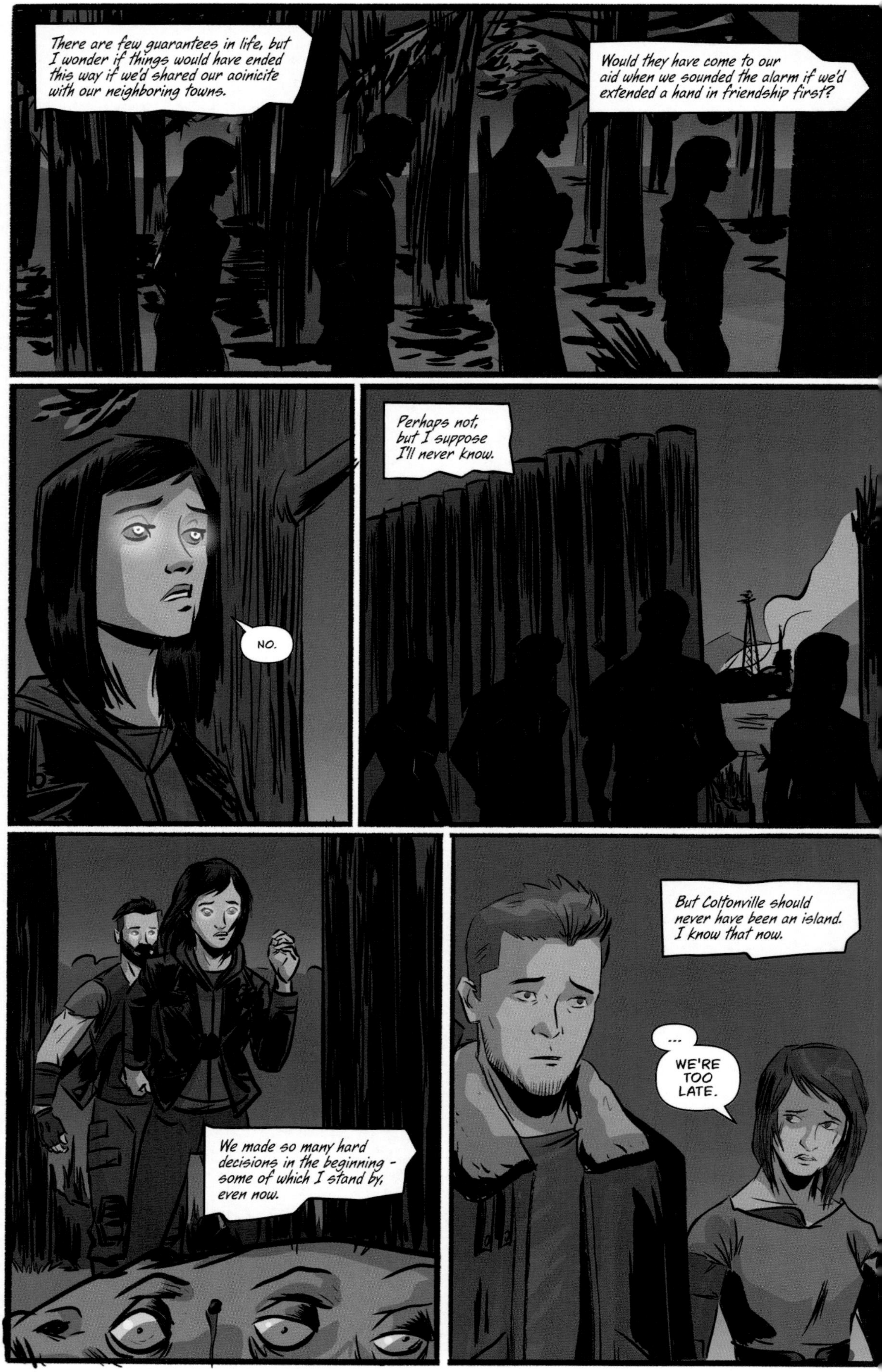
There are few guarantees in life, but I wonder if things would have ended this way if we'd shared our aoinicite with our neighboring towns.
Would they have come to our aid when we sounded the alarm if we'd extended a hand in friendship first?
NO.
Perhaps not, but I suppose I'll never know.
We made so many hard decisions in the beginning - some of which I stand by, even now.
But Coltonville should never have been an island. I know that now.
...
WE'RE TOO LATE.

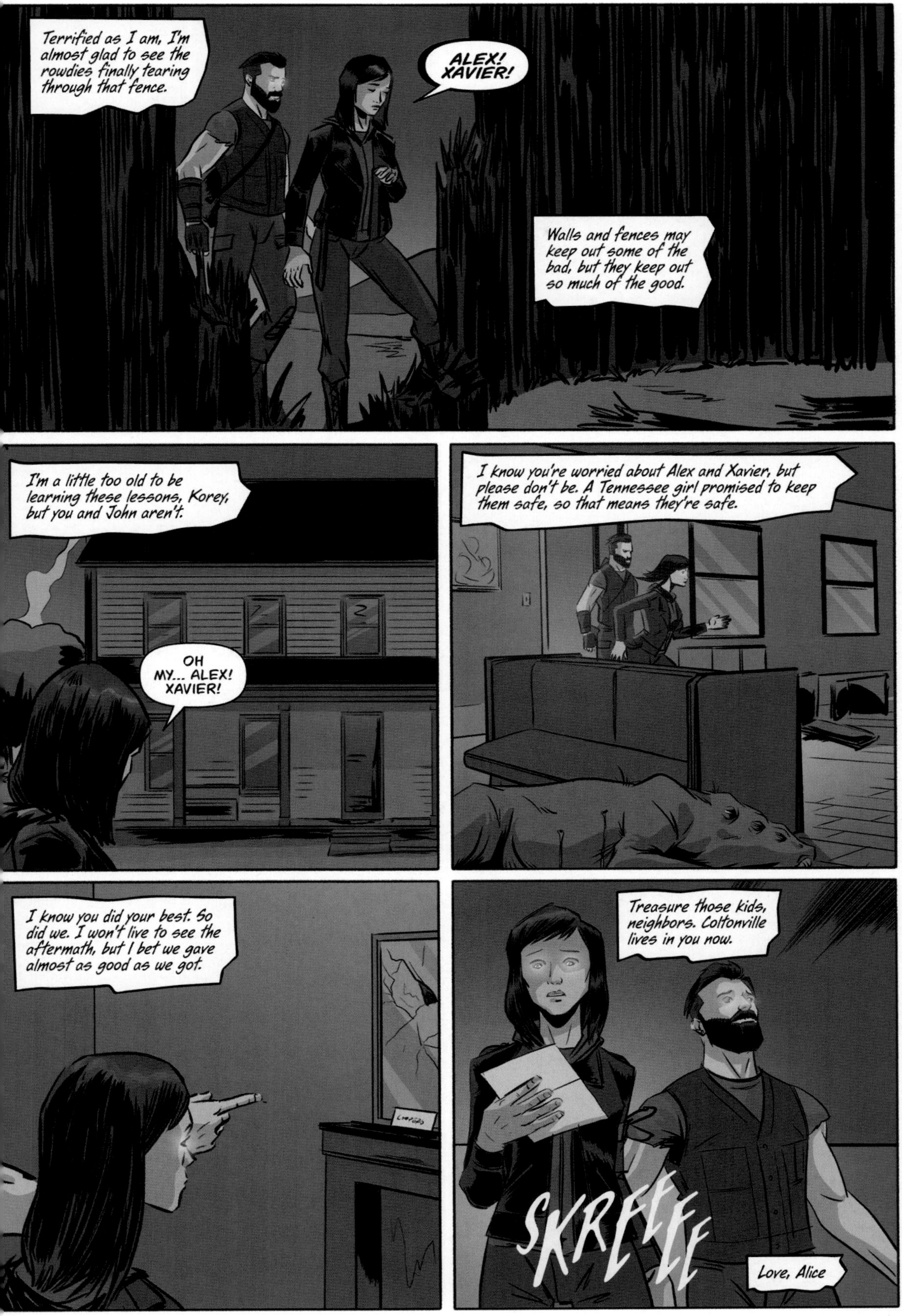

Terrified as I am, I'm almost glad to see the rowdies finally tearing through that fence.
ALEX! XAVIER!
Walls and fences may keep out some of the bad, but they keep out so much of the good.
I'm a little too old to be learning these lessons, Korey, but you and John aren't.
OH MY... ALEX! XAVIER!
I know you're worried about Alex and Xavier, but please don't be. A Tennessee girl promised to keep them safe, so that means they're safe.
I know you did your best. So did we. I won't live to see the aftermath, but I bet we gave almost as good as we got.
Treasure those kids, neighbors. Coltonville lives in you now.
SKREEEE
Love, Alice

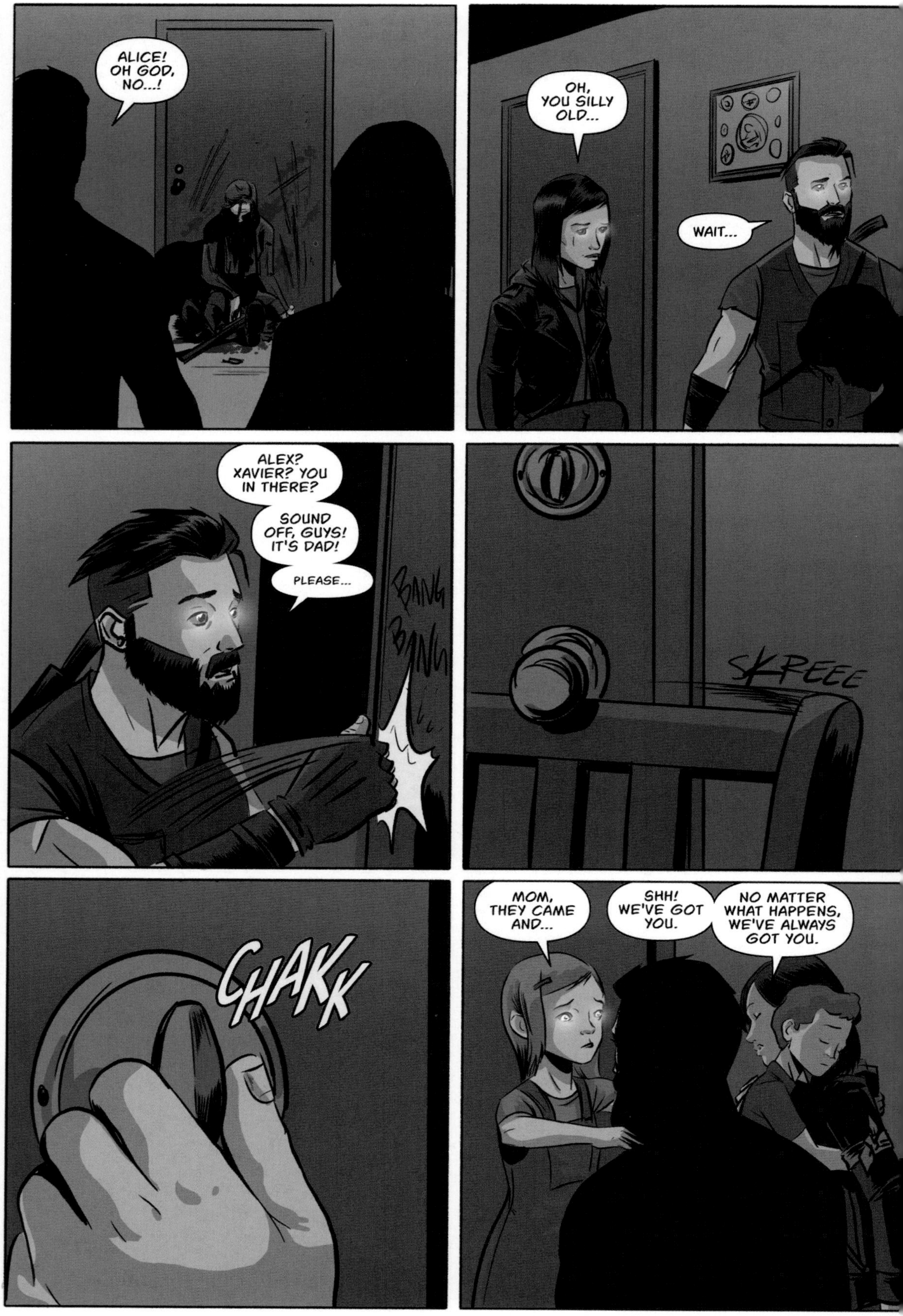
ALICE! OH GOD, NO...!
OH, YOU SILLY OLD...
WAIT...
ALEX? XAVIER? YOU IN THERE?
SOUND OFF, GUYS! IT'S DAD!
PLEASE...
BANG BANG
SKREEE
CHAKK
MOM, THEY CAME AND...
SHH! WE'VE GOT YOU.
NO MATTER WHAT HAPPENS, WE'VE ALWAYS GOT YOU.

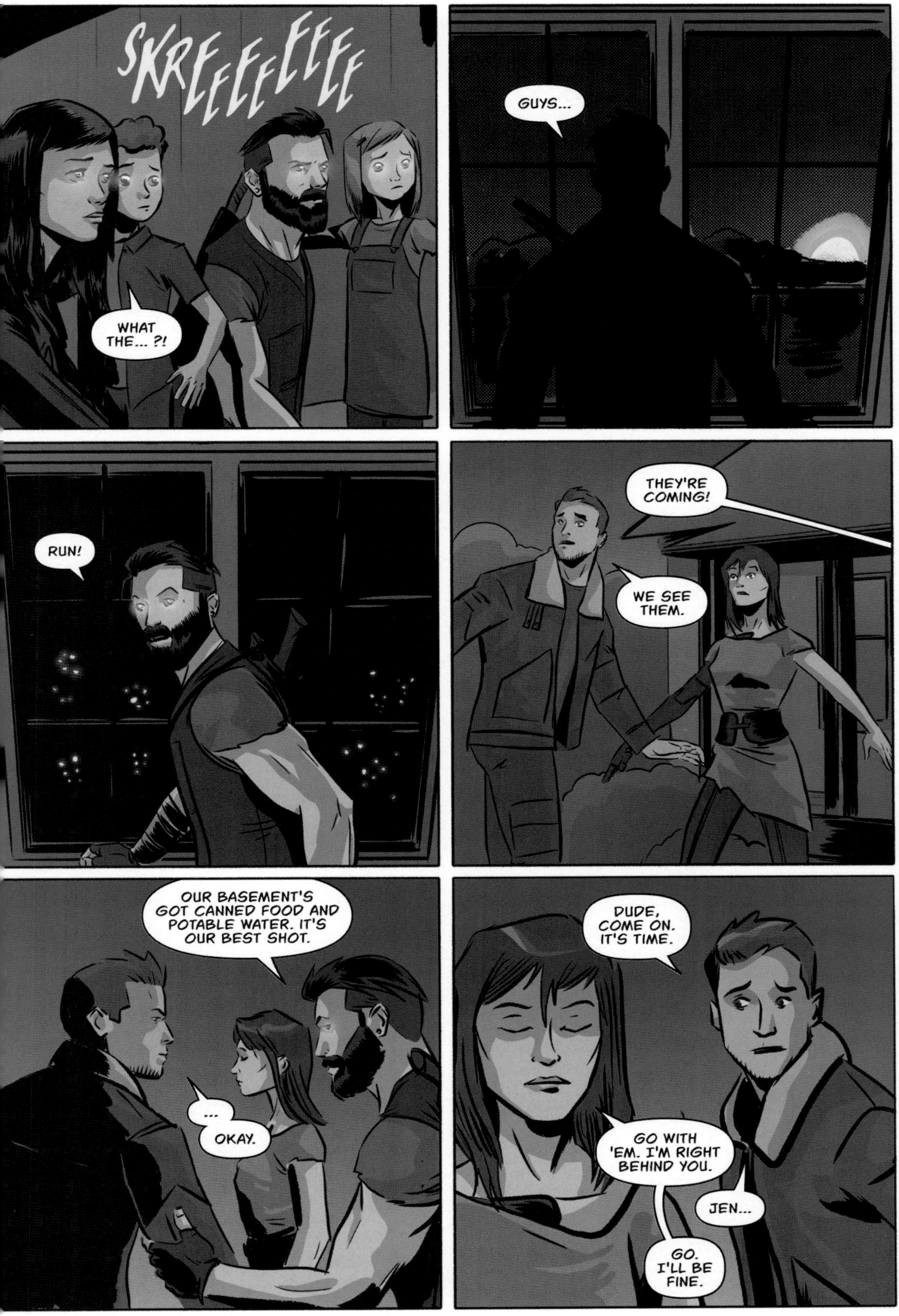
SKREEEEEEEEE
WHAT THE... ?!
GUYS...
RUN!
THEY'RE COMING!
WE SEE THEM.
OUR BASEMENT'S GOT CANNED FOOD AND POTABLE WATER. IT'S OUR BEST SHOT.
... OKAY.
DUDE, COME ON. IT'S TIME.
GO WITH 'EM. I'M RIGHT BEHIND YOU.
JEN...
GO. I'LL BE FINE.

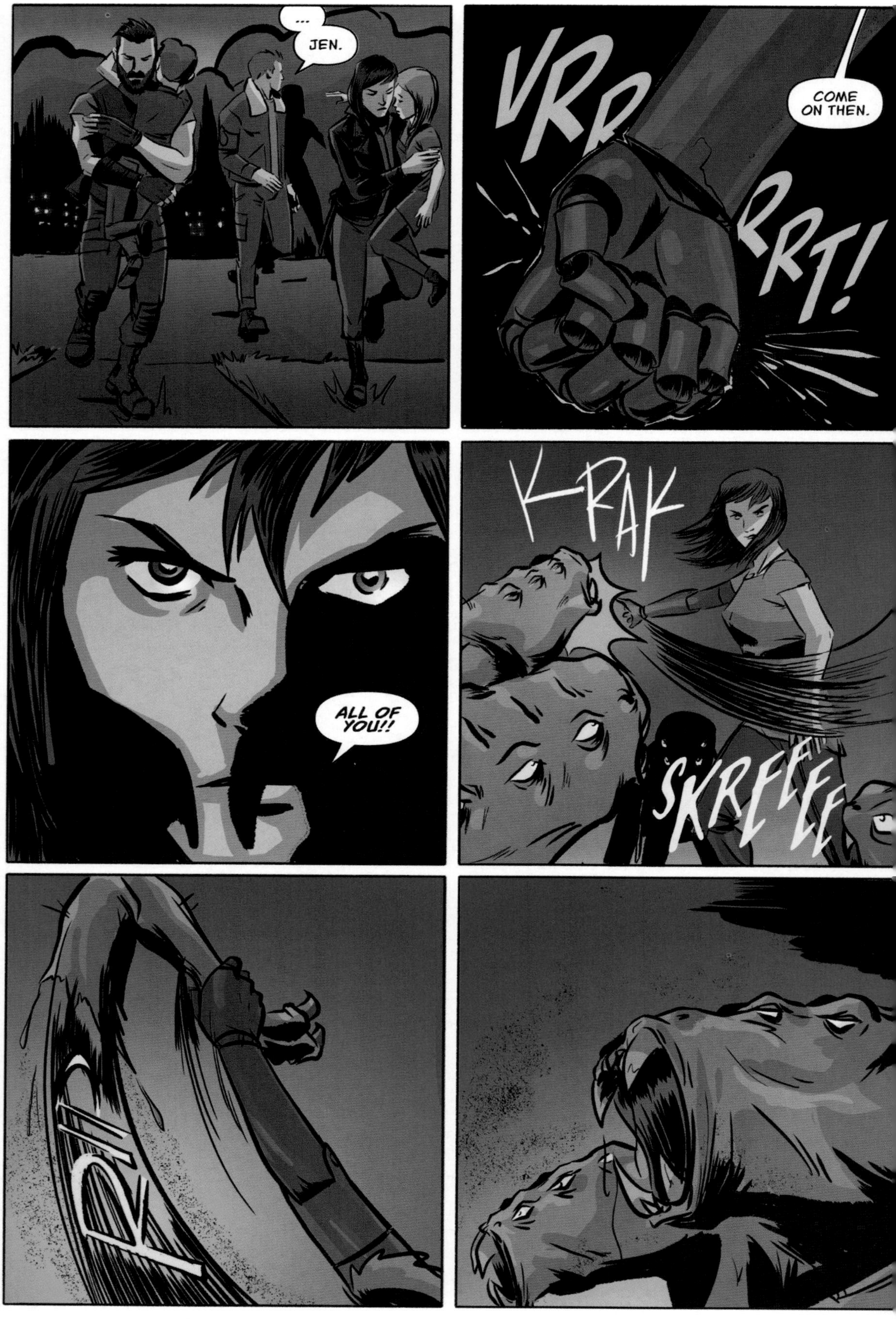
...
JEN.
VRRRRRT!
COME ON THEN.
ALL OF YOU!!
KRAK
SKREEEEEE

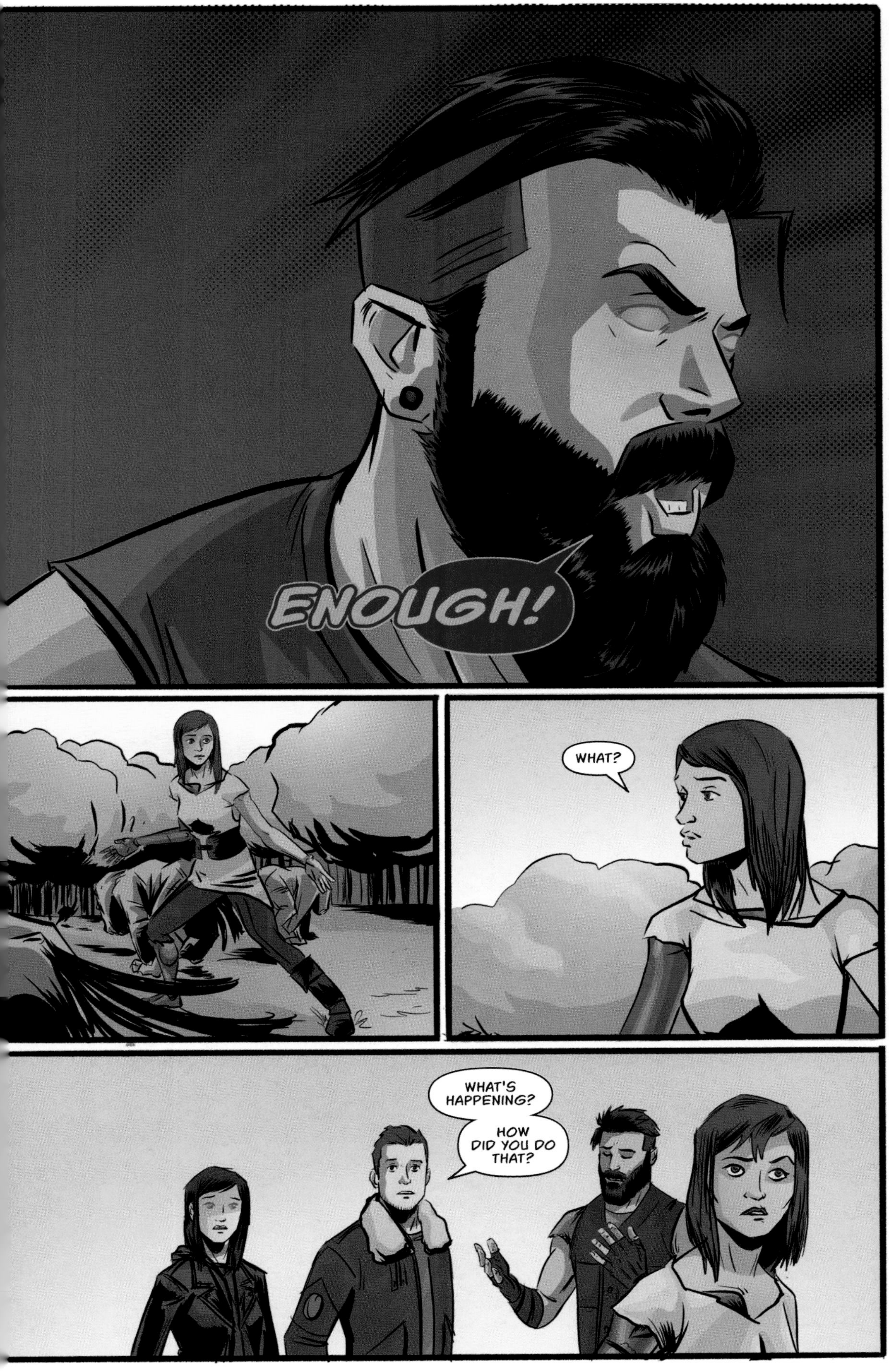
ENOUGH!
WHAT?
WHAT'S HAPPENING?
HOW DID YOU DO THAT?

I-- I DON'T KNOW.

HARRY DID SOMETHING LIKE THAT BEFORE. HE STOPPED THEM ATTACKING US.

COME ON-- YOU SPOOKED THEM, BUT THEY'LL BE BACK.

YEAH, I THINK YOU'RE RIGHT. I THINK THEY'LL BE BACK FOR SURE. LET'S GET TO THE BASEMENT.

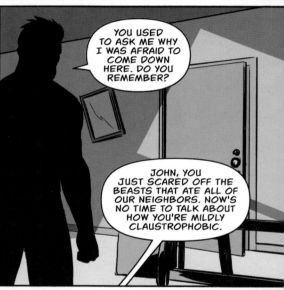

YOU USED TO ASK ME WHY I WAS AFRAID TO COME DOWN HERE. DO YOU REMEMBER?

JOHN, YOU JUST SCARED OFF THE BEASTS THAT ATE ALL OF OUR NEIGHBORS. NOW'S NO TIME TO TALK ABOUT HOW YOU'RE MILDLY CLAUSTROPHOBIC.

NO, SEE IT'S ABOUT THAT. ABOUT HOW I DID THAT. I THINK-- I THINK I HAVE A THEORY ABOUT THE ROWDIES. ABOUT WHAT THEY *ARE*.

GO ON?

REMEMBER THE ROWDY ATTACK... THE BIG ONE? ABOUT THREE YEARS AGO.

SURE. IT WAS ONE OF THE FIRST TIMES THE TOWN REALLY NEEDED TO USE TO ECHO DEFENSE SYSTEM. FOUR ROWDIES GOT THROUGH THE GATES. WE LOST TWO MEN BEFORE WE REPELLED THEM.

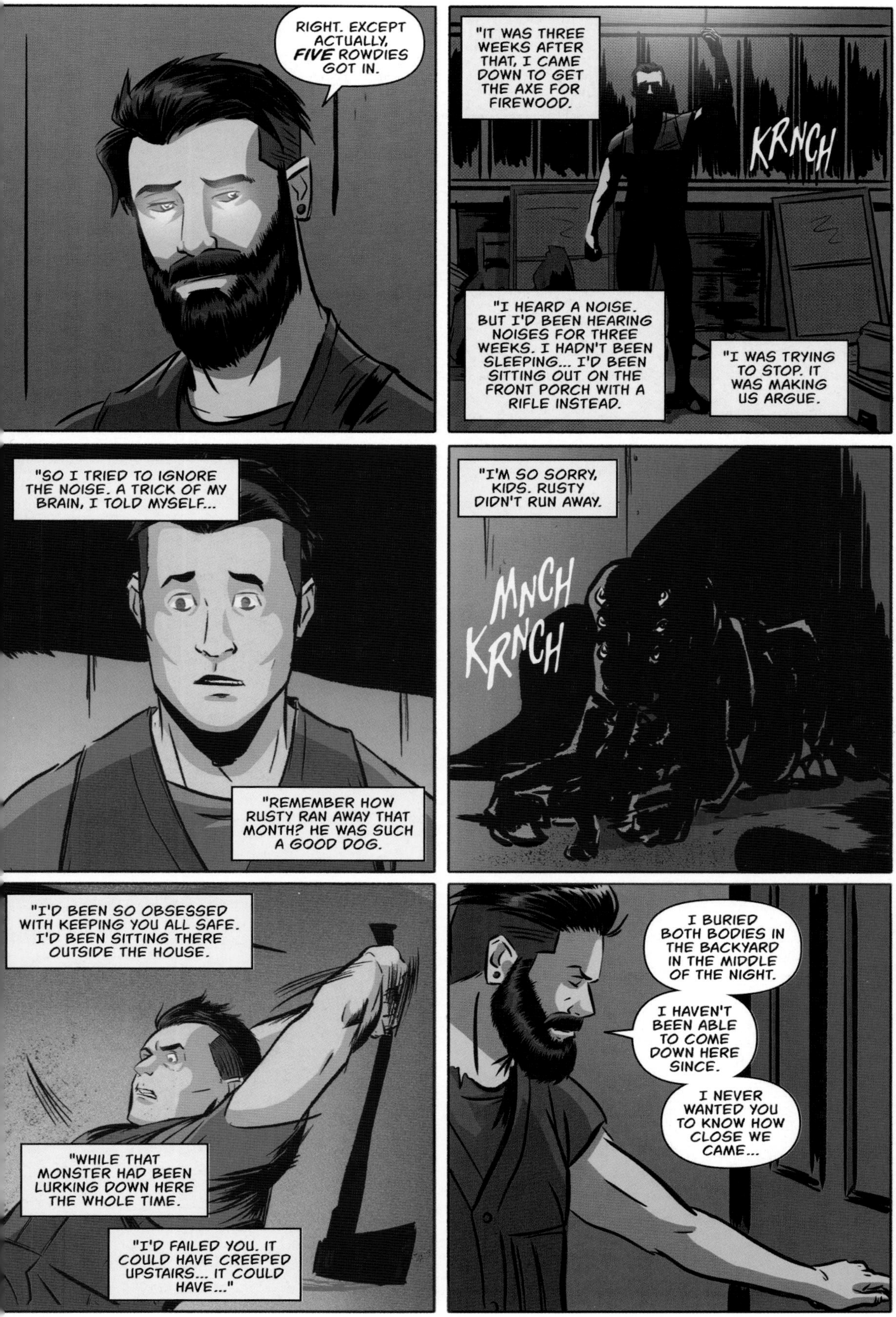
RIGHT. EXCEPT ACTUALLY, FIVE ROWDIES GOT IN.
"IT WAS THREE WEEKS AFTER THAT, I CAME DOWN TO GET THE AXE FOR FIREWOOD.
KRNCH
"I HEARD A NOISE. BUT I'D BEEN HEARING NOISES FOR THREE WEEKS. I HADN'T BEEN SLEEPING... I'D BEEN SITTING OUT ON THE FRONT PORCH WITH A RIFLE INSTEAD.
"I WAS TRYING TO STOP. IT WAS MAKING US ARGUE.
"SO I TRIED TO IGNORE THE NOISE. A TRICK OF MY BRAIN, I TOLD MYSELF...
"REMEMBER HOW RUSTY RAN AWAY THAT MONTH? HE WAS SUCH A GOOD DOG.
"I'M SO SORRY, KIDS. RUSTY DIDN'T RUN AWAY.
MNCH
KRNCH
"I'D BEEN SO OBSESSED WITH KEEPING YOU ALL SAFE. I'D BEEN SITTING THERE OUTSIDE THE HOUSE.
"WHILE THAT MONSTER HAD BEEN LURKING DOWN HERE THE WHOLE TIME.
"I'D FAILED YOU. IT COULD HAVE CREEPED UPSTAIRS... IT COULD HAVE..."
I BURIED BOTH BODIES IN THE BACKYARD IN THE MIDDLE OF THE NIGHT.
I HAVEN'T BEEN ABLE TO COME DOWN HERE SINCE.
I NEVER WANTED YOU TO KNOW HOW CLOSE WE CAME...

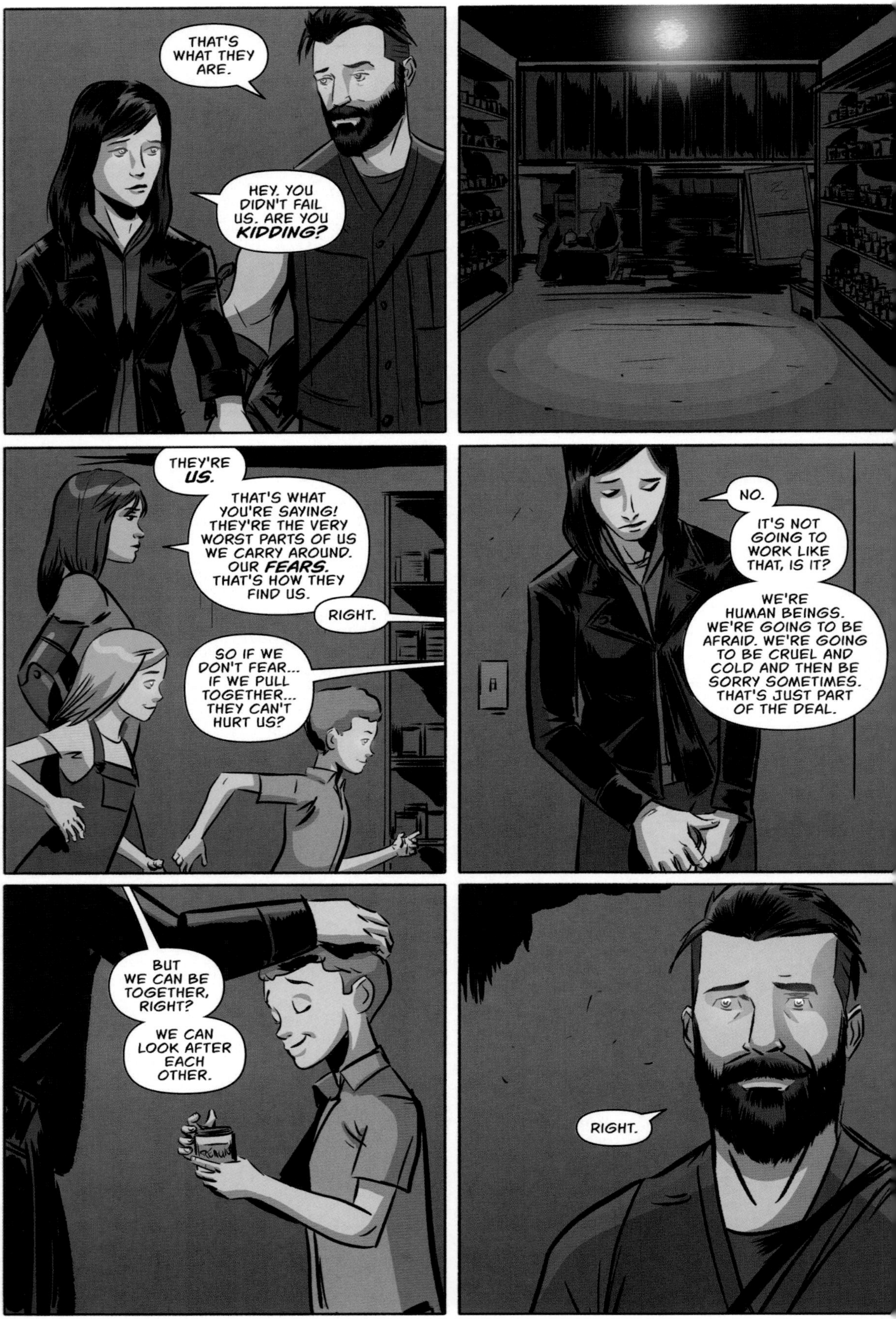
THAT'S WHAT THEY ARE.
HEY. YOU DIDN'T FAIL US. ARE YOU KIDDING?
THEY'RE US.
THAT'S WHAT YOU'RE SAYING! THEY'RE THE VERY WORST PARTS OF US WE CARRY AROUND. OUR FEARS. THAT'S HOW THEY FIND US.
RIGHT.
SO IF WE DON'T FEAR... IF WE PULL TOGETHER... THEY CAN'T HURT US?
NO.
IT'S NOT GOING TO WORK LIKE THAT, IS IT?
WE'RE HUMAN BEINGS. WE'RE GOING TO BE AFRAID. WE'RE GOING TO BE CRUEL AND COLD AND THEN BE SORRY SOMETIMES. THAT'S JUST PART OF THE DEAL.
BUT WE CAN BE TOGETHER, RIGHT?
WE CAN LOOK AFTER EACH OTHER.
RIGHT.

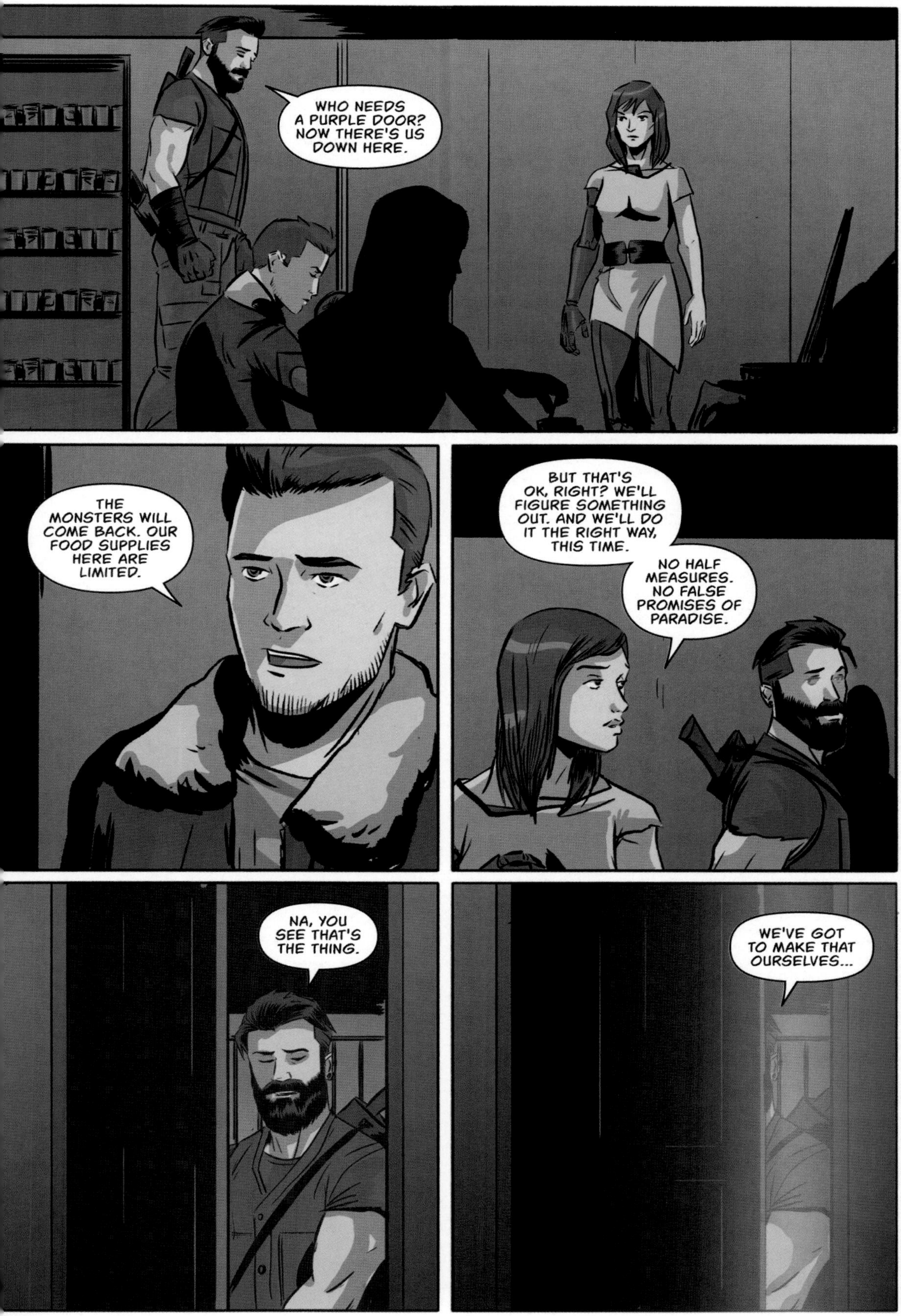
WHO NEEDS A PURPLE DOOR? NOW THERE'S US DOWN HERE.
THE MONSTERS WILL COME BACK. OUR FOOD SUPPLIES HERE ARE LIMITED.
BUT THAT'S OK, RIGHT? WE'LL FIGURE SOMETHING OUT. AND WE'LL DO IT THE RIGHT WAY, THIS TIME.
NO HALF MEASURES. NO FALSE PROMISES OF PARADISE.
NA, YOU SEE THAT'S THE THING.
WE'VE GOT TO MAKE THAT OURSELVES...

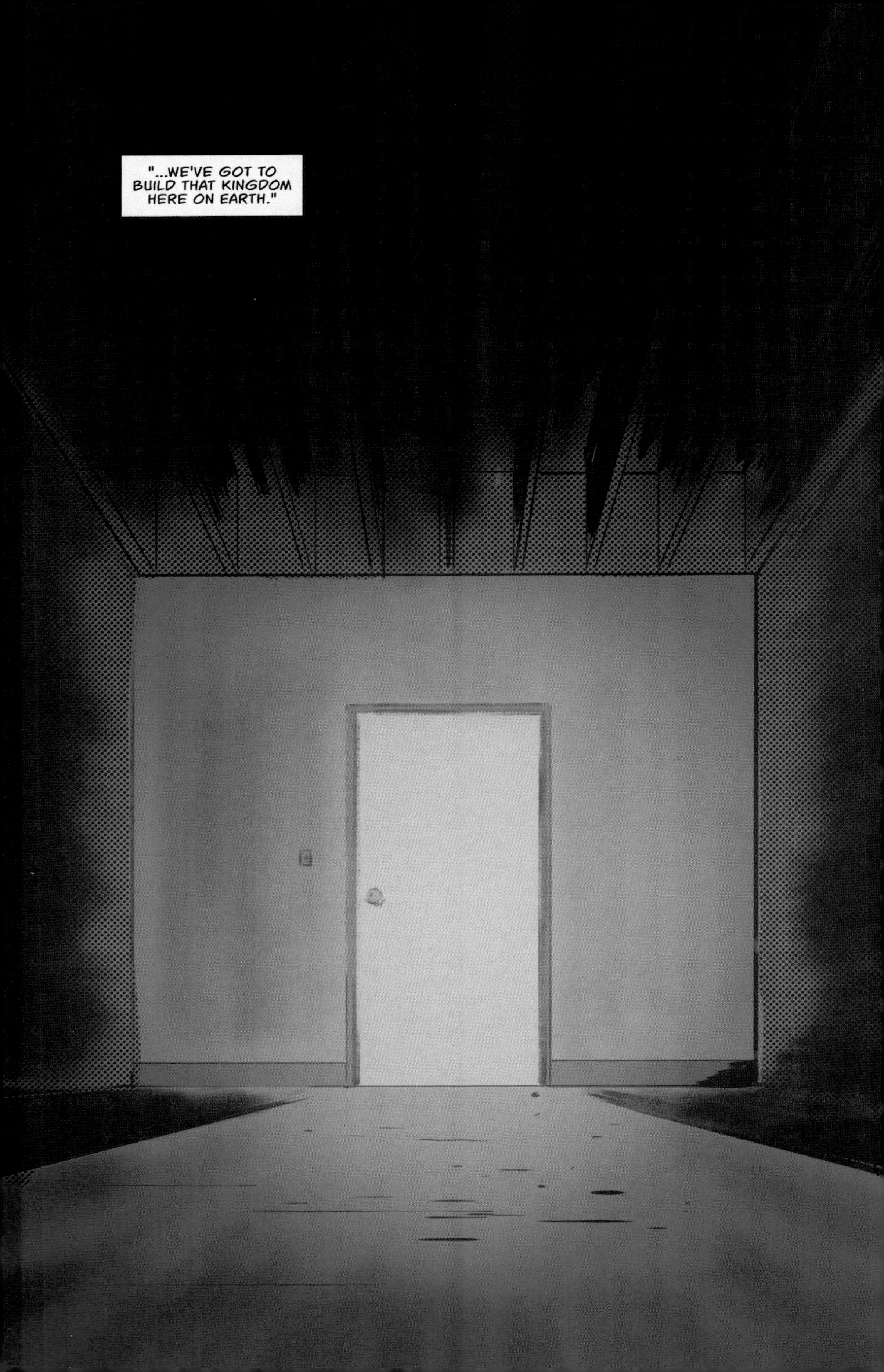
"...WE'VE GOT TO BUILD THAT KINGDOM HERE ON EARTH."

Pin Up By Jen Ledger

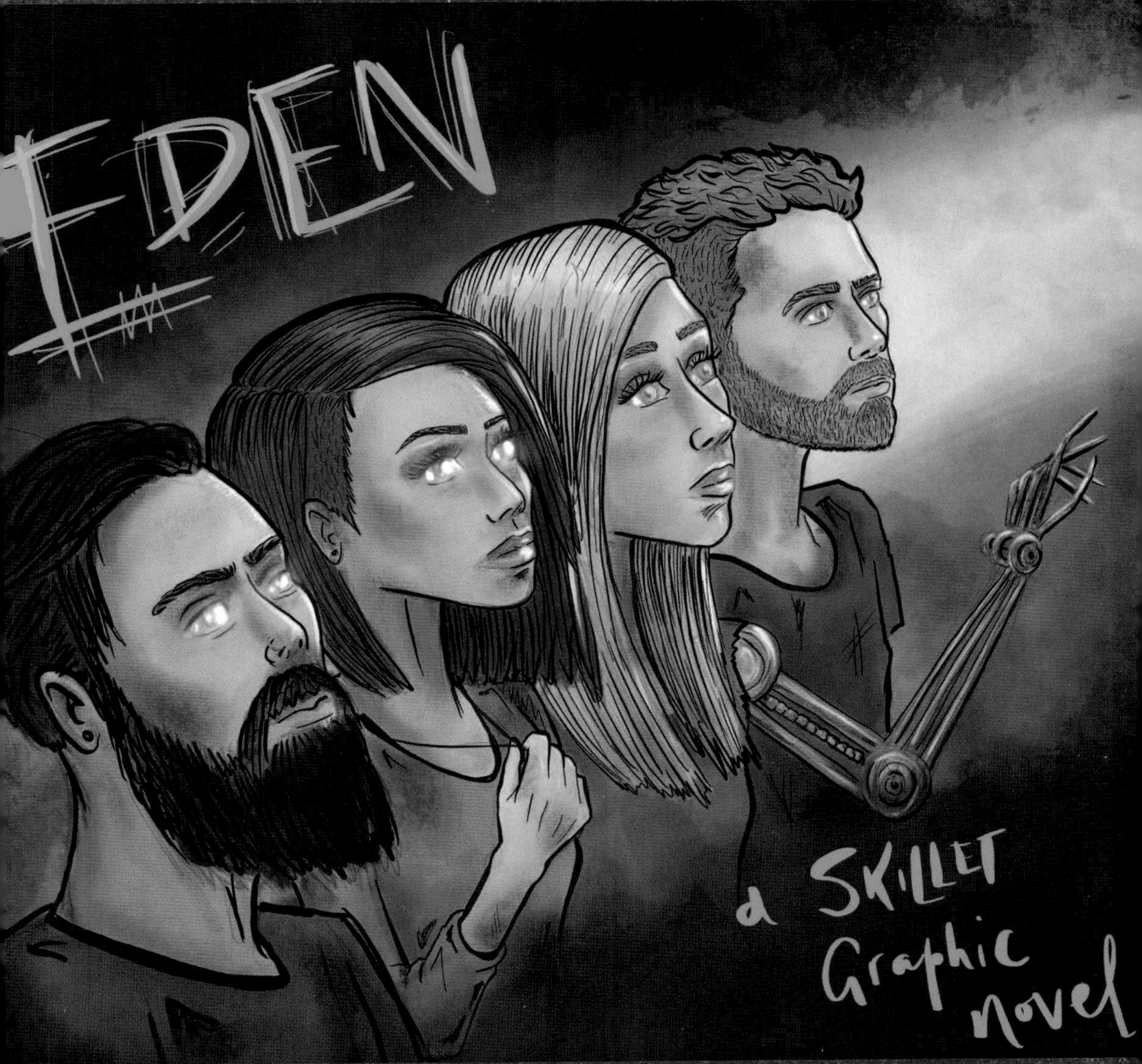
EDEN
a SKILLET Graphic novel

Pin Up By John Cooper